Scan for ???? except for
PIS/MIS papers.

Mass Media and National Development

Mass Media
and National Development

The Role of Information in the Developing Countries

Wilbur Schramm

Stanford University Press, Stanford, California
Unesco, Paris

Published in 1964
by the Stanford University Press,
Stanford, California, and the
United Nations Educational,
Scientific and Cultural Organization,
Place de Fontenoy, Paris-7^e

© *Unesco 1964*
Printed in the United States of America
MC.C.64/D.56/A

Unesco Foreword

This study forms part of the continuing effort of the United Nations and Unesco to help develop the mass media of communication. A new impetus was given to this effort when, in 1958, the General Assembly of the United Nations called for a "program of concrete action" to build up press, radio broadcasting, film, and television facilities in countries in process of economic and social development. To draw up the program and assess the resources required, the United Nations requested Unesco to carry out a survey.

Unesco conducted this survey by means of a series of meetings in which mass media experts, professional organizations, and government representatives joined in preparing a development program for each region. The first meeting, for Asia, was held at Bangkok in 1960; the second, for Latin America, at Santiago, Chile, in 1961; and the third, for Africa, at Unesco Headquarters in Paris in 1962. The reports of the three meetings provided the substance of the survey submitted by Unesco to the United Nations.

The General Assembly in December 1962 unanimously adopted a resolution "expressing its concern that the survey discloses 70 per cent of the population of the world lack in adequate information facilities and are thus denied effective enjoyment of the right to information." The General Assembly added that "information media have an important part to play in education and in economic and social progress generally and that new techniques of communication offer special opportunities for acceleration of the education process." Consequently, governments were invited to include in their economic plans adequate provision for develop-

ment of national information media and to take this factor into
account in their programs for the United Nations Development
Decade. Public and private agencies, particularly Unesco, were
urged to support this effort.

The General Conference of Unesco at the end of 1962 authorized
the publication of a study designed to help give practical effect to
the mass media development program. An expert was to be com-
missioned who, drawing on the results of the three regional meetings held during 1960–62, would examine the role of the mass
media in promoting economic and social progress.

Dr. Wilbur Schramm, Director of the Institute for Communication Research at Stanford University (U.S.A.), agreed to undertake the study. He is the author or editor of many books on mass
communication and has served as an adviser to governments in
this field. As a participant in all three regional meetings organized
by Unesco, he was well equipped to make make an international
correlation of the results.

It is as an independent expert that Mr. Schramm here examines
the role of the mass media in promoting national development, and
as such he assumes responsibility for the opinions expressed. His
study will, it is hoped, enhance the scholarly understanding of a
relatively unexplored subject and also help the developing countries in the practical application of this knowledge for the welfare
of their peoples.

Preface

The United Nations Conference on Freedom of Information, in 1948, called freedom of information "one of the basic freedoms," and free and adequate information "the touchstone of all the freedoms to which the United Nations is dedicated." It is now generally understood that before there can be free and adequate information in any country, there must be adequate development of mass communication. Therefore *all* countries, new or old, industrialized or not, highly developed or underdeveloped, are properly concerned with the development of their communication systems.

But one aspect of communication development is of special concern to the new and emerging countries. This is the contribution that effective communication can make to economic and social development. Free and adequate information is thus not only a goal: it is also a means of bringing about desired social change. Without adequate and effective communication, economic and social development will inevitably be retarded, and may be counter productive. With adequate and effective communication, the pathways to change can be made easier and shorter.

The following pages take for granted the general desirability of free and adequate information, and concern themselves primarily with this second aspect of communication development. They are concerned with the part that information can play, if used wisely, to speed and smooth what Julius Nyerere called the "terrible ascent" of the developing nations of the world toward social and economic modernity.

The author acknowledges gratefully the help of many people in

many countries in his efforts to write on this very large topic. Liter-
ally hundreds of individuals have contributed to this book, and it
is possible to mention only a few of them by name.

The Department of Mass Communication of Unesco—and its director, Mr. Tor Gjesdal—has supported this work generously and
thoughtfully. Mr. Julian Behrstock, Dr. Henry Cassirer, and Mr. E.
Lloyd Sommerlad, of that Department, gave the manuscript a detailed and most helpful reading. Mr. Alfredo Picasso-Oyague, of
the same Department, worked far beyond the call of duty in assembling data and putting in the author's hands information for
which otherwise he might have searched long and vainly. The rap-
porteurs of Unesco's three continental conferences on development
of the mass media—Mr. Sommerlad, for the Asian conference at
Bangkok; Mr. Jorge Fernandez, Director of the Centro Interna-
cional de Estudios Superiores de Periodismo, in Quito, Ecuador,
rapporteur of the Latin American conference, at Santiago, Chile;
and Mr. François Itoua, Editor in Chief of Radio Congo (Brazza-
ville), who served as rapporteur of the African conference, held in
Paris—all were kind enough to examine the manuscript at an early
stage, in relation to the findings of their conferences and their particular parts of the world. Dr. Douglas Ensminger and Mr. W. Bert
Johnson, of the Ford Foundation in India, were kind enough to
read and comment on the manuscript in the light of their long experience with economic development. Dr. Y. V. L. Rao, Associate
Director of the Press Institute of India; Mr. Richard Bertrandias,
President of RTV International, Inc., of New York, which specializes in the problems of developing countries; and Dr. Eugene
Staley, economist of the Stanford Research Institute, himself author of standard books on economic and social development—all
read and commented most helpfully on the work. A most special
debt of gratitude must be acknowledged to Dr. Fernand Terrou,
the distinguished scholar and director of the Institut Français de
Presse, who not only examined the manuscript but also contributed
the section on institutional and legal problems. Thanks also are
due Dr. C. Ray Carpenter, of Pennsylvania State University, Mr.
Robert B. Hudson, Vice-President of the National Educational

Television and Radio Center, and Dr. Lyle Webster, former Director of Information of the United States Department of Agriculture, who discussed many of the problems of this book as members of a research team in Asia, headed by the author. Among my colleagues in the Institute for Communication Research, of Stanford University, Dr. Richard Fagen, Dr. Edwin B. Parker, and Dr. Richard F. Carter all read the manuscript, and Dr. Carter, in particular, furnished detailed comments and criticism. The Stanford University Press furnished useful critiques, and its customary thoughtful and meticulous editing. Mrs. Linda Miller typed most of the manuscript twice and parts of it three times, and thus became, doubtless through no wish of her own, a considerable authority on the contents and a most useful copy editor. Finally, the author wishes to express his appreciation to the Ford Foundation for continuing support of international studies at the Institute for Communication Research, and in particular for making possible the released time during which much of the research and writing on this book was accomplished.

All these people and institutions are blameless for the faults of the book, but it would have been poorer without them.

W. S.

Contents

Mass Media and National Development

Introduction:
The Human Meaning of Underdevelopment

The Ifes

In west central Africa lives a family which, in its own small way, illustrates some of the problems that will concern us in this book. We shall call them the Ife° family. Their real name doesn't matter, nor is it important to know exactly where they live, except that they are in a part of the world that is commonly called "underdeveloped."

There are five in the Ife family. The mother and father are in their middle thirties. They have two living children out of five born to them. One child died of a fever when he was little more than a year old; the other two died at birth. The two surviving children are a boy of 13 and a girl of two. The fifth member of the family is Mr. Ife's father, who has come to spend his last years with them because he is too old and sick to work. They treat him very kindly even though he is a bother to take care of and is an unproductive member of the family who has to be fed but can't contribute to the family income or the chores.

The first thing you are likely to notice about the Ife family is the warmth of their life together, the affection they seem to feel for each other, and in particular the kindness they show to the old and useless grandfather. Another thing you are likely to notice is the way they savor the little happy things of life, how they throw back their heads and laugh with their whole bodies. One doesn't hear

° Pronounced EE'-fay. The name has no reference to the city of Ife, Nigeria.

full-bodied laughter very often these days, but one still hears it in Africa, and from families like the Ifes. And a third impression you are likely to bring away from the home of the Ifes is that you have seen bright, quick, talented people, despite the fact that they have talked of nothing farther than ten miles from their home, and despite the primitiveness of their home surroundings and their ways of working.

You will perhaps feel that the Ifes are not very ambitious; they don't seem to be striving to be "upward mobile." That may puzzle you, when you think of their native ability. But when you get to know them better you will realize that they are very often sick. They have dysenteries, malaria, and hookworm, and are constantly attacked by tropical parasites. They are sometimes hungry. They will hide this from you, but if you watch them eat you will realize that they probably average no more than 1,700 or 1,800 calories a day, compared with 2,500 to 3,000 for Europeans or North Americans. They usually go without lunch, and soothe their hungry stomachs with nuts they can hold in their mouths and suck for hours. Their diet has very little meat, except occasional chicken or a small animal hunted down in the woods. They eat cassava root, beans, peanuts, rice, or fruit, when they can get it, and whatever else is available to supplement these staples. It is a low-protein, high-carbohydrate diet, and thus helps to keep down the hunger pains, but it does not make a person energetic, ambitious, and hard-working.

Furthermore, Mr. Ife hasn't much choice of occupation. There is no industry in his village where he might get a job. He would like to be a government service worker, but this possibility is closed to him because he has never learned to read and write. He makes his living—like most of the other villagers—by clearing a small farm plot out of the bush, working it with home-made implements, planting it for one year, then letting it lie fallow for three or four years, while the poor washed-out soil regathers some of its mineral content. The second year, he goes to another farm plot, the third year to still another one, and so forth. He lives in a house just like the other houses in the village—mud walls on a bamboo framework, thatched roof, and cooking stove made of round stones. When the termites eat the wood frame, the house falls, and he has to build another one. He would like to have a galvanized iron roof, but an expenditure like that is pretty hopeless for a man who, in the course of a year, handles perhaps $50 in cash, and out of that must try to buy food supplements, clothing, tobacco, beverages, and medical help.

Yet one comes away with the idea that Ife is someone pretty special. The clearness and sharpness of his mind impress you even when he talks about such a homely subject as planting, or the qualities of a thatched roof. More often than one would expect, he talks about the past. He has never read a book of history, of course, and yet he is deeply interested in the past of his people. He points out that his people have had an interrupted past, because of the long period of colonialism, and that what happened, who lived, who did what, before they were colonies, is now faint in their memories. He speculates, for example, on what the buildings were that are now ruins on the hill north of his village. There is no doubt that Ife has deep and rich interests that education could cultivate.

He is deeply interested in mechanical things, too, although he sees very few of them. One day he watched for hours a pump that a government engineer was using. When the workers left the pump, he began to take it apart to see how it worked; they angrily chased him away when they saw what he was doing. If he were an educated man, in a developed country, he too might be an engineer.

He has leadership qualities, too. The people in his village often come to him for advice and guidance. Yet his leadership is of very little use to his hard-working and ambitious country, because the news of national development is so faint and faraway. National news, development policies, don't mean much to that village. Some of the villagers are not quite certain even that the country is independent.

There is talent and ability in the rest of the Ife family. The mother is skilled in weaving colorful and artistic frames and baskets out of the vines that grow near the village. The 13-year-old boy has a remarkable memory; he can hear a native song once and then sing it through perfectly. It is a pity that he never got further than the third grade in school. He had to walk six miles through the bush to reach the school, and in the third year he suffered badly from worms and malaria, and would sleep with his head on the desk half the school day. The teacher didn't like that, and his relationships at school got worse and worse, until finally he quit school and began helping with the farm work. He had learned to read simple material, of course, and after he quit school he occasionally asked his father whether they should not try to get a newspaper to read. But there was no money for that, and no books to borrow, and the boy's reading skill gradually slipped away for lack of practice. He can still write his name, and occasionally his father asks him to do that trick before admiring visitors.

There is a lot more to tell about the Ifes, but it all adds up to the same point: this family represents incompletely used resources. When you have seen them, you come away thinking if they could only get a better diet so they would have more energy—if they could only get medical care for their worst illnesses—if someone would only explain to them very clearly and persuasively why they should boil their water—if only they could be educated so as to get the fullest use of their talents. If only a bright boy did not have to be lost to schooling and literacy in the third grade! If only Ife were not wasted on subsistence agriculture, where he has no special talent, instead of being educated to the point where his bright and curious mind and his leadership qualities could be adequately employed for his own good and that of his neighbors! If only an able family like this could participate actively in the country's effort to develop into nationhood!

These are some of the thoughts that go through your head after you have met the Ifes. But now let us move some thousands of miles and look at another family.

The Bvanis

Bvani° is not their real name, but it is convenient to call them that. They live in southern Asia, in a very old country where the past is

° Buh-VAH'-nee.

more clearly remembered than it is in the Ifes' country. The Bvani family, therefore, lives with a rich heritage of religion, philosophy, poetry, and art. Many of the monuments of their past are still standing in their original glory for everyone to see. But economically the Bvanis' country is almost as underdeveloped as is the land of the Ifes.

There probably isn't much difference between how much the Ifes get to eat and how much the Bvanis get, although their food is different. The Bvanis raise rice, the basic dish for all their meals. Sometimes they eat rice by itself; sometimes they combine it with beans and with hot sauces made from peppers and other spices. Occasionally they have some poultry or meat to go with it. There aren't many days when their intake of calories is over 2,000.

The Bvani family gives the impression of being more vigorous and in better health than the Ife family. They are fine looking people—short, dark, clear-eyed, with wide, intelligent faces. They have probably had fewer chronic, debilitating diseases than have the Ifes. But the Bvanis are used to having epidemics sweep across their country. They have lost children to smallpox and cholera, as well as to the complications of childbirth.

There are five Ifes and 14 Bvanis. Their family life seems so different. All the Bvanis live together in four one-room houses, in a little compound separated from the rest of the village by a low wall. They are really three families. The patriarch of the Bvanis lives with his wife, whom they call Little Mother, in the corner house of the compound. Like the other houses, it is made of packed earth, dried and smoothed, and baked by the sun until it is like cement. Like the other houses, it has only one room and is almost without furniture. In the two adjoining houses, the two sons of the patriarch live with their wives and children. The patriarch is in his fifties, which is old for that country. The two sons, alert, intelligent men, are in their late thirties, a few years older than their slim, dark-eyed wives. There is one other house in the compound, recently emptied by death, now waiting for the marriage of the oldest son of one of the younger Bvanis.

When the boys of the family marry, they bring their wives home to live in the compound. When a girl marries, she goes to live with her husband's family. This is the pattern called the joint family. It is hard to be lonely in the family compound. The children of the several families play together. The men work together. The great, placid, white buffaloes and bullocks share the compound with the humans. In the daytime, the women chatter with each other. In the evening they sit outside, the men smoking, an occasional song rising, the patriarch recalling a legend of the Bvani people, the children's eyes round and white in the darkness. They rise at dawn and go to bed soon after dark. In the warmer parts of the year they all sleep outside in the compound, the humans and the animals together in the open air under the brilliant sky.

The Bvanis pool their wealth, such as it is, and farm together their few acres of land. When a family decision needs to be made, they go to the patriarch. He muses and ponders, and what he finally says becomes family policy. There is very little argument over such things, although sometimes the boys shake their heads in disappointment. The patriarch is a benevolent ruler, but a tough one. Only very rarely are his decisions challenged; when the younger men do not agree with him, they have the choice of conforming or leaving. Two of the Bvani sons did, in fact, leave. The patriarch had sent these two boys to school. They came home with new ideas, especially ideas about jobs and money. At home they found little sympathy for these thoughts. So one day they went to the city to look for jobs and never came back. This was a bitter experience for the patriarch. He never mentions these two boys in public.

As a matter of fact, the present patriarch has been in his position of eminence only a few years, since his own father had lived to an incredible age and had held his power until the day he died. So the present patriarch had waited year after year to inherit the honor. He had seen his own brothers die, his sons grow up and marry, and their sons grow up until they were almost ready to marry. All this time he had to serve his aged and rather crotchety father. As the years passed, he became more and more frustrated. Now, *his* oldest son defers to *him,* serves *his* whims, and waits.

Tension is now somewhat greater in the Bvani compound because change is pushing into the village. For one thing, the government is sending out community development workers to try to make agriculture more productive. They talk to the younger Bvanis, who come home and report to the patriarch.

"These men say we can raise a bigger crop of rice if we do it this way," say the young men.

"And why should we raise more rice?" asks the patriarch.

"They want us to raise more and sell it for money."

"Money is trouble," says the old man.

"With it you could buy Little Mother a new dress."

"She has a dress. And where would she put another one?"

"With it we could send the children to school."

"And have them go to the city and leave us?" asks the patriarch. There is bitterness in his voice. Since the two brothers ran away to the city, no Bvani has gone to school. The young men realize this is no time to talk further about the changes suggested by the government.

Perhaps if the patriarch were younger, you think . . . Or if the system were organized so that the young men had more to say about the decisions . . .

Change comes hard in that village. The old men are the decision makers, and they usually make conservative decisions. There is a tight caste system, which limits the kinds of jobs any man can aspire to. There are rather rigid customs as to what kind of work a woman can do and what her influence can be. The government has been trying to break down these rules, but it is hard to do by law; the old customs linger. The whole village system tends to enforce what has been, and to oppose what might be. You will hear in the village what happened when one of the neighbors of the Bvanis, a few years ago, went sharply against village traditions and the advice of the old men. He seemed to be making a good thing of it, but he lost his friends. They quit talking to him. Their wives quit talking to his wife. One night, by accident or design, the bullocks got into his field. After a while he went back to the old ways.

Thus the village has its own way of enforcing its customs. But the better you get to know the patriarch of the Bvanis, the more clearly you realize that his opposition to change isn't pigheaded or obstinate. Rather, it is prudent. He has learned to operate on a very narrow margin. A poor crop, he knows, means famine. Over the years he has learned a relatively sure and safe way to farm. He learned it from his own father. He watched his neighbors practice the same method. He became skilled in it through 50 years of trial and error. These lessons he trusts. These teachers he knows. He has no reason to trust a government man from far away, who comes with strange and unfamiliar suggestions of change. What is old, what is tried, what is near, what he himself has done, is safe. What is distant and new, he distrusts. Now that he bears the whole responsibility for the family, he has more reason than ever to take no chances.

Furthermore, some of the suggestions for change he hears in the village offend his deepest beliefs. He has a strong feeling about man's relation to nature; it does not seem right to him that man should deliberately try to manipulate nature to make it serve *him*. He has similar strong beliefs about killing living things. Beliefs like these come from some of the holiest men and from the greatest writings of his nation.

And furthermore he is caught in the village system. The village has its way of enforcing its norms. It is vastly easier and more pleasant to go with the old norms than to try to introduce new ones.

Nothing short of a change in the social patterns would make it very easy for change to come to the Bvanis.

The elder Bvani is a more impressive man than he seems on first sight. He is short, thin, wizened by age and heat, pockmarked by the smallpox that nearly killed him when he was 15, but he still moves with dignity and cuts a figure in the village. In his decisions he is thoughtful. In his dealings with his extended family he is firm but benevolent. He speaks surprisingly well, often in the cadence of the great poems of his people. Many of these poems he remembers from having heard them in his youth. Many of the ancient legends he remembers, too, and recalls them for the children. He is illiterate, but far from unlearned. Indeed, he has a great fund of folk wisdom, proverbs, and common sense. He hasn't been far from home, and he has never made a trip into science or modern politics, but what he has seen—what has actually passed before his senses—he has experienced intensely and is able to talk about with vigor and charm. In no sense is he a slow or a stupid man; he is merely a limited man.

We might call the Bvanis limited people—limited by their conservative leadership, the tight social system, and the traditional norms of their village, limited in the education and information they are able to seek and the innovations they are permitted to try, limited in the extent to which they can use their native intelligence and vigor in the aid of national development.

It is even clearer in the case of the Bvanis than in the case of the Ifes that economic development requires also a social transformation. And a social transformation is basically a set of human transformations—people to be educated and informed, attitudes and values to be changed, human relationships, customs, social behavior to be reviewed and rethought. Economic development in that country requires that farms should be made more productive, so that part of the human resources can be moved from agriculture into industry. But even such a simple thing as a Bvani boy leaving a farm family for a job in the city, as millions of his countrymen will do in the next ten years—even such a simple act as that raises a set of hard human problems and challenges the social system. Within every economic problem lie human and social problems. We can state it as a kind of axiom:

> *If national economic development is to occur, there must be a social transformation, and in order for this to happen, human resources must be mobilized and difficult human problems must be solved.*

THE HAVE AND HAVE-NOT COUNTRIES

We have begun with the Bvanis and the Ifes because they are the people this book is about. They represent the people of the developing countries, where the winds of change now blow so strongly.

In the language of the United Nations, a "developing" or an "underdeveloped" country is one in which the annual per capita income is $300 or less. That is all we mean when we speak of an "underdeveloped" country. Such a country is not underdeveloped in every respect: it may be underdeveloped economically but highly developed in some of its personal relationships (like the Ifes') or in art and philosophy (like the Bvanis'). *Not all* of such a country may be economically underdeveloped: in the Bvanis' nation there are a small number of rich landowners and a few great industries, scattered among the tiny farms and the poor people; and in the Ifes' nation, where most of the people cannot read and write, a few men have earned advanced degrees from some of the oldest universities in Europe. It makes little sense to think of the Ifes and Bvanis as "underdeveloped people," although they do represent incompletely used resources. They are limited in what they can do by the society around them, by their poverty and lack of education. Develop the economy and the society, and you will see different behavior in the people.

Thus, "underdeveloped" is not a pejorative term. It means simply that economic growth (and the social changes that must accompany economic growth) have not yet passed a certain point. And to be called a "developing" country is a badge of honor, because it means that a nation has undertaken to lift itself up by its own strength out of the stage of economic underdevelopment and to do in a few decades what in earlier history has usually taken centuries.

Suppose all the peoples of the earth were divided into two groups: citizens of countries where the average per capita income is $300 a year or less (the "underdeveloped" countries), and citizens of all other countries. And suppose it were possible to assemble these two enormous groups of people in some vast open place so that one could go up in a jet plane and look at them. Then one would see an astonishing thing: the assembly of the economically underdeveloped nations is twice the size of the other group!

Two-thirds of the earth's people live in national states where an average family of five can count on less than $1,500 a year, in cash, goods, and services. In many countries it is far less than that. Where the Bvanis and the Ifes live, an average family of five can count on no more than $300 total per year. At least two-thirds of this must go for food, leaving less than $100 for clothing, shelter, medical expenses, education, and the little amenities of life. The difference between this order of income and the average income in an economically advanced country may be as great as 25 to 1. Deshmukh points out that less than one per cent of all the people in India have an income equal to, or greater than, the *average citizen's* income in the United States.[1] This is one of the central facts of our time.

Where are the two-thirds of the world's people whose per capita national income is less than $300? (See Table 1.)

They cover Africa except for the Union of South Africa. They cover all South Asia except Singapore, all East Asia except Japan, all Central Asia except the Soviet Union's extension into the Asian heartland. The two most populous nations, China and India, are thus included. Also included are Latin American countries except Argentina, Chile, Colombia, Costa Rica, Cuba, Jamaica, Panama, Trinidad, and Venezuela; most of the Pacific Islands, but not Australia or New Zealand; almost all the Middle East; and such European countries as Albania, Bulgaria, Portugal, and Yugoslavia. These are the earth's Underdeveloped Lands.

What distinguishes the Underdeveloped Lands from the others? → Geography? The division is almost but not quite by continents. For example, most of Europe is well developed, but parts are not; most of Asia is underdeveloped, but Japan has proved that an Asian country can be highly productive. Climate? A majority of the less-developed countries are in warm latitudes, but not all of them. In the past some of the most prosperous countries, including some like Egypt, Syria, and Greece that are less prosperous today, have been in warm climates. Resources? There is no monopoly of natural resources in developed countries. Switzerland, for example, is much poorer in natural resources than, say, Indonesia or Brazil. Room to expand? The United States, the Soviet Union, Australia had it, but so do many of the countries of Africa and Latin America. And the most prosperous country of Asia is one of the most crowded countries in the world.

[1] Numbered notes (primarily source citations) will be found at the back of the book, on pages 299–309.

TABLE 1. Countries of the World, Arranged by Per Capita Gross Domestic Product at Factor Cost, 1958 Expressed in U.S. dollars

$100 or Less	$101–$300	$301–$600	$601–$1,000	$1,001–$2,000
Aden	Algeria	Argentina	Austria	Australia
Afghanistan	Barbados	Chile	Denmark	Belgium
Angola	Brazil	Colombia	Finland	Canada
Bhutan	British Borneo	Costa Rica	Germany, Fed-	France
Bolivia	(now Saba)	Cuba	eral Repub-	Luxembourg
Burma	Br. Guiana	Cyprus	lic of	New Zealand
Burundi	Cameroun	Greece	Iceland	Norway
Cambodia	Cent. Afr. Rep.	Guadeloupe	Netherlands	Sweden
Chad	Ceylon	Ireland	Venezuela	Switzerland
Congo	China (Taiwan)	Israel	West Berlin	United
(Leopold-	Congo	Italy		Kingdom
ville)	(Brazzaville)	Jamaica		
Dahomey	Dominican Rep.	Malta and Gozo		Over $2,000:
Ethiopia	Ecuador	Martinique		
Gambia	El Salvador	Panama		United States
Haiti	Fiji Islands	Puerto Rico		of America
India	Gabon	Singapore		
Indonesia	Ghana	South Africa		
Kenya	Guatemala	Spain		
Laos	Guinea	Trinidad		
Mozambique	Honduras	and Tobago		
Muscat and	Hong Kong	Uruguay		
Oman	Iran			
Nepal	Iraq			
New Guinea	Ivory Coast			
(Australia)	Japan			
Niger	Jordan			
Nigeria	Korea, Rep. of			
Pakistan	Lebanon			
Papua	Liberia			
Portuguese	Libya			
Guinea	Madagascar			
Portuguese	Malaysia			
Timor	Mali			
Rwanda	Mauritania			
Sierra Leone	Mauritius			
Somalia	Mexico			
Sudan	Morocco			
Tanganyika	Nicaragua			
Thailand	Paraguay			
Togo	Peru			
Uganda	Philippines			
Upper Volta	Portugal			
Vietnam,	Reunion			
Republic of	Rhodesia/			
Yemen	Nyasaland			
West Irian	Ryukyu Islands			
	Saudi Arabia			
	Senegal			
	Surinam			
	Syria			
	Tunisia			
	Turkey			
	UAR			
	Zanzibar, Pemba			

Source: Yearbook of National Accounts Statistics, 1962 (United Nations, 1963). Does not include per capita gross domestic product data for the centrally planned economies.

⇢ Race? It is true that a majority of countries settled chiefly by the white race are economically well developed. But many white countries are not well developed; and people of all races and colors have now distinguished themselves in the tasks necessary for development.

⇢ Newness? The Underdeveloped Lands do contain a high proportion of new nations, including many former colonies that have recently gained independence. But this is by no means true of the less-developed nations. For example, Ethiopia traces its history to the Queen of Sheba, and has been independent for centuries. And some of the less-developed countries were world leaders one to three thousand years ago.

There is only one distinction that is universally applicable: The more highly developed states have experienced the Industrial Revolution, or their version of it; the underdeveloped ones have not, or have experienced it in a limited way or only in limited sectors of their population. In many cases, the less-developed states have not been ready for an industrial revolution. The remarkable collection of ingredients that helped Europe through its own Industrial Revolution have not been present everywhere. In Western Europe, the way was prepared by the Renaissance, widespread political freedom, swift advancement in literacy and education, development of commerce and capital, fairly high percentages of entrepreneurs and innovators in the population, and ideas favorable to the effort that had to be made.[2] The Revolution was exported quickly to the transported Europeans in North America, and later to those in Australia and New Zealand. Still later, Japan, the Soviet Union, and Argentina passed through their own industrial revolutions. The fact that some of the late-comers have been able to make the climb faster than the 75 to 100 years it took to accomplish the task in the nineteenth century has greatly encouraged the states that are now looking up enviously at the economic mountains.

The presently underdeveloped nations were either furthest from the center of the Industrial Revolution when it was at its height in the nineteenth and early twentieth centuries or were in poor shape to make use of it. Now these nations are anxious to make up for lost time. We are looking at a dramatic chapter in the history of the world. Two-thirds of the world's people are preparing—or at least their leaders are trying to prepare them—to go through an industrial revolution. If they succeed, they are going to change the face of the earth.

But why *now*? Some people have always been poorer than others. Education has usually been a privilege of the rich. Health has always been better in some places than others. Privilege and social differences have written themselves over all the pages of history. Why, then, should these problems concern so many people *just now*?

One reason is that more people know about the problems. Vastly extended communication has made the situation clear. Roads have come to villages. Automobiles have taken people over the roads. Jet airplanes have connected nations and cities. Mass media have reached down from the cities to the villages. In many ways, therefore, the men and women in the villages have been able to compare their ways of living with those of the city people, and the underdeveloped states to compare their standard with that of the economically developed states. It is hardly possible any longer to take refuge in the comforting idea that "everyone else probably has the same problems we have." The gap between the have and the have-not peoples is too wide to ignore.

The *end of colonialism* and the emergence of so many new states have now given many of the less-privileged peoples a real chance to do something about their own economic situation. These new states are in a hurry—or at least their leaders are. They refuse to remain underprivileged. They want to share with the advanced countries the good things of life. But they see, perhaps even more clearly than do the more advanced countries, the breadth of the gap between the underdeveloped and the highly developed economies. Therefore, their concern is how to shorten the agonizingly long time usually required for economic development.

Seeking to speed up the process, the new states have usually sought help from the more highly developed ones. They have asked the older and more advanced states to share their experience and skills, and in many cases to invest capital or provide financial aid. The fact that they have usually received this aid reflects, of course, in large degree, the *competitiveness of great power blocs* in today's world. But it suggests also the revival, on a considerable scale, of a *world conscience.*

In part the world conscience has been stimulated by a revulsion against colonialism. Improved communications have helped bring this about, just as they have helped to inform the have-not peoples how the others live. Everywhere, there has been a remarkable flood of mass media coverage of the new countries. There has been a great increase in travel from the highly developed countries, and in the last 25 years the stationing of troops overseas, often in out-of-the-way places, has made it possible for otherwise untraveled young men to see how other people live. Educational systems in many advanced countries have shifted their emphasis from the past toward the present, and as a result are doing a better job of covering today's world.

In addition to these developments there has come to be a rather general feeling that the blessings of science should be shared. Science is a possession rather different from the treasures of the great powers in previous eras, and scientists are different from buccaneers and conquerors. Scientists themselves usually feel that their knowledge should be shared. Unlike land and gold, scientific knowledge *can* be shared without depleting the central treasury. All these factors together have resulted in what history will probably call an emergence of conscience on a broad scale and a point of view that would doubtless have been incomprehensible to some of the economic robber barons of the past—a genuine concern with the economic condition of the have-nots of the earth.

Still another reason for this concern is a growing sense of *interdependence* in the world. It isn't "one world," but it is more nearly one than ever before. Stability is now seen to depend on more than one or two nations. A few trouble spots may upset a far wider balance. There are no more great population movements, such as the one that peopled the Western Hemisphere, to take care of economic strain and provide economic opportunity; it is now clear that potential problems must be handled where they are. The United Nations has given the underdeveloped countries a new voice and importance in world affairs, and an opportunity to state their problems and to build up friendships and alliances. In the modern world no country is commercially self-sufficient; therefore, the flow of resources and products into and out of the less-developed lands is itself a significant factor in interdependence. For all these reasons, it has become next to impossible to sweep the economic problems of the poor countries under the rug. What happens to the new states of Africa, Asia, and the Middle East, and to the somewhat older but underdeveloped states of those continents and of Latin America, is now of the greatest concern to the powerful nations of the world, because of the delicate balance of relationships and the wide network of interdependence.

Beyond all these elements, however, there is a new sense of *capability* in the world—a sense that we have the tools and skills to do something about old scourges like poverty, ill health, illiteracy, and primitive living conditions. Partly this is the result of great accomplishments in biological, chemical, and physical sciences and their medical and engineering applications. It has become relatively easy now to eradicate many diseases and parasites that have been curses of the less-privileged societies. New sources of energy are available, and new ways to mechanize and extend human labor. In addition to the great growth of confidence in science, there is a new confidence in industrial skills and experience. Industry has moved beyond the stage where it was a gamble, and where only a few men could be successful with it. There are ways to organize production and distribution which are now well understood and widely tested, and this knowledge exists among many people in the industrialized countries. There is also a greater confidence than before in the ability of humans to change and improve society. This is born partly of the knowledge of economics gained, during recent years, by studies of many countries and systems; partly of the growing understanding of social psychology and social organizations; partly of growing skill in, and improved tools for, communicating effectively with large numbers of people. In other words, social engineering is no longer entirely a mystery or a suspect activity. If the problems in the less-privileged societies are gigantic, the tools, skills, and knowledge which can now be applied to those problems are also substantial. As a result, there is a general belief now that the job of widespread economic and social development can be done. It will be difficult, it will be expensive, but it is no longer impossible.

All these circumstances have contributed a sense of destiny to the thinking about national development. Need the destiny of man be war, poverty, disease, and ignorance? Are not the visions of world peace, well-being, health, education, and information—visions that were once found only in Utopian books—at last within the power of man to bring about? May it not be the destiny of generations now living to see these supposedly Utopian visions made real?

These are the reasons why most of the nations of the world are now deeply concerned over economic and social development.

THE HUMAN PROBLEM

When the leaders of the developing countries talk about what it means to be underdeveloped, and explain why their nations are working so hard to develop economically, they almost always couch the argument in human terms.* A difference of a hundred

---

* For example, Tom Mboya says: "Africa is one of the underdeveloped continents of the world. Socially, Africa is underdeveloped in the sense that its tribal components have not yet found a proven basis for collective action. . . . Furthermore, Africa is socially underdeveloped because there is almost no social and cultural traffic between English- and French-speaking Africa. The culture imposed on us sticks like burrs. . . . Economically, Africa is underdeveloped in the sense that mass poverty is universal. This poverty is not entirely due to poor natural resources, and hence it could definitely be lessened by methods already proved successful in other parts of the world. It is reflected in deficiencies like the shortage of schools, social services, hospitals, universities, and technical institutions. It is further reflected in the number of our women who die in childbirth, the universality of malnutrition, high incidence of various diseases, low wages, and in the contrast between the luxury and affluence of Europe and North America on the one hand, and the slum conditions and poverty prevailing in Africa on the other." (Council on World Tensions, *Restless Nations,* pp. 43–45.)

dollars in per capita national income, a difference in energy equivalent to one ton of coal, or a difference of 10 per cent in the number of adults able to read a newspaper or hear a newscast—these differences are reflected not only in productivity and balance sheets, but also in the lives of human beings.

"What these people have in common," said Forrest D. Murden, speaking of the Underdeveloped Lands, "are their problems and their history of misery. They are poor; they are diseased; they are hungry; they are badly housed; they can neither read nor write; they die young; they are increasing by more than a million a month."[3]

That is one side of the human problem of underdevelopment today. The Ifes and Bvanis illustrate it. They get 1,800 calories a day to eat; if they lived in northern Europe they would get 3,000. The Ifes are in a region where there is, on the average, one doctor for 35,000 people; in countries like Czechoslovakia and the Soviet Union, doctors are 60 times as plentiful in proportion to the population. The Ifes and Bvanis can expect their children to live about 35 years, on the average; if they were in an economically advanced country, they could expect a life span twice as long. Schooling, literacy, participation in public affairs—in all these respects and others also, the Ifes and Bvanis are at a disadvantage in comparison to the people of countries that are more advanced economically. This is what it means to be underdeveloped.

But this is only part of the human meaning of underdevelopment today. For change is in the air, and the Ifes and Bvanis of the world are being invited into modern life. It will not be easy for them to accept. They are ill-equipped as yet, by reason of illiteracy and ignorance, to take part in it. It may be that they would be happier not participating in the struggle of national development or marching in the parade of modern life, but this is unrealistic. There is no cave where the people of an underdeveloped country may hide from modern life. If they try to hide from it, they will have nothing to say about what form it takes, and it will seek them out in the form someone else has given it.

In an eloquent passage in *The Discovery of India,* Jawaharlal

Nehru admits the evils of certain kinds of industrialization and the attractiveness of some patterns out of the past, but still commits himself to "a qualitative changeover to something different and new." "We will change the static character of our living," he says, "and make it dynamic and vital, and our minds will become active and adventurous. New situations lead to new experiences."[4] This is the challenge which the present day offers to the people of the Underdeveloped Lands—to make of their static traditional society something "dynamic and vital . . . adventurous and new."

There is still another side to the human problem as it exists today in the Underdeveloped Lands, for the country has a problem broader than that of the Ifes and Bvanis. Each developing country needs desperately to mobilize its human resources. These *are* the Ifes and Bvanis. They know little beyond their villages, little of science, little of modern agriculture, little of their country's efforts at economic development, little of the responsibilities of nationhood. Despite their innate abilities, fine qualities, and leadership potential, they make a weak base on which to build a modern nation. Unless they change, they will have to watch technological growth from the sidelines; social change will happen to them, rather than their playing an active part in bringing it about; they will be a part of the relatively inert mass out of which the leaders of development in their country are trying to fashion something "dynamic and vital."

Countries in a hurry cannot afford the luxury of such an inert mass. They require the active and informed cooperation of their village people as well as their city people. Their human resources are indispensable. Therefore they are going to have to speed the flow of information, offer education where it has never been offered before, teach literacy and technical skills very widely. This is the only way they can rouse and prepare their populace to climb the economic mountains. And the only way they can do it and keep the timetable they have in mind is to make full use of modern communication. That is why we have written this book.

1. The Role of Information in National Development

No one who has seen modern communication brought to traditional villages will ever doubt its potency. Once in an isolated village in the Middle East I watched a radio receiver, the first any of the villagers had seen, put into operation in the head man's house. The receiver promptly demonstrated that knowledge is power. It became a source of status to its owner; he was the first to know the news, and controlled the access of others to it. For him and all others who heard, the noisy little receiver became a magic carpet to carry them beyond the horizons they had known. But the most impressive demonstration of the impact of that radio was the scene when a group of villagers—who had previously known higher government chiefly through the tax collector or a soldier—heard for the first time a spokesman of their leaders invite them to take part in governing their country. The surprise, the incredulity, the rather puzzled hope in their faces made an unforgettable picture.

 No one who has heard the happy shouts with which a cinema van is greeted in an African village is ever likely to forget the experience. Less quickly, less dramatically, the impact of communication is seen when a road is newly opened to a village. Strangers come in with goods to sell and ideas and news to exchange. Villagers travel to the nearest city and bring back new standards and customs.[1] And change begins.

There is little doubt that modern communication can be influential in a developing culture. To see how it contributes to economic and social development, we shall have to look briefly at the development process itself.

The basic dynamic

The essence of economic development is a rapid increase in the economic productivity of society. All theories of economic development agree on that, and we are going to concentrate on some of the common elements rather than on the differences among the several theories. Productivity is the key. The most productive sector of modern society is the industrial sector. Industry has built a great engine to produce more and more with fewer and fewer workers. Taking advantage of the increasing division of labor and the specializing of skills, industry has organized the separate acts of work into a cooperative and cumulative process, multiplied man's little strength by the great energy of water power or combustion or electricity or nuclear power, and extended man's limited power of attention and supervision by mechanizing—in our time, *automating* —as many tasks as possible. The same number of men, organized into industry, can produce an immensely greater amount of goods than they could make by hand.

Therefore, the attention of development economists has been on the problem of how to husband resources so as to invest in this most productive part of society. Capital must be invested to generate more capital. Unless some very rich natural resources can be drawn upon, or an extraordinary amount of help can be secured from richer countries, investment capital can hardly be accumulated without saving. Thus, the basic dynamic of economic development is: save and invest in productivity.

Some economists state this as the "iron law" of economic growth: Growth is a function of national investment, the productivity of the investment, and the population increase. Let us take an example. Suppose that a country is able to save and invest 7 per cent of its income, which is a fairly common figure for many developing countries. And suppose that the average productivity of the investment is 25 per cent, meaning that the investment will earn an additional

25 cents on the dollar. Then the stage is set for economic growth at the rate of 1.75 per cent per year (investment *times* productivity). But suppose that the population is also growing at the rate of 1.75 per cent per year (the world average of population increase is about that). Then the economic growth will merely keep pace with the population. If the population is growing faster than 1.75 per cent per year, the country will be relatively poorer for all its efforts at economic growth. If the rate of increase in population is *less* than 1.75 per cent, then the country will grow economically.

Suppose that a country can save and invest 20 per cent of its income and get an average productivity return of 30 per cent. Then it is set to grow at the rate of 6 per cent per year. If it can hold its population growth down to, say, 1.75 per cent per year, its national per capita income will increase about as fast as—for example—Brazil's income has been growing.

We have made the process seem simpler than it is. There are many subtleties in how to save and how to invest which we cannot consider here. Furthermore, as we shall see, investment in industry is necessarily related to investment and development in other sectors of society. But the basic questions are those we have suggested: How much can a country invest in the most productive parts of its society, and how far can it stay ahead of its rate of population growth?*

The other sectors

A developing country cannot afford to put all its investment income into industry, however, no matter how productive it is. The goal of planning is a balanced and related growth in all the sectors of society.†

---

* It is noteworthy that three-fourths of the underdeveloped countries are above the world average of population growth. About three out of five of all the new humans are born in Asia. This is the kind of galloping population growth Heilbroner was thinking of when he said (p. 69) that Asia, merely "to maintain her present low level of living standards, must increase her aggregate product by 60 per cent between now and 1975, and by an additional 75 per cent between 1975 and 2000."

† Colin Clark and Jean Fourastié, among others, have set the pattern for talking of developing societies in terms of three sectors: the *primary* sector, con-

TABLE 2. Proportion of the Population Engaged in Agricultural Occupations, in Countries at Different Stages of Economic Development

Per Capita National Income $300 or less	Per Capita National Income $301 to $600	Per Capita National Income over $600
%	%	%
Brazil 58 (1950)	Argentina .. 25 (1947)	U.K. 5 (1951)
Mexico 58 (1958)	Italy 28 (1961)	Belgium ... 12 (1947)
UAR 64 (1947)	Hungary .. 38 (1960)	United States 12 (1950)
Pakistan ... 65 (1954/		Canada ... 12 (1961)
56)		Germany,
India 71 (1951)		Federal
Turkey 77 (1955)		Republic. 14 (1960)
Thailand .. 82 (1960)		Sweden ... 17 (1960)
		Netherlands 19 (1947)
		France 26 (1957)

Source: Food and Agriculture Organization of the United Nations, *Production Yearbook 1962* (Rome, 1963).

Thus, for example, agriculture (the primary sector) must be modernized so that fewer cultivators can grow more food and some of the agricultural population can be released to work in industry (the secondary sector). In many highly developed countries, be-tween 10 and 20 per cent of the labor force can feed the rest of the population; an underdeveloped country, on the other hand, may have 90 per cent of its workers on the farm and still be unable to feed its population adequately (see Table 2). The plain truth is that agriculture in many less-developed countries is not very pro-ductive, as Table 3 demonstrates. Behind its lack of productivity are ancient methods of farming, scarcity of fertilizers and pesti-cides, a lack of agricultural machinery, a high proportion of subsis-tence farming, and attitudes unfavorable to change. Yet a develop-ing country has a great deal to gain by modernizing its agriculture,

---

cerned with the production of raw foodstuffs and other raw materials from the soil; the *secondary* sector, concerned with the transformation of raw materials by industry; and the *tertiary* sector, concerned with the relatively nonmaterial tasks of economic life. Clark has specified these sectors in great detail; Fouras-tié, on the other hand, conceives of them as somewhat fluid groupings of ac-tivities. See Colin Clark; and Fourastié, *Le Grand espoir du XX siècle* and *La Productivité*.

TABLE 3. Rice Yield per Hectare for Different Countries in 1961/62
(*Yields in 100 kilograms*)

Country	Yield	Country	Yield
Australia	66.3	Indonesia	18.4
Italy	54.6	Burma	16.8
Japan	47.0	India	15.1
France	40.6	Guatemala	14.0
United States	38.2	Thailand	13.9
Argentina	34.4	Nigeria	12.6
China (Taiwan)	32.1	Iraq	10.7
Rumania	29.2	Cambodia	10.5
Mexico	25.6	Sierra Leone	9.3
Malaysia	23.8		

Source: Food and Agriculture Organization of the United Nations, *Production Yearbook 1962* (Rome, 1963).

and thereby raising its productivity. Not only will this release workers for industry; it will also contribute to the general health and vigor of the country. In many countries where foods, fruits, or fibers are chief exports,[2] it will contribute to investment capital.[3]

To support both agriculture and industry, a country must build up the part of its society that some economists call "social overhead," which includes basic transport, irrigation power facilities, and communications. Table 4 illustrates how closely the consumption of energy (part of the social overhead) is related to the stage of development. Behind all these developments there must be a

TABLE 4. Commercial Consumption of Energy by Countries at
Different Stages of Economic Development
(*In megawatt hours per capita*)

Per Capita National Income $300 or less		Per Capita National Income $301 to $600		Per Capita National Income over $600	
Thailand	0.3	Argentina	7.1	Netherlands	17.8
Pakistan	0.6	Italy	8.4	France	19.5
India	1.0	Hungary	11.0	West Germany	26.8
Turkey	1.8			Belgium	32.8
Egypt	2.1			Sweden	33.2
Brazil	2.9			United Kingdom	39.8
Mexico	5.7			United States	66.0

Source: N. Ginsburg, ed., *Atlas of Economic Development* (Chicago: University of Chicago Press, 1961, p. 80).

mobilization of human resources. Education, the chief activity in mobilizing human resources, is sometimes considered a part of the tertiary sector, sometimes considered by itself as a part of the task of human mobilization, which obviously cuts across all the sectors of society. The sector location matters little. What does matter is that education, literacy training, mechanical skill training, health improvement, adequate living facilities, all must be a part of the development plan if a country is to use its human resources at their full strength. Table 5 illustrates, by means of literacy, the close relationship of human resources development to economic development.

TABLE 5. Adult Literacy: Distribution of Countries in Two Major Groups According to Degree of Adult Literacy

	Number of Countries	Literacy			
		0–25%	26–50%	51–75%	76–100%
Three largely underdeveloped regions—Asia, Africa, and Latin America—with two-thirds of the world's people	104	56%	20%	15%	9%
Four largely developed regions—North America, Europe, USSR, and Australia and New Zealand	33	0	0	15	85

Source: Calculated from figures in *Illiteracy at Mid-Century* (Paris: Unesco, 1957).

The point we are making is that agriculture, social overhead, and human resources have to be developed to a certain level before any country is ready to make the "big push" through industry.[4] It is not necessary to decide which is the prime mover—whether, for example, the modernizing of agriculture affects industrial development, or industrial development affects the development of agriculture. Undoubtedly each affects the other. The same kind of interaction exists between industry and social overhead and the development of human resources. The point is that they must go forward together.

A development plan is therefore usually a compromise between essential needs in different sectors. Nigeria, for example, which is in a relatively early stage of development, is presently putting about equal investments into agriculture and industry—about 14 per cent of the total planned investment each. She has planned very heavy investment in social overhead: 21 per cent of the plan investment in transportation and 15 per cent in electricity, among others. Considerable investments are also being made in the tertiary, including 10 per cent in education, 3 per cent in health, and 6 per cent in town and country planning. Altogether the present plan calls for investing 15 per cent of income, 8 per cent of which is expected to come from savings and the rest from foreign aid or outside investment.[5]

As the Nigeria plan suggests, development must go forward on a broad front. The process of development is really a broad transformation of society. It is not sufficient merely to build factories and turn out machine tools, for industry cannot get far ahead of its support. On these supporting developments—the radical change in agriculture, the creation of social overhead, the mobilizing and upgrading of human resources, and the like—it is worth noting here that they are all slow developments. They cannot be accomplished quickly. This is not only because they are expensive and difficult, but also because they require a large degree of human change.

It takes a long time to modernize traditional agriculture, not so much because the task is expensive as because it requires teaching new skills and new attitudes, and persuading cultivators to give up ancient practices and strongly held beliefs. Providing modern transportation, communications, power, and other social overhead takes a long time because it is very costly and requires a number of highly skilled workers and managers, who are in short supply and must be trained. Education is slow not only because it is costly to train and pay teachers and build schools, but also because education is by nature a slow process. As a French word for education, *formation,* suggests, education aims at the formation of a new person, with new horizons, new skills, new goals. It does indeed take a long time. All the kinds of human change required for economic development take long, and are costly and difficult. And yet, as Millikan and Blackmer argue so persuasively, "the paramount requirement of change in any society is that the people themselves must change."[6]

As we see it, this is the point where modern communication becomes so important to economic development. For the task of the mass media of information and the "new media" of education is to speed and ease the long, slow social transformation required for economic development, and, in particular, to speed and smooth the task of mobilizing human resources behind the national effort.

MOBILIZING HUMAN RESOURCES

In one sense, many developing countries have already mobilized their human resources. They are using these resources to move heavy loads, to break the soil, or to do other tasks which, in more advanced economies, would be done by machine. A horde of men scraping a new airfield or cutting a new road with hand tools, long lines of women carrying baskets of dirt or stones on their heads—the scene is commonplace in many parts of the world. In populous countries where machines are scarce, muscle power is the cheapest and most readily available form of energy. But it is at best only a stopgap—mobilization for the needs of yesterday, not for those of tomorrow. It is not the kind of mobilization that is required to climb the economic mountains. When machines come in, as they inevitably will, they will take over from muscle power. It is for this new age, when humans will operate machines rather than do the work of machines, that developing countries must prepare their manpower.

Frederick Harbison recently studied the manpower problems of 75 countries, and summed up this way:

The progress of a nation depends first and foremost on the progress of its people. Unless it develops their spirit and human potentialities, it cannot develop much else—materially, economically, politically, or culturally. The basic problem of most of the underdeveloped countries is not a poverty of natural resources but the underdevelopment of their human resources. Hence their first task must be to build up their human capital. To put it in more human terms, that means improving the education, skills, and hopefulness, and thus the mental and physical health, of their men, women, and children.[7]

Education, skills, and hopefulness: in other words, what they know, what they can do, and the attitudes they hold toward national development in general—these are respects in which the people must change before the nation can change.

Take, for example, a country like Malawi (Nyasaland), which is no better or worse off than certain other new nations. It has three million people. As recently as 1960, fewer than 800 Nyasas had completed secondary school, and only a small percentage of these had been to a university or college. Even though Malawi has its own government and legislature, this meant that nine out of ten high-level jobs in government had to be filled by foreigners, as did most of the jobs in private industry that require the equivalent of a secondary education. In the entire country there were only a half-dozen or so African doctors, one lawyer, one engineer, and no scientists. There was not one native man or woman trained to be a secretary.[8] Obviously, Malawi and countries like her must invest heavily in upgrading their human resources before they can build a technical and industrial economy.

The United Arab Republic has a quite different problem of human resources. It has actually more highly trained people of certain kinds than it can use. It has so many college graduates that the government cannot find suitable jobs for them at home, and encourages them to teach and work in countries where college graduates are scarcer. The UAR has more students in universities, in proportion to its population, than has the United Kingdom, and twice as many, proportionally, as the Federal Republic of Germany. On the other hand, the proportion of children in elementary and secondary education is rather low. Literacy is low. And despite the surfeit of college graduates there is a severe shortage of technicians and management personnel.[9] India is in a similar position. Her colleges are bulging with students, a very large number of whom are studying humanities or law (but very few of whom ever intend to practice law). On the other hand, the country is short of technicians and skilled labor, and its overall literacy is only about 25 per cent. The UAR and India represent the countries that will probably have to reorient and redirect some of their educational and training programs.

An enormous amount of skills training and education must go on, in any new nation that yearns to go upward. This runs the gamut from literacy training to the production of research scientists. It includes skills as diverse as scientific farming, machine tool operation, repair of radios and motor vehicles, construction, accountancy, secretarial work, plant and office management, nursing, medicine and public health, engineering, marketing, and journalism. Supporting these there must be a broad base in education: a substantial proportion of the population able to read and write and figure, and take an active part in government.

Philip Coombs calls education in a developing country "an important investment industry."[10] There is no longer much doubt among economists as to the need to upgrade the labor force in a developing country and, in order to do so, to invest substantial amounts in education. Without getting ahead of our story, we can point out that mass communication has a role in this aspect of development. What can it do to speed the process and make the investment go further? For example, where can it substitute for the teacher not yet trained, or support the teacher not well enough trained? Where can it share the best teaching over vastly wider areas than one teacher could ordinarily cover? Where can it extend the opportunity to learn, beyond the school, to the home and community?

The kind of training that must go into a developing country is different from that in an economically advanced country, for one thing because it involves the creation of new work roles. One example is the role of management. Less-developed countries have typically been accustomed to individual work—the individual cultivator, the craftsman, the home industry. The coming of industry and large-scale construction brings in the problem of complex working groups, using a variety of tools and machines. These require skilled management. Management in a developing country is to some extent different from management in a well-developed country because it is conducted always against the backdrop of rapid change. Someone has described it as akin to riding a galloping horse that grows to elephant size as it runs. The changing pieces of industrial life must be fitted together as they grow. In a developing country the elements of industrialization are not produced seriatim. One is not able to build factories, then train the labor force, then build desirable attitudes in the workers, then buy machine tools and build houses. These activities, and many other related ones, are all going on at the same time. One of the problems of management is therefore to fit them together as efficiently as possible. Raw materials, machines, and workers must be ready when, but not too long before, the factories are ready. People must learn to read and go through school, but only when there is going to be opportunity to make productive use of their new skills. Transportation plans must mesh with industrial plans, and both with plans for developing natural resources. Saving and long-term investment must be encouraged, but reward, as least a partial reward, must not be withheld too long. These and other delicate relationships are the problems of management. The more skilled the management at every level from national planner to foreman, the more efficiently the pieces will mesh, and the more satisfied the participants will be. It is hardly necessary to point out that efficiency in these management roles requires efficient two-way communication; the more complex the task, the more complex the communication must be.

Management in a program of national development is different from some other kinds of management also, because the essential part of it consists of managing *innovation*. The developer is constantly trying to make a change. He is dealing with people whom he wants to do something *for the first time*. He is dealing with workers who are unfamiliar with the job; he wants some farmers to change their basic practices and others to leave the farm; he is dealing with people who rely on folk wisdom when he wants them to learn to solve problems; he is dealing with a country that is used to living in the past and present, although its policy is to live in the future. Innovation, therefore, calls for a number of "middleman" roles: persons who can perform in both traditional and modern cultures, persons who can transmit modern culture and technology to people who have grown up in traditional values and beliefs, propagandists and agitators for national development, and the like.[11] Needless to say, people who are skillful in these roles are not plentiful in many developing countries.

In mobilizing human resources for national development, skill training and attitude change usually go side by side. An example of this is the improvement of public health. An industry where half the workers may be absent on a given day because of malaria, or where the vigor and attentiveness of workers is often reduced by intestinal parasites, is not likely to be highly productive. It is much less profitable to train a skilled worker in a country where the average life span is 35 years than in one where it is 65. In one case, the cost of training will buy perhaps 15 years of service; in the other case, 40. To improve the health and vigor and extend the life span of the population requires not only the provision of medical and pharmaceutical services, but also the teaching of new health habits, which in turn require in many cases the adoption of new attitudes. For example, recall the fairly widespread religious or philosophical objection of people in traditional cultures to the killing of living things. This prohibition applies sometimes to specific animals, sometimes to all animals, sometimes even to insects and parasites that are dangerous to health or that stand in the way of improved farming and of better living in general.

Therefore the mobilizing of human resources requires a great deal of attention to what the population knows and thinks of national development, and especially to the encouragement of attitudes and social customs, and the provision of knowledge, which will be favorable to development.

Consider the problem of national saving, which, as we have said, is essential to the accumulation of investment capital. In many of these countries, as Maurice Zinkin has said, "thrift is not a virtue, but a vice, fit only for a merchant."[12] Traditional social patterns and structures are not capital-creating. The agricultural villager tends to live at a subsistence level rather than in a money economy. He prefers to bring up a large family for "old-age insurance," and to use his money, when he has any, for a daughter's wedding or a feast or some other reward more immediate than bank accounts or insurance policies.

As a matter of fact, the attitudes in most traditional cultures tend to be hostile to change and lacking in economic motivation. Kusum Nair concluded after her study of the village people of India:

In these circumstances introduction of new techniques from outside will help only to a limited extent. Unless the desire for change and for appreciably higher living standards takes root in the peasant communities, these techniques will often not be accepted or exploited fully—as has been the case with the Japanese method of paddy cultivation, for example. This technique was introduced in the paddy growing areas about a decade ago. But rarely has it been adopted in its entirety anywhere.[13]

And John Condliff says in the same vein:

The revolution of rising expectations [will need] a good deal of translation into economic motivation before it can become an effective force for economic development. . . . Motivation implies a change in values. Until the average man and woman in the developing countries wants education for his children enough to make the sacrifices . . . it is not likely that there will be much development. Education and abundance must be desired enough to sacrifice leisure and such customs as expensive marriage celebrations. Foresight and planning must become personal.[14]

The fear and distrust of innovation in traditional communities was illustrated by what happened to the Bvanis' neighbor who was first in the village to try out a new way of farming. In part this attitude is grounded in fatalism—the belief that man cannot make any change in his destiny or master his environment, and the related idea that suffering and resignation are to be sought rather than struggled against. In part it is grounded in the low margin available for experiment: one unsuccessful innovation in a family that is barely able to raise enough food by present methods may mean starvation. Therefore, the tendency is to stick to the methods proved by centuries of use, inefficient and unproductive though they are. These things help to explain why so few innovators come to the fore in traditional societies, and why new ideas and behaviors often get an unfavorable reception.

Interwoven with such counterproductive attitudes are counterproductive customs and social patterns, among them the widespread custom of going deeply into debt for wedding dowries, festivals, and funerals, and the observance of an excessive number of holidays, which are hardly consistent with the national determination to progress economically. Another example is the caste system, which greatly restricts the kinds of work a man can do and the extent to which he can associate and cooperate with other men. India has moved against this system both on moral and on economic grounds. In many countries that do not have an elaborate caste system, however, there is a general distaste for manual labor. Far from believing in "the dignity of labor," the people of these countries tend to consider hard work degrading, undesirable, something to be avoided. In particular, educated and high-status people tend to feel that any kind of manual labor is beneath them.

Mobilizing human resources requires the substitution, wherever possible, of productive attitudes and behaviors for unproductive ones such as we have been mentioning. By productive attitudes we mean those favorable to cooperation, especially to cooperation in a long-term national effort; social patterns that make cooperation and mobility easy; attitudes favorable to innovation, to work, to good health practices, to saving, and to the achievement of delayed rather than immediate rewards.

Perhaps the most stimulating treatment of attitudes supportive of national development is David McClelland's *The Achieving Society*.[15] This reports a series of studies on an attitude constellation which McClelland calls "need achievement." People who rate high on "n-ach" are likely to be ambitious, hard-working, upwardly mobile; they tend to value innovation, to be willing to take risks, to assume responsibility. Unlike the merchants in underdeveloped countries who insist on a fast deal, they are people who are willing to postpone the reward in order to earn a larger reward at a later time. These values are obviously related to economic development. McClelland tests them in a series of historical case studies, and in current surveys. He finds evidence that such attitudes existed in many of the fast-developing cultures, and were related closely to industrial development in our own time.

But how does one implant need-achievement values in a population? McClelland believes that they are learned most often in a child's early years and arise out of a family situation of low father dominance and high achievement standards. He also points out that these are typically middle-class attitudes in Europe and North

America, and that they are much like the set of attitudes which Max Weber called the Protestant Ethic.[16] It is clear that they were developed in a number of cultures in fairly recent times, and if they were developed once, there is good reason to think they can be developed again.

So here are additional tasks for information within the overall task of mobilizing human resources. People must be given the knowledge they need in order to decide on such basic questions of belief and behavior as we have mentioned. There must be adequate channels for leadership and an opportunity to bring the debate, if any, out into the open. There must be information designed to encourage productive attitudes, social patterns, and customs. This raises a question of ethics and responsibility.

A QUESTION OF ETHICS AND RESPONSIBILITY

Let us recall the Bvanis and Ifes. We can see many ways in which social change could operate to meet their aspirations more fully, make better use of their talents and potentialities, improve their health, widen their horizons of knowledge, and in general make them more effective and—we hope—happier citizens. At the same time we can see that their social systems have built into them such resistance that change is likely to come hard and to be somewhat painful.

Therefore, we must ask a basic question. What are the ethics of the kind of action we are talking about in this book? What are the ethics of using what we know about modern communication to assist social and economic change, even though we are aware that some people in any country will resist some of the changes that are desirable? What are the ethics of using modern communication to do the tasks we have just been talking about—encouraging "productive" attitudes even though counterproductive ones may be strongly held, encouraging different kinds of farming even though farmers distrust innovation, encouraging better health habits in the face of fatalism and unwillingness to kill living things, encouraging people to work hard and save when they don't seem to wish to?

Let us put the question in the ugliest way: Are we advocating that mass communication should be used in the developing countries to *manipulate* people? To readers in some countries, this may seem a "straw man," unnecessary to demolish. We hope these readers will bear with us while we make clear, for other readers, how we stand on the question.

In the first place, change is inevitable. The developing countries have decided for change. They have decided that for the good of their people and the destiny of their nations they must modernize their society. These decisions have been made by responsible leadership in each of the countries. The leaders in most cases have sought aid and advice from international organizations and more experienced nations. Change is coming to those developing countries, and the questions are not whether, but how fast, by what methods, and in precisely what directions.

It is very hard to argue against change based on assumptions that, other things being equal,

—knowledge is better than ignorance;

—health is better than disease;

—to eat is better than to be hungry;

—a comfortable standard of living is better than poverty;

—to participate actively in one's nation is better than to be isolated from it.

One could continue with a long list of such statements that constitute the social basis of national development. And, as we have said, it would be difficult to find many people, in highly developed countries at least, willing to argue against such principles.

But these decisions, it seems to us, are clearly for the people of the developing countries to make. Even on such matters as health, food, comfort, and knowledge, a developing nation must decide what *it* wants to do: how fast, how far it wants to go, and whether it wants to do some things at all. Our belief is, however, that without adequate information such a decision is bound to be not a national decision at all, based neither on popular will nor on sound evidence.

Choices are possible, of course, only within certain boundaries. Once a nation opts for modernizing its society and developing economically and socially, then certain choices cannot be avoided. For example, a developing country, as Staley remarks, cannot choose "fine highways and public buildings and a cradle-to-the-grave social security system" without choosing also measures that lead to greater productivity.[17] It cannot choose to import the mechanical side of modern civilization while retaining old social institutions that are inconsistent with industry. But within such limits it is still possible for the people to decide how their own lives shall be redirected, what form the necessary social changes shall take, when and how fast they should proceed. However, they need to know *what* choices are possible, *what* limits are upon choice, and what *opportunities* lie beyond a given choice, if they are to make any use of *local* choice whatsoever.

There is an essential difference between the act of "manipulating" people and the carrying of facts, discussion, persuasion, and argument, which are parts of the process by which consensus is attained in any free society. Obviously, communication can be used to some extent for manipulation, if the owners of the channels choose to use them for that purpose. But just as obviously, the greater and freer the flow of information, the less likely it is that manipulative communication will have any effect. The basic social effect of free information is to liberate rather than to manipulate man. It is to free him from ignorance and from one-sided manipulation. This is what the United Nations Commission on Human Rights meant when it called information one of the basic rights. The process of national development illustrates it admirably. An adequate flow of information is required for knowledge to be shared between those who have more of it and those who have less on any given subject. An adequate flow of information is needed if the ordinary people of a country, the Ifes and the Bvanis, are to be brought into the decision process.

An adequate flow of information in a developing country is necessarily more than a flow from the top of the political hierarchy to the Ifes and Bvanis at the bottom. It must carry the Ifes and Bvanis the information they need to play their parts in a modern society. This is true. But it must also provide channels by which these people may discuss with their fellow villagers and with other villages what policies and practices they shall adopt; and it must provide channels by which the needs and wishes of the villagers may be carried up the hierarchy to form a part of higher-level decisions. Thus, far from suggesting that we "manipulate" the Bvanis and Ifes of the developing countries, we are suggesting that they be brought actively into the decision making and given an opportunity to participate fully and effectively in the process of modernizing their society, building their nation, and improving the lot of their people.

All social change is accompanied by tension. But when change is accomplished, tension is often relieved. This is the observation that Rao made in his study of two Indian villages, of which one had begun to modernize and the other was on the verge of doing so.[18] The village in which change was imminent was full of tension and frustration; the other was quieter, busier, more satisfied, more purposeful. Furthermore, swift change is often less painful than slow and gradual change. Margaret Mead, after a restudy of Manus 25 years later, advanced the hypothesis that if change is generally desired, if it cuts across an entire culture and includes all aspects of the culture, then there may be "less social disorganization and individual maladjustment than if changes occur piecemeal over a long period."[19]

The flow of information is of the greatest importance in regulating the level of social tension. Communication is a kind of temperature-controlling agent. It can raise the social temperature, for example, by raising aspirations when the developing economy is not ready to satisfy them. It can reduce temperature by providing explanation, holding out rewards, speeding up development, by permitting change, in Dr. Mead's words, to "cut across an entire culture," above all by making the people as well as the leaders heard.

To be sure, an effective communication system can be used to "manipulate" people if the system is under the control of people who wish to use it that way. It can also—and should—be used for a quite different purpose: to bring the people of the developing countries into the decisions of development, to give them a basis for participating effectively, to speed and smooth the changes decided upon. The point is that national development is people changing themselves. It is not entirely an impersonal, inflexible process. If the flow of communication will permit, the people can have a great deal to do with setting goals and deciding when and how they should change and what they want their society to change into. For, as Keynes said in his famous toast to the Royal Economic Society in 1945, economists "are the trustees not of civilization, but of the *possibility* of civilization."

WHAT INFORMATION DOES

When human society was primitive tribes huddling in caves against the cold and the ever-present dangers, even that society had certain essential information needs in addition to the sort of everyday information exchanged in courtship, family life, children's play, or casual conversation. The tribe had to post a watchman to scan the horizon and report on dangers and opportunities, for instance to bring word when a hostile tribe came into view or when a herd of animals was seen within hunting distance. When information like this came back to the tribe, there had to be some arrangement for deciding what to do. A leader, or a council of leaders, would have to make a decision (often after debate or discussion), explain the situation, issue orders, and allocate responsibilities. Not all tribal policy was decided by a council in response to an unexpected emergency, of course; much of it was determined by a code of beliefs, customs, and laws, many of them older than the oldest living man in the tribe. A highly important task, therefore, was to teach these beliefs, customs, and laws, and the necessary skills of tribal life, to new and young members of the group. The parents taught the children, and the priest and the elders taught the younger members. These three information roles, then, were clearly to be seen in early society: the *watchman* role (to scan the horizon and report back); the *policy* role (to decide policy, to lead, to legislate); and the *teacher* role (to "socialize" the new members, by which we mean to bring them into the society with the skills and beliefs valued by the society). Underlying these relatively formal functions, as we have said, was a layer of everyday communication without which the tribe could never exist—the expressions of friendship and love, the challenges, arguments, and discussions; the bartering and trading; the dancing, singing, storytelling, and other informal communication that gave color and cohesiveness to the society.

Now, what happens to these information functions when society grows large and complex and achieves what we call "civilization"? The same essential functions still remain. The exchange of information has become less simple: some activities that were informal and casual have been formalized; some things that were once done by individuals now require social institutions; machines have been inserted into the communication process to see, listen, speak, and write for man, and around these machines some of the largest of the information institutions have grown up—the mass media. But the same information functions continue to be the basic ones. The job of watching the horizon is now largely assigned to the mass media of news, with all their reporters, news agencies, telecommunications, printing, and broadcasting facilities. The job of arriving at social consensus, establishing policy, and directing action has been given mainly to government, but such organizations as political parties and the mass media enter powerfully into the process of shaping public opinion and action. What used to be done by a few men in a brief conversation now may take months of discussion, involve millions of people, and perhaps require nation-wide campaigns; but the task is still what it was in tribal days —to decide on policy and to lead. The task of socializing new members of society now has, in considerable part, been turned over to the schools and to such teaching media as textbooks, educational radio and television, instructional films, and encyclopedias. The need for knowledge and training is no longer restricted to childhood. Institutions of adult education and specialized instruction (such as agricultural extension) have had to be created. More complex, more sophisticated, perhaps—but still society requires the same information services.

Underneath these services, the underlying stratum of social communication is basically as it was in tribal days, although here, too, some parts of communication have grown large and complex and formal. Men and women still greet their friends in the street, but it has also become common to greet a distant friend by letter, telegraph, or telephone, and for a national leader to send greetings by broadcast to a whole population. Men still make deals and trade things, but around the old system of barter has grown up a vast complex of communication for buying, selling, and borrowing, for advertising, and for carrying price reports. Similarly, much of the responsibility for public entertainment, which used to call forth the folk song, the ballad, the legend, and the tribal dance, has been handed over to the mass media and to other formalized devices such as the theater, the circus, and large-audience athletics.

In the centuries between the tribal culture and modern civilization, therefore, the information functions have not changed, but, rather, devices and structures have been developed to enlarge and extend those functions. Writing was developed so that society's fund of knowledge did not have to depend on personal contacts or old men's memories. The art of printing was developed so that a machine could duplicate man's writing more cheaply and more swiftly than man himself could do it. Around this machine grew up all the institutions of printing and publishing, and public schools. Later, machines were developed so that what man could see would not be limited so radically by space or time. First came the camera, films, and projector; then photo-engraving; then film studios, distribution, and theaters. Machines were created to let man hear and be heard at great distances, and around them developed the enterprises of telephone, sound recording, and radio. When the hearing machines were combined with the seeing machines, we had the basis for sound films and television. In other words, between the day of the tribe and the time of modern civilization, society has found out how to share and store information so as to surmount much of space and much of time, to keep history from being lost, and to enlarge an effective society from a few dozen to many millions of people.

It is no more possible to think of modern civilized society existing with the type of information exchange a primitive tribe used than to think of a primitive tribe existing with the kind modern society uses. Every stage of society has its appropriate stage of communication. The tribe taught its young at the parent's knee, but this was no longer sufficient when the lessons were long and complex and the students were many. Feudal society could exist without printing from movable metal type, but when a large proportion of society became interested in government, then they needed—and got—print to read and schools to teach them to read it. Or, to put it another way, until large numbers of men could read, and had suitable material to read, there was little likelihood of very wide participation in government. Whether information creates some of the other structures and forms of society, or the other structures and forms of society create a certain stage of communication development, is a futile argument. Undoubtedly there is a powerful interaction: new developments in communication affect society, and new developments elsewhere in society affect communication. The important thing is that a certain level and stage of communication development have to accompany a certain stage and level of social development generally. Without a sophisticated and efficient development of communication, the base of population, cooperation, industrialization, education, and skills needed in modern industrial society cannot possibly be established. It goes without saying that underdeveloped countries have underdeveloped communication systems too.

Information in a developing nation

A new nation, at the time it decides for development, begins with a communication system which is somewhere between that of the tribe and that of modern civilization. Most typically, its villages are drowsing in their traditional patterns of life, its cities are beginning to thrum and echo with mass media and jet planes. But the new nation has a need that neither the tribe nor modern civilization has—the urgent requirement to change, swiftly, broadly, but as painlessly as possible. And it can draw on resources that the tribe never could imagine—modern communication techniques, already in use in many parts of the world.*

As national development gets under way, it is not the functions of communication that change, but rather the *amounts* of communication. For example:

The watchman function. When development begins, the watchman is asked to survey a wider landscape. The elite in the cities and the farmers in the traditional village suddenly find themselves very much interested in each other. The city realizes that the village and its work must be modernized before the base of national industry can be greatly enlarged. The villagers realize that the city has certain things they want. Similarly, the village and the national government, previously connected chiefly by the tax collector, discover each other in a new light. Where even the name of the national leader may have been unknown, villagers begin to edge into politics, and to ask for help in modernizing. Where the tax collector had gone, now the government sends extension teachers and technical specialists. Fifteen years ago, most of the new nations were not greatly concerned with foreign relations, except perhaps with the colonial power, if any. Now they find it necessary to be active on the stage of world politics, and also to seek out the knowledge and help of countries that are technically more advanced. In other words, the horizon widens, and the developing country needs an enormously greater amount of information from the horizon.

The policy function. A developing country finds that it must spread its essential decision making more widely. For one thing, it wants the active participation of its people. Beyond that, it is asking its people to make individual decisions that are of the greatest difficulty and importance. In effect, they are being asked to decide for modernity, and to change their lives and beliefs

---

* If it seems an extraordinary act of fortune that such resources should be available just when such a need becomes apparent, let us remind ourselves that if modern communication were not available, perhaps the sense of need would be less urgent. The urge to develop economically and socially usually comes from seeing how the well-developed countries or the more fortunate people live. With fast transportation and mass media to bridge the gap between village and city, rich country and poor country, it is now impossible for one culture *not* to know how the others live.

accordingly. They are being asked to accept new goals, new attitudes, new customs, new responsibilities. This will require both information and persuasion. Furthermore, the information must flow and the changes must be discussed, not only through a downward channel from the leaders to the villagers, but also *upward* to the leaders, and *laterally* so that people can talk things over and arrive at group decisions. More people need to talk to one another. Local needs and local voices have more need to be heard. In other words, the base of important policy making has to be broadened.

The teaching function. When development is going well, almost everybody in a country is learning.[20] Almost every developing country is trying to accomplish a rapid increase in the school population, the education and extension services, and the information media. Every sector of society has new skills to learn—agricultural, mechanical and electronic, health, literacy. The country uses information to raise the thirst for more information: to encourage people to seek advice from a village worker or a technical specialist, to encourage them to send their children to school or to learn to read. In most developing countries, literacy training is a major battleground. It is sometimes hard to understand what a difference literacy makes in the pace and drive of development. The man who learns to read acquires far more than the ability to use the printed media. For him, as Daniel Lerner says in an eloquent passage, literacy becomes "a prime mover in the modernization of every aspect of life . . . the basic personal skill that underlies the whole modernizing sequence."[21] He acquires a bridge to a wider world. Illiterate respondents in the Columbia survey of Middle Eastern development said of their literate compatriots: "They live in another world."[22] And this is essentially the teaching function of national communication when a country begins to develop—to open to all the people the door to the wider world of modern technical knowledge and public affairs.

Perhaps the most general way to describe what the enormously increased flow of information does in a developing nation is to say that it provides a *climate* for national development. It makes the expert knowledge available where it is needed, and provides a forum for discussion, leadership, and decision making. It helps to raise the general level of aspiration. The process of modernization begins when something "stimulates the peasant to want to be a freeholding farmer, the farmer's son to want to learn reading so he can work in the town, the farmer's wife to stop bearing children, the farmer's daughter to want to wear a dress and do her hair."[23] Change will not take place smoothly or very efficiently unless people want to change. It is generally the increasing flow of information that plants the seed of change. It is also the widened background of information that furnishes the climate for "nation-ness" itself. By making one part of a country aware of other parts, their people, arts, customs, and politics; by permitting the national leaders to talk to the people, and the people to the leaders and to each other; by making possible a nation-wide dialogue on national policy; by keeping the *national* goals and the *national* accomplishments always before the public—thus modern communication, wisely used, can help to weld together isolated communities, disparate subcultures, self-centered individuals and groups, and separate developments into a truly *national* development.

A FEW CASE STUDIES

It may be interesting now to look at a few case studies of information at work in national economic and social development. Unfortunately there are only a few major studies of this kind. This is partly because of the prevailing economic determinism of developmental studies, and partly because information has simply been taken for granted. Communication is fundamental to all social process; it is really *society interacting*. Therefore, information is typically treated as part of something else—part of commerce, for example, or part of education, or part of politics. Only recently has the notion become widespread that the informational aspects of national development will themselves repay study, and in the next few years we can expect some of the careful case studies that we need so badly.[24]

A Middle East case

Of the existing case studies, the best known is Daniel Lerner's *The Passing of Traditional Society: Modernizing the Middle East.*[25]

In 1950 and 1951, the Bureau of Applied Social Research of Columbia University conducted a total of 1,600 long interviews with individuals in six Middle Eastern countries: Iran, Egypt, Turkey, Syria, Lebanon, and Jordan. The interviews were designed to find out as much as possible about the exposure of each person to the communication media, and about many of his attitudes, particularly those related to the political and social development of his country. Dr. Lerner was one of the members of the Bureau who supervised the field work in the Middle East. In 1954, after he had left Columbia, he was invited to reanalyze the data from the interviews and to prepare a book on the entire study. He revisited the Middle East, talked with many of the interviewers and some of the persons who had been interviewed, and wrote *The Passing of Traditional Society.*

As he observed events in the Middle East and tried to relate them to his 1,600 interviews, he was reminded, he said, of the "titanic struggles whereby, over the course of centuries, medieval lifeways were supplanted by modernity" in Western Europe.[26] He therefore centered on the process that he called "modernization" although fully aware that it is a relative term: what is modern today will no longer be modern tomorrow.

Europeanization some years ago penetrated the upper levels of Middle East society, and affected mainly leisure-class fashions. *Modernization* today reaches a far wider population and touches public as well as private aspirations. "Central to this change," says Lerner, "is the shift in modes of communicating ideas and attitudes—for spreading among a large public vivid images of its own New Ways is what modernization distinctly does." Europeanization used the *class* media; modernization, the *mass* media. The mass media, he says, are what chiefly make the difference between the effect of these two social movements.[27]

As Lerner analyzes the history of modernization in the countries with which he is dealing, he sees the process occurring in three phases:

Urbanization comes first, for cities alone have developed the complex of skills and resources which characterize the modern industrial economy. Within this urban matrix develop both of the attributes which distinguish the next two phases—literacy and media growth. There is a close reciprocal relationship between these, for the literates develop the media which in turn spread literacy. But, historically, literacy performs the key function in the second phase. The capacity to read, at first acquired by relatively few people, equips them to perform the varied tasks required in the modernizing society. Not until the third phase, when the elaborate technology of industrial development is fairly well advanced, does a society begin to produce newspapers, radio networks, and motion pictures on a massive scale. This, in turn, accelerates the spread of literacy. Out of this interaction develop those institutions of participation . . . which we find in all advanced modern societies.[28]

On the basis of demographic data, he suggests that 10 per cent is probably somewhere near the "critical minimum" of urbanization; only after urbanization reaches that point does the literacy rate begin to rise significantly. Thereafter, literacy and urbanization rise together until they reach about 25 per cent, after which literacy continues to rise independently of urban growth. These percentages may or may not apply elsewhere than in the Middle East, but they suggest the order of events.

Behind this historical pattern, Lerner discerns a psychological pattern. He suggests that the man who changes in a developing society is usually a "mobile personality." By this, he means a person who has a high capacity to identify with new aspects of his environment, and who can take in stride the new demands upon himself that are "out of his habitual experience." The mobile personality is high in empathy; he can see himself "in the other fellow's situation." This is the type of person who becomes "the cash customer, the radio listener, the voter," who accepts and advocates change. And, says Lerner, this is "the predominant personal style only in modern society, which is distinctively industrial, urban, literate, and participant."[29]

So the first element in the social dynamic of development, as Lerner sees it, is an infusion of modern or "mobile" personality. The second element is what he calls "The Mobility Multiplier: Mass Media." Geographic mobility used to be almost the sole vehicle of spreading social mobility. Certainly one of the chief elements in the development of America was the mass migration

into a new and challenging situation. But in our own day the
"earlier increase of physical experience through transportation has
been multiplied by the spread of *mediated* experience through
mass communication."[30] The media, he says, have "disciplined
Western man in those empathic skills which spell modernity. They
also portrayed for him the roles he might confront and elucidated
the opinions he might need." In our century, they are "performing
a similar function on a world scale."[31]

This is the dynamic of social development as Lerner sees it:
a nucleus of mobile, change-accepting personalities;[32] then a growing mass media system to spread the ideas and attitudes of social
mobility and change; then the interaction of urbanization, literacy,
industrialization, and media participation to bring modern society
into being. His conclusion, therefore, is that mass communication
serves as "the great multiplier" in development, the device that
can spread the requisite knowledge and attitudes immeasurably
more quickly and widely than ever before.[33]

An Asian case

Lerner—and, indeed, everyone else who has looked into the matter—found a very high correlation between the measures of economic growth and the measures of communication growth.* That

* All studies of the topic show a high correlation between the development
of mass media and indexes of economic development. For example, here are
Unesco's figures (from *Mass Media in the Developing Countries*, Paris, 1961,
p. 17):

	Per Capita Income	Literacy	Urban-ization	Industrial-ization
Newsprint consumption per capita.	.83	.82	.69	.68
Newspaper circulation per capita..	.83	.79	.75	.51
Cinema seats per capita	.80	.68	.86	.82
Radio receivers per capita	.86	.72	.71	.78

Schramm and Carter found correlations of .72 and .74, respectively, between a scale of economic development and other scales representing the development of mass media receiving and propagating systems in 100 countries.
Lerner (*The Passing of Traditional Society*, p. 63) found high correlations
among all four of the measures, urbanization, literacy, media participation, and
political participation, in 54 countries. Greenberg (pp. 76–78) found for 32
countries correlation of .72 between literacy and per capita income, and .66
between per capita income and circulation of daily newspapers. Harbison (p.
147) recently reported a correlation of .888 between enrollment in secondary
schools and universities and gross national product per capita.

is, as national per capita income, urbanization, and industrialization increase, so does literacy, and with it the circulation of newspapers; so do the broadcasting facilities and the number of radio
receivers, and all other measures of media participation.

Y. V. L. Rao,[34] a young Indian scholar, decided to take a harder
look at this relationship. What is the prime mover, he asked? What
moves what? Does economic development make possible communication development, or do improved communication facilities
(and the increased flow of information resulting therefrom) make
possible economic and social development?

To gather some evidence on this problem, he studied two Indian
villages. When he conducted the field work in 1962, Village A was
already developing out of its traditional pattern. It had a variety
of small industrial units that offered employment and income to
a number of persons who otherwise would have had no viable
alternative to working on the land. Village B, on the other hand,
was still in the traditional stage of culture, relying heavily on the
barter system, observing the occupational restrictions enforced
by caste, and working the landlords' farms. Village B, as he points
out, was not wholly without signs of development, but the differences were very great between the two villages in this respect,
whereas in size, location, social composition, and so forth, there
was very little difference. Thus, Rao felt, it was possible to make
a meaningful comparison between the traditional and modernizing
villages.

As nearly as Rao could reconstruct what had happened, a key
to the difference was a road that was put through from Village A
to a neighboring small city.[35] Over this road came strangers, publications, and films; and over it residents of the village traveled for
the first time to see urban life. When a small industry was brought
to the village, the people were ready for it.

When information comes from the outside to an isolated community, it triggers change, says Rao. This information and the economic advantages accruing from it are first made use of by the
wealthy and powerful. Gradually, however, "the changes are
noticed by the mass and questions are asked. Where information

channels are available, these questions are answered and others begin to take advantage of the opportunities available. . . . Where the channels of information are varied and broad-based (newspapers, radio, etc.), the changes resulting from economic, social, or political ideas creeping into the community are smooth. Where the channels of information are tight and controlled by the few, changes are difficult to make and often lead to a worsening of the factions."[36]

The amount of information available and the wideness of its distribution is thus a key factor in the speed and smoothness of development. If it is freely available, says Rao, competition for new jobs and opportunities takes place in a climate of realistic knowledge rather than suspicion and jealousy. The "stresses and strains created by new knowledge and the opening of new opportunities act as spurs to activity rather than idle chatter only if all pertinent information is readily available."[37] The existence of parallel sources of information is also important, because these channels act as checks on each other. Lack of such sources and opportunities to check leads the villager to distrust his leadership and to engage in destructive talk or activity. Rao found much more such talk and tension—and much less information—in the traditional village than in the developing one.

But if sufficient information is available, then it contributes to a spiral of developmental activity. It helps farmers to improve methods and produce more. It also helps some of the excess manpower on the farms to transfer to other more productive jobs. More productivity leads to improved income, to widening consuming habits, to increased economic activity within the village (such as shops and restaurants), to new appetites for consumer goods, to a seeking after new opportunities, and so on in a chain of related development.

Similarly, this process acts as a spur to education. As Rao says, "the educated are able to read, get jobs, talk about many things. Reading is another symbol of prestige."[38] Educated people make possible more sophisticated industries. Educated people want a library. This is another example of spiral of development: economic and social development make education more attractive; education contributes to further economic and social development.

Lerner sees communication as the great multiplier of ideas and information for national development; Rao sees it as the great smoother of transition. When enough information is available, he points out, division of labor tends to take place smoothly. When new industrial roles are created for which there are no scriptural or traditional norms, the media fill in the gap with new norms and new ideas. Gradually the flow of information leads to broadening of the horizons, and if the information is sufficient this will tend to happen without a bitter struggle between traditional isolationism and the new national and international viewpoints.

Like Lerner, Rao considers the development of empathy and the mobile personality key psychological variables in bringing about change, but he points out that information contributes to these attitudes as well as being stimulated by them. He also points out that ability to think in abstract terms and general confidence in the future are attributes of great importance, which contribute to and are furthered by an increase in the flow of information and further economic growth.

What, then, is the prime mover? There is actually none. Each element acts on the others. "While it is true," he says, "that economic development leads to an increase in the flow of information through the greater purchasing capacity of the people, reflected in subscriptions to newspapers, magazines, and specialized journals as well as the ownership of radio sets and travel, it is also true that increased information in turn furthers economic development. It is futile to attempt to treat this interaction between communication and economic development as a causal relationship and isolate the chicken from the egg. The *interaction* is constant and cumulative."[39]

An African case

For Africa there is no such study as the two we have just reported, in which the relationship of communication to economic elements is studied directly. There is, however, a remarkable study of conditions at the birth of mass communication in Africa, and of the variables involved in understanding and using communication at that stage of development. The study is by Leonard Doob, a psychologist on the faculty of Yale University.[40]

When Lerner studied the Middle East, the change from oral to mass media communication was already well under way. When Doob studied Africa, however, the change was merely beginning.

"Africans themselves, living in a wide variety of societies, have evolved their own forms of communication, which for them at the time were adequate (except perhaps for the almost complete absence of the permanent flexible record provided by writing)," says Doob. "As they accept more and more practices and values from the West, they come to be intimately dependent upon the extending and especially upon the mass media of the culture they absorb. Modern Africa contains a mixture of traditional and novel communication systems because those systems so sensitively reflect and affect the changes in progress."[41]

Doob's observations tend to confirm those of Lerner and Rao— the great importance of information at the time of culture change and the interactive pattern by which communication developments both affect and are affected by other social and economic developments.

Much of Doob's detailed and sensitive study is concerned with the need to understand the conditions that exist at the confrontation of the new and the old communication systems. On the one hand, there is the undoubted potency of the new media, and the overwhelming welcome they receive. "The writer, like anyone who has had the experience," Doob says, "can testify to the shouts of joy which go up in a village when a mobile cinema van arrives."[42] On the other hand, there is an essential need to be "local" in using the media—to be aware of local culture and symbol systems. Doob writes:

Again and again films are reported to fail because they are not adapted to the audience at hand. An educational picture produced in Nigeria and aiming to instruct mothers on how to bathe a baby offends women in Uganda: a child, they say, should not be shown naked, and his head must be washed first, not last (Spurr, 1952, p. 38). Even what appears to be universally acceptable cartoons can cause trouble. Some Congo soldiers during World War II, meeting Donald Duck for the first time, threw stones at the screen because they thought they were being ridiculed. "Animals don't talk," they shouted. "Whoever saw a duck in uniform?"[43]

It is possible, however, he points out, to adapt familiar communication patterns to the new media. For example, when radio was introduced into what was then the Gold Coast, the introducers

sought deliberately to fit it into an African framework. They believed that its initial prestige depended in large part on the kind of translation that was used, since people allegedly had confidence only in "the deep vernacular . . . a highly figurative and allusive form of language which requires a knowledge of the doings of mythical figures, the traditions, the folklore, the proverbs and rough country humor passed orally from one generation to another." A format was used which resembled the pattern of the linguist who transmits messages between the chief and his people. . . . A "signature drum" announced the start of a transmission, the way a drum in the village assembles the people; programs began, as linguists open a meeting, by greeting dignitaries (such as the paramount chief and the village headman) and by offering good wishes for the sowing and protection of crops.[44]

Used with due understanding of the cultural environment, the media prove their effectiveness. And yet Doob cautions against any undue confidence that they will at once bring about the cultural changes at which they are directed. He cites an example wherein Moslem men in northern Nigeria became convinced through communication that "drinking water ought to be boiled and filtered. Within their homes unboiled, unfiltered water, however, may continue to be drunk, since the kitchen is not their domain and their wives, especially those in purdah, cannot be easily reached by adult-education officers."[45] He cites examples in which useful information can be learned without changing values or behavior, and other examples in which people, without changing their values, can still decide to get vaccinated.[46] He speaks of the tiny flow of information into the rural regions of a country when mass communication is only beginning. Yet even this channel may be significant, as he illustrates with the story of a group of adult males in a Nigerian village who were rounded up for an interview on public affairs. "Only one old man," he said, "could be found who had any knowledge about world affairs, including some recent developments in the field of atomic warfare. To all the rest it seems the mass media had failed to communicate such information, but with him they had been successful, undoubtedly because he alone in the village had a radio. Under some circumstances such as a crisis, this limited success might be crucial: the man could pass on information, and, if his status were high . . . he could become an influential recipient-disseminator."[47]

Not only are there problems of content in introducing the mass media; there are equally severe problems of distribution. Doob repeats a comment by a government publisher in Africa, that whether the roads are flooded so that lorries are unable to deliver the newspapers has more to do with the effect of the editorials than the way the editor writes. He points out also that for almost all of Africa every single piece of mass media equipment must be imported.

But having described some of the birth pains of mass communication, he returns to the potential strength and activity of the new baby. "Communication could not be discussed without referring . . . to almost all behavior," he said. "Communication in Africa could be appraised only by mentioning most of the significant aspects of African society." At the moment when Africa starts to move out of traditional toward modern society, "communication is a critical problem at the very center of existence."[48]

A Latin American case

In the literature of research on Latin America there is no major study in which economic and communication development are the chief variables. There is, however, a study of a remarkable experiment in social change, in which communication was obviously important. The chief experimenter, Dr. Allan R. Holmberg, set down his conclusion with regard to the functions and importance of communication in carrying on the developmental process.[49]

The experiment was conducted in a hacienda of about 35,000 acres, high in the Andes of Peru. "Attached to the land but owning none of it," as Holmberg says,[50] were 1,850 Quechua-speaking Indians. They lived under a system that might be described as feudalism. The hacienda belonged to the state, and was rented out to the highest bidder every ten years. The renter, or *patrón*, was thus able to behave like a feudal baron. Economic, political, and judicial power rested almost entirely in him. He was entitled to three days a week farm labor from one adult member of each family, in return for the family's right to occupy a tiny subsistence farmstead on the mountainside. He was also entitled to a considerable amount of free service from the farmers and their families as grooms, cooks, shepherds, household servants, and watchmen. Standards were at a bare minimum, health and nutrition very low, education almost wholly lacking, and community cooperation almost nil.

This was the situation when Cornell University leased the hacienda, in 1949, as an experimental site. The problem was to find out whether, without any large infusion of funds, the Indians could be helped to develop economically and socially. The problem had to be solved, also, without a great number of personnel. Except for the Peruvian government agencies normally operating in that area, no more than two Cornell graduate students and two Peruvians were at any one time assigned to the hacienda for purposes of the experiment.

The program of change centered on three major areas: economics and technology, nutrition and health, and education. In the course of developing these, it was necessary to make changes also in social organization. Some of the most disliked features of hacienda life—for example, free service required as cooks and servants—could be eliminated at once. A clinic and modern health practices were introduced. Schooling was made attractive, so that most of the children instead of a mere handful attended. Farm production was almost doubled, so that more money was available for other changes. Control was gradually shifted to an elected group of hacienda residents. It is a temptation to talk about these changes in detail, but let us say merely that the accomplishments were quite remarkable. In the preceding 400 years, the hacienda had hardly changed in any respect. But in the eight years after 1949 so much progress was made that in 1957 Cornell was able to transfer the lease to the elected officers of the hacienda. After four centuries of feudal peonage the residents were finally the masters of their own land, their own government, and their own destiny.

From our present point of view, however, the most significant conclusions of the study have to do with the further needs of the hacienda as it develops toward modernity. It became apparent that if the hacienda were to continue to progress, some serious communication problems would have to be solved. Holmberg says one of the greatest needs is the development of community solidarity. To meet this need, interests, activities, and communication must be developed to cut across the lines of kinship and neighborhood groups. Beyond this, to understand its own problems, the little mountain village must learn much more about the towns and villages of its own area, so as to emulate the good things they have done. Perhaps most important of all, for the long term, is the establishment of better communication with the outside world. Physical access to the mountain villages is improving rapidly, says Holmberg, but information is still badly circumscribed. When orders and communications from district and provincial offices are delivered to the hacienda, they usually have little effect. The officials seldom visit the village to explain. Trade or fiesta contacts with neighboring towns do not extend the horizons very much, because the Indians are treated by the mestizos of these towns as social inferiors. The real problem, therefore, is *to bring the mountain villages into the life and attitudes and stored knowledge of the nation.*

One of the best ways to broaden these channels of information is to make more use of the mass media. But, as Holmberg says,

The improving of communication media involves more than simply teaching people to read and write, or imparting information through the written word. Many isolated villagers of the sierra have not learned to look at photographs in such a way as to grasp their full meaning. For example, the showing of a public health film at Vicos revealed that the picture had failed to convey its intended message, for each scene was understood as a separate incident. The audience was wholly unable to see any connection between the film and its own life, and it misunderstood any features that were not completely realistic. When lice were depicted as larger than life, the conclusion was that they were an entirely different species of animal. Except for religious fiestas, few rural villagers had seen any variety of drama, and the functioning and purpose of radio are known only to a few individuals. While radio, newspapers, and films may play a leading role in the process of accelerated modernization—and the establishment of regional newspapers and radio stations would be a major step forward—in the early stages only patient face-to-face explanation and demonstration can provide effective channels of communication.[51]

Like Doob, therefore, Holmberg warns his readers that the introduction of mass media, though important, is not easy or automatic. But, he concludes, it is worth doing:

While there are many other aspects of community development that can be tackled in any program of induced social change, giving special attention to the three key areas—economic life, leadership, and communications—has the advantage of bringing about other changes. Increased economic contacts between the village and the outside world will lead to a growth of knowledge about outside markets, more effective techniques, use of available resources, and opportunities for putting special skills to work. Widening the channels of communication with the outside will make the rural villagers better aware of the government services that are available to them and will encourage them to play a more active role in their dealings with local, provincial, and national governments. Similar gains can be expected in other areas of sierra life.*

Doob's statement that communication is "at the very center of existence" for developing Africa provides a conclusion for this part of the book. Our point is that communication is *always* at the very center of existence, for *any* society, developing or not. Wherever dangers or opportunities need to be reported, decisions need to be made, new knowledge needs to be distributed, or change is

---

* Holmberg, pp. 105–6. For supporting evidence of the potency of the mass media in Latin American development, see Wagley. The rapid development of mass media during the last few decades, he says, is "at once a result and a cause" of the Brazilian economic and social revolution (p. 205). See also Deutschmann, a study of media exposure in a Colombian mountain village. Deutschmann found that even in this relatively little developed village, the mass media were coming in and were having an apparent effect on some farming decisions; even some illiterates appeared to show signs of having been exposed to the media.

imminent—there information flows. These needs are especially urgent and widespread in developing countries, where the tasks assigned to the communication media are vastly greater than before the time of development. If the flow of information and the channels of communication are not adequate to these tasks, they must be built up to the level of need. Therefore, let us now examine the adequacy of information and its channels in the developing countries.

2. The Flow of Information in the World

The currents of information in the world today are nearly as predictable as the currents of air that we call the winds. Frequently an event or a series of events disrupts the information flow as a storm disrupts the meteorological chart. But underneath these disruptions are repetitive patterns as regular as trade winds. We are going to consider some of these patterns, and we shall find, unfortunately, that they are not especially favorable to new and developing countries in urgent need of information. The questions before us are: How does information get to people in developing countries, and what is the level of useful information at the points where developing countries most need that information?

THE FLOW BETWEEN COUNTRIES

The flow of information and informational materials between countries also is governed to a considerable extent by certain basic realities. For one thing, the great avenues of exchange are mostly owned by a few countries. The five major world news agencies are owned, publicly or privately, in four nations. Ownership of long-distance telecommunication facilities is not quite so restricted as that of agencies, but is still in a relatively few hands. Furthermore, less than one-third of the countries of the world are major producers and custodians of the technology and technical knowledge on which modern society depends. The concentration of technology, wealth, and power in a relatively few countries makes any of their policies and actions important and therefore newsworthy to other countries, and ensures that they will produce a lion's share of useful technological information. And finally, the concentration of wealth in certain countries makes it easier for their people to travel, to support the industries and enterprises of communication, and to produce the equipment which an efficient flow of information requires. All these circumstances are reflected in the pattern of flow between countries.

The flow of news

What are the characteristics of the world-wide flow of news? In every country, of course, the newspapers and newscasts devote the majority of their attention to news of that nation. The proportion of national news ranges usually from 60 to 90 per cent. Only a minority, but a significant minority, of items comes from outside the country.

The most extensive study recently made of the world news flow dealt with 13 nations on five continents, including both highly developed and developing countries. From each of these nations, three daily newspapers were selected—a "prestige" paper (e.g., *The Times* of London), a large-circulation "popular" paper (e.g., *The Daily Express* of London), and a "provincial" paper (e.g., *The Scotsman,* of Edinburgh)—or the nearest possible approximation to that combination in the press system of a given country.[1] Each of these papers was studied for the same month in the spring of 1961. The space devoted to news from various foreign countries was recorded, and so also was the handling of news events of general importance. From the data that resulted, it was possible to get a sense of the news flow among these countries and continents. Some of these data are shown in Figure 1.

In certain respects these results are surprising. Some of the countries never appeared in the news columns of the other 12 countries at any time during the test month. Some of the countries received less than a column in the papers of the other 12 during the month. Attention to foreign news was dominated, throughout, by four countries—the United States, the Soviet Union, the United King-

FIGURE 1. Proportion of foreign news in representative newspapers of 13 countries devoted to the other 12 countries during one month in 1961. A blank indicates less than 1.5 per cent.

Printed in papers of:	News of these countries:												
	Argentina	Australia	Brazil	Egypt	France	India	Italy	Japan	Pakistan	Poland	U.K.	U.S.	USSR
Argentina			6		15	3	6	2			11	43	12
Australia					13	2		2			32	41	12
Brazil	6			2	14	2	4	2			9	43	18
Egypt			2		30	2	2	2	2		12	34	15
France	2		3	3			12	2		2	21	49	20
India		2			10		2	4	11		19	35	15
Italy					29	4					24	29	13
Japan					16						12	49	23
Pakistan					16	13		2			17	33	13
Poland					26		3				8	26	30
U.K.	2	2	3	2	22	3	2	2	2	3		43	33
U.S.	3	3	3	2	20	8	3	3	2	3	22		25
USSR	3		3	3	22	3	6	6	3	8	17	33	

dom, and France. At least three of the four received more attention in the press of Argentina than did nearby Brazil; in the press
of Brazil than did nearby Argentina; in the press of India than did
nearby Pakistan; in the press of Pakistan than did nearby India;
and so forth. Clearly, the world flow of foreign news deals chiefly
with a group of highly developed countries which are also dominant in world politics.

It is clear also that news flows from the highly developed to the
less-developed countries. It flows from Europe and North America to the other continents. It flows from the United States and the
Soviet Union to all other countries.[2]

It is possibly more than coincidence that the four countries that
dominate this news flow are also the homes of the five world news
agencies. The Associated Press and United Press International
are United States agencies; Reuters is British; Agence France
Presse is French; and Tass is Soviet. We might expect these agencies to emphasize the news from home, and this most of them do,
if we can rely on a sample of the Asian wires provided by them
for two consecutive days in the spring of 1961.[3] AP and UPI concentrate on the United States about as much as Tass concentrates
on the Soviet Union. Reuters represents strongly the United Kingdom and the United States. AFP, however, in this Asian wire emphasizes the United States, the United Kingdom, and the Soviet
Union more than France itself. However, the total effect of these
five news wires is about the same as the previously described
newspaper content. Figure 2 should be compared with Figure 1.
From time to time, events like the outbreak of fighting in Laos,
revolution in Hungary, attack upon Suez, volcanic eruption in Bali,
and war in Korea attract much of the attention away from the
usual sources of news in the great powers. But if any such event
goes on for very long, or assumes a threatening quality, it soon
involves one or more of these great powers. And thus, day in and
day out, the highly developed countries, and particularly a few
of them, dominate the news.

To point out merely that the countries that get the most news
coverage (except for great news events like Laos or Suez) are

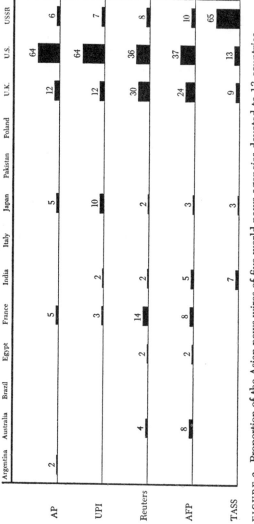

FIGURE 2. Proportion of the Asian news wires of five world news agencies devoted to 13 countries during two days in 1961. A blank indicates less than 1.5 per cent.

also the ones that own the world news services is far too simple an explanation. The potency of these countries in world affairs; their possession of the nuclear weapon; the strength of their economies, and the relation of these through trade and finance to the economies of all other countries; their eminence in science and industry—all these things ensure that almost anything of serious significance that happens in one of these countries is likely to be of interest or concern to smaller countries throughout the world. In a very real sense, many of the dangers and opportunities which a tribal watchman used to look for from his vantage point on the nearest hill are today to be found in the highly developed countries, and it is not surprising, therefore, that the newspapers of less-developed countries should provide a great deal of news from these countries. Furthermore, the more highly developed a country, the more highly organized its newsgathering facilities, so that it becomes easier in such countries to find and report news of interest. And in reporting their own countries *in extenso,* the news agencies are doing what they are best equipped to do and what their foreign clients expect of them. Therefore, many reasons beyond a nationalistic quality in world news agencies help to determine why news emphasis is not distributed equally throughout the world.

As a matter of fact, the heaviness of news flow from a *few* countries is less disturbing than the thinness of the flow from *many* countries. Analyzing the flow of one agency's news from Latin America in February of 1962, Hal Hendrix, Latin American editor of *The Miami News,* came to the conclusion that if this wire file were the only source of enlightenment for the rest of the world, then Latin America would be considered to consist mainly of Cuba. From several countries there was no news whatsoever during the month. From Bolivia, there came only the announcement of the arrival of Prince Philip; from Peru, only shorts about a plane crash and a bus wreck; from Chile, nothing more than a note that Billy Graham, the evangelist, was conducting his meetings in Santiago. Studying another news service from Latin America, Al Marlens, news editor of *Newsday,* found only one news story from Brazil during the whole month. The news was full of facts, but, said the critics, not very illuminating. Marlens reviewed the detailed and voluminous coverage of Cuba and asked, with commendable understatement, how much this coverage would "increase a North American's *understanding*" of events in that country.[4]

Jacques Kayser, in *One Week's News*,[5] reports on how 17 well-known newspapers from 17 countries handled 18 news events which were judged to be of international interest or significance.

Kayser found great differences in the amount of coverage and the nature of coverage different papers gave each of these stories. But more surprising is the fact that many of the stories were not covered at all, during the week, in many of the papers. Only three stories—the Korean war, the deputies' conference, and the French cabinet crisis—were reported in all 17 papers. The Moroccan situation and Bevin's resignation were reported in all except one paper. Eight of the 17 stories were carried in less than half the papers in the list. One paper—*O Estado*—carried all except one story. But another paper—*Ta Kung Pao*—carried only four of the 17 stories. The average was between 10 and 11. In other words, the average reader of one of these papers had no chance to read about six or more of these events.

What is the result of this kind of coverage? Some years ago, the International Press Institute asked a distinguished Indian correspondent and a distinguished American correspondent to examine and report the treatment of their own countries for one month in the newspapers of the other country. Neither correspondent was very happy with what he found. We can convey the tone of the reports by brief excerpts.

India in the U.S. press:[6]

Coverage perfunctory and haphazard . . . Editors interested evidently in only four broad classifications of news from India—bizarre or outlandish news, news having some bearing on the East-West struggle and communism, news connected with American economic aid, and news of disasters . . . Too often editors publish only the first few lines and jettison the rest . . . The domestic political scene in India is practically a closed book . . . But for the inevitable pieces about untouchability or the caste system or child marriages, nothing much is published in the daily press about Indian social affairs.

The United States in the Indian press:[7]

As bizarre as the average American's impression of India . . . The news is given, but not the story behind the news . . . The picture of the United States is both inadequate and unbalanced . . . It suffers from narrow channeling and a dearth of Indian correspondents in America. . . . Aspects of life in the United States which are most objectionable to Indian feelings are played up in the Indian press out of all proportion to their importance in the American scene.

We must conclude that the flow of news among nations is thin, that it is unbalanced, with heavy coverage of a few highly developed countries and light coverage of many less-developed ones, and that, in some cases at least, it tends to ignore important events and to distort the reality it presents.

Flow of persons and personal messages between countries

Other things being equal, the flow of persons, letters, telegrams, and telephone messages into and out of developing countries is relatively less than for highly developed countries. This is not surprising, inasmuch as all the mechanisms and facilities of tourism and travel are better developed in the advanced countries, and well-developed systems of commerce and industry provide more reason to visit a country on business. But some of the differences are quite large.

For example, according to the last comparable figures (1961), India was receiving annually about 109,000 tourists. This is one foreign visitor for every 3,970 Indians. France, on the other hand, received annually slightly more than five million visitors—about one for every *nine* Frenchmen.

Here are comparable figures on tourism in different countries:

> Uganda, one visitor for every 872 Ugandans
> Japan, one for every 776
> Turkey, one for every 219
> Poland, one for every 202
> Thailand, one for every 176
> UAR, one for every 126
> Chile, one for every 106
> United Kingdom, one for every 38

In tourism and foreign travel, of course, "other things" are not always equal. Some countries have more tourist attractions than

TABLE 6. Number of Pieces of Foreign Mail and of Foreign Telegrams
per Year per Capita in Selected Countries

Country	Pieces of Mail	Telegrams
Indonesia	.18	.01
India	.37	.02
Nigeria	.97	
Turkey	1.1	.03
Chile	1.6	.14
Poland	2.3	.03
United Arab Republic	3.5	.003
Morocco	3.6	.08
France	8.4	.16
United Kingdom	17.1	.34
Norway	17.5	.41

Source: *United Nations Statistical Yearbook, 1962.*

others. Some (for example, the European countries) are in the
midst of thick clusters of foreign population. Some present fewer
language problems than others. But in general, there is clearly a
smaller flow of persons into the underdeveloped countries, and
fewer people in these countries can afford to travel abroad. Therefore there is less opportunity for personal contact and communication with foreigners.

The same thing is true of the flow of mail and telegraph messages, as Table 6 illustrates. In this case, as with tourism, things
are not necessarily equal. For example, countries like Morocco
and the United Arab Republic, with strong economic ties or political and social interests abroad, have a larger flow of mail than one
might expect from their level of economic development. But in
general, the pattern holds: The well-developed countries have developed wider horizons of personal contact. The developing countries are still in process of doing so.

Flow of informational materials between countries

By informational materials, we mean not only books, periodicals,
and films, but also the raw materials of information and education:
printing paper; raw film; projection and photographic equipment;
radio and television receivers, parts, and transmitting equipment;
printing equipment; sound recording equipment; scientific instru-

ments; models, maps, charts, and other teaching equipment; and the like. All these are in much better supply in the highly developed countries, and there are usually some difficulties in the way of importing them into less-developed countries.

We can illustrate the unequal supply of these materials by noting that in 1960, Indonesia, India, and the Philippines together produced about 350,000 radio receivers. In the same year, Japan, the Soviet Union, and the United States produced about 35 *million* radio receivers, and about 10 million television receivers. In the developing countries there is a need for more radios; in the industrialized countries there is a supply of them, and a capability of increasing production if export sales demand it. In greater or less degree this is true of all kinds of informational materials we have mentioned. What is it, then, that stands in the way of a large flow of such materials from the developed to the less-developed nations?

Basically, it is the inability of the developing countries to pay for all they need to import. International and bilateral aid will extend to some extent their ability to purchase, but the only real solution is to build up their productivity and national incomes. Meanwhile, inability to pay is translated into shortages of foreign exchange. Before an importer may be permitted to purchase foreign exchange, he usually must obtain a license for the desired import. This makes it possible for the government to control the flow of exchange and to assign priorities to different uses of it. It is not astonishing that steel, machine tools, energy sources, electronic equipment, and other props for industry should often draw higher priorities than materials of enlightenment. Considering political realities, it is not astonishing even that instruments of war and national defense should draw higher priorities than books or magazines or laboratory equipment for chemistry courses.

Beyond these basic exchange controls designed to make efficient use of scarce financial resources, many countries also impose import controls on some informational materials. They also levy tariffs on many such imports. Usually these measures are intended to produce revenue or to protect domestic manufacturers and sellers. Once the materials are imported, they are often subject to a sales tax—either wholesale or retail, or both—which is intended to raise revenue for the government. The effect of all these tariffs and taxes, of course, is to raise the cost to the ultimate consumer and to cut down the flow of imports.

A few years ago Unesco made a world-wide survey of tariff and trade regulations affecting the international flow of information materials. Of the 92 countries surveyed in the Unesco report, published as a manual entitled *Trade Barriers to Knowledge*, 57 were in the developing regions. While adopting fairly liberal policies with regard to publications, most of them severely restricted the importation of materials required by the mass media.

Thus, of these 57 countries, four imposed duties on newspapers and magazines ranging from 2 to 9 per cent of the value, and two charged consular fees of 8 per cent. On books, two countries levied duties of from 9 to 33 per cent, one charged a duty of 15 U.S. cents a kilo, and two imposed consular fees of 8 per cent. The remaining countries exempted publications from duties.

Newsprint and other printing paper were not so liberally treated. On these materials, 40 countries levied duties ranging variously from 5 to 40 per cent ad valorem, or from 1 to 5 cents a kilo. In some cases there was a small tax by weight plus an 8 per cent ad valorem charge.

Fifty-six of the 57 countries levied duties on unexposed film. These ranged from 12 cents to $2.03 a kilo, or from 0.1 to 0.5 cent a foot. Two countries also charged consular fees of from 20 to 30 per cent ad valorem. Fifty-five countries taxed film projectors, with duties varying from 14 to 80 per cent, or from 51 cents to $4.02 a kilo.

Fifty-five countries likewise imposed duties on radio receivers. These ranged from 12 to 100 per cent, or from 51 cents to $5.36 a kilo. Information on television receivers was available from 18 countries, all of which charged duties on them. These varied from 12 to 45 per cent, or from $1.19 a kilo to $1.44 a kilo plus 100 per cent ad valorem.

Almost all of the 57 countries restricted the importation of information materials through foreign exchange controls or licensing, or both.

Unesco has contended strongly that

Restrictions upon the free flow of knowledge can and should be lifted. . . . These restrictions have, in fact, been applied in many cases fortuitously rather than by design. . . . The general trend toward economic control engulfed materials of education, science, and culture, along with other commodities. Yet the revenue derived by governments from duties imposed on such materials is relatively small, nor in most cases is there any serious danger of competition with domestic industry. Whatever slight sacrifice may be involved in freeing this sector of trade, it is more than outweighed by the enhanced opportunities for educational advancement and mutual understanding."[8]

What this means to the developing countries

The effect of these imperfect links between countries is to emphasize and help to perpetuate the difference between the developed and the less-developed nations. The nations that are already rich in informational materials find it far easier than do the underdeveloped nations to add to their stock of these materials. The nations that already have the widest and most frequent interpersonal contacts find it easier, because of the dispersion of travel and of messages, to add to those contacts. The nations that already have the most news available to them also dominate the world flow of news, so that the news of underdeveloped countries is relatively little heard, and the underdeveloped countries learn all too little even about each other. Where informational materials, personal contacts, and news of similar countries are most needed, there they are hardest to obtain.

THE FLOW WITHIN COUNTRIES

Even in the most highly developed country, information is more readily available in the great cities than in the rural regions. Great newspapers, libraries, periodical kiosks, universities, experts and scholars, lectures, meetings, clubs, galleries, adult courses and evening schools—these are easily found in London, Paris, or Moscow, but not so readily at hand in villages 200 miles away. The same comment might be made of Cairo, Bombay, Lagos, and Lima, as compared with villages 200 miles away. But the significant point to note is how greatly the supply of information drops off between city and village in an underdeveloped country, and how relatively little it drops off in a highly developed country.

This can be illustrated by the results of two public opinion surveys made in the Western Hemisphere. In 1953, an international organization financed a study of readership and foreign news knowledge in a national sample of adults in the United States. One comparison this made possible was of the news knowledge between city dwellers and people who lived in the small towns and rural regions. Here are the results of some of the questions asked of people who lived in cities of more than 50,000 and people who lived in settlements of fewer than 2,500.[9]

	Proportion of Correct Answers	
	More than 50,000 Population	*Fewer than 2,500 Population*
The British Foreign Secretary recently visited the United States. What is his name?	48	41
Will you tell me what recent disaster left thousands homeless in the Netherlands?	79	82
Who is Prime Minister of the United Kingdom now?	81	76

Some of these questions may not have had as large a proportion of correct answers as newspapers and newscasters might have expected, but in any case there appears to be very little difference between the level of such news in the cities and in the rural regions in the United States.

Compare with this a survey made in 1960 of a nation-wide sample of Brazilians. In this survey, the urban population was compared with the people in towns of under 2,000:[10]

	Proportion of Correct Answers	
	Urban Population	*Rural Population*
Who is the outgoing President of Brazil?	80%	50%
Who is the outgoing President of the United States?	35	5
Who is the leader of Cuba and the Revolution? ...	35	6
With what countries should Brazil cooperate (percentage who had an answer)?	49	17

In Brazil, therefore, there is considerable difference between news knowledge in the cities and the villages, a difference that extends even to knowing who the President of the country is.

The rapid decline of information level as one moves away from the cities in a developing country was demonstrated by Damle, when he studied the incidence of different kinds of information in villages at different distances from the city of Poona in India.[11] The nearest village was on the very outskirts of the city; the farthest 80 miles. The others were, respectively 11, 20, 24, 26, and 72 miles from Poona. Linear distance did not perfectly predict the amount of information, because some villages were more easily reached than others by road, and in some the social structure was better suited than in others to seeking and spreading information. But between nearby villages, the group of villages at an intermediate distance from Poona, and the farthest villages, the differences were dramatic. The village of Patan, 72 miles from Poona, was almost devoid of contact with the outside world. There were no literates in the village; there had been one, but he had gone to the city to get a job. Only four persons had ever seen a train, and no resident had ever been as far as Poona. Only the *Patil* (head man) knew, at the time of the study, that Nehru was the political leader of India, and that was all this *Patil* knew about national politics. Knowledge of world politics and India's foreign policy was nil. Of modern ideas on caste and religion, nothing was known. No newspapers, periodicals, or radio came into the village.

Closer to the city, information was more common. The names of Nehru and other national leaders were known by many people in the two nearest villages, but in two of the farther villages the majority of people did not even know that India was independent. Knowledge of foreign countries, of the division of the world into two camps, of foreign leaders, of India's foreign relations and policies—these were little known anywhere, and such knowledge was practically nil beyond the two nearest villages. Comparatively few people anywhere knew about details of the five-year plan and of community development plans, but this knowledge had reached *some* people as far away as the middle group—the 20-mile-distant group—of villages. Modern ideas of caste, religion, and equality were well known in the nearby villages, slightly known if at all in the middle group, completely unknown in the distant villages. Thus, as one moved outward from the life of the city, the curtain gradually fell on the modern world and modern knowledge, until one found the distant villages almost untouched and uninformed by modernity.

Professor Damle made this study in the middle 1950's. If he were to go back over the same territory today, he would doubtless find that the modern world has penetrated further into the villages and that much more is known about national development and politics. But the general nature of the pattern still holds: whereas in a highly developed country information is diffused relatively evenly among villagers and city dwellers, in underdeveloped countries there is a sharp decline in the supply and amount of information between the cities and the villages. Why should there be this difference?

The two communication systems

Lucian Pye, in a penetrating study of communication patterns and governmental patterns in non-Western societies, points out that most non-Western societies have two distinct levels of communication—the urban or elite level and the village or mass level. He says:

In the urban centers are the media of mass communication, based on Western technology, serving the most Westernized elements of the society and most closely related to the dominant or national sphere of politics. Outside these centers, the communication process is still largely dependent upon the traditional level of technology, and in its operation it mainly serves the needs of the less Westernized people, and a more or less formally structured political process.

As a consequence of this basic cleavage, ideas and themes that dominate the political communications among an important element in the society may not be reflected in communications among other groups in the population. News about a dramatic event may travel very rapidly throughout the society—the speed with which most Indian villages learned of Gandhi's death is often cited as an example of the efficiency of a word-of-mouth process of communication—but interpretations that give context to such events are far less effectively communicated. It is true that at the village level there is often a person who receives one of the urban newspapers and thus becomes an important source of information. However, the barrier of illiteracy is great and the frame of reference employed by newspapers in communicating to an urbanized audience is often one that is not meaningful to those in the village. Possibly more significant is the fact that the urban process of communication is generally not very responsive to what takes place in the various village systems. It is often the case that the media of mass communication are far more sensitive to the sphere of international communications. This may not be a surprising fact since the most Westernized groups are the main audience of these media, but it is important for understanding the character of these countries. Rather than appealing to the vigor and the values of a folk culture and rejecting the values of the foreigner, as is common with extreme nationalists in the West, these groups often express their aspirations by judging the outside world by its own values.

In addition to this fundamental division, the pattern is usually further complicated by the fact that communication at the village level is largely dependent upon a word-of-mouth process which results in countless subsystems, each limited to the chain of personal contacts of its participants.[12]

Professor Pye's comments fit with the observations of others who have tried to describe the information system of developing countries. In all such countries, the mass media become much less available outside the cities. Damle, for example, found that neither radio nor newspapers apparently made much contribution to the store of knowledge except in the nearest villages. This is to be expected because illiteracy rapidly decreases the market for printed media outside the city, lack of electricity makes it hard to use electronic media, and a shaky transportation system makes it hard to deliver anything. But even when the mass media do come to the villages, they usually are not of and for the villages. Rural and small-town newspapers and local radio are uncommon in developing countries. Therefore, it is the *urban* newspaper and the *city* or the *national* radio that come to the villages. As Pye says, the villages and the cities do not have anything like equal access to the same communication systems, but, rather, two communication systems are perpetuated—the city-centered mass media, which are efficient and quick but concerned with urban matters, and the interpersonal systems of the villages, which are slow and limited in range, and help to isolate the villages, but deal with the topics that most concern the villagers.

Nevertheless, all available evidence points to a fundamental change in information levels as soon as mass media come in. Ler-

TABLE 7. Ability of Egyptian Male Villagers to Distinguish between
Plebiscite and Election, Related to Their Exposure
to Newspaper and Radio

	Answered Correctly	Did Not Answer Correctly
Read newspapers	13.9%	27.7%
Did not read newspapers	4.6	53.8
Listened to radio	15.5	60.0
Did not listen to radio	3.0	21.5

Source: G. K. Hirabayashi and M. F. El Khatib, "Communication and Political Awareness in the Villages of Egypt," *Public Opinion Quarterly,* 22 (1958), 357–63.

ner has written of the importance of the first radio receiver in a village. More recently, we have a measure of political knowledge in an Egyptian village as related to mass media exposure. Hirabayashi and El Khatib[13] studied five small villages about 50 miles north of Cairo. They found out who read newspapers and who listened to the radio, and then asked some questions about political personalities and issues. They asked their respondents to explain the difference between an election and a plebiscite. This explanation requires a certain amount of political sophistication, and therefore it is interesting to see how use of the media relates to ability to answer the question. Table 7 gives the results they reported. It says that among villagers who could distinguish between a plebiscite and an election, there were three times as many newspaper readers as nonreaders, five times as many radio listeners as nonlisteners. About half of the newspaper readers as compared with one-twelfth of the nonreaders could answer the question, and about one-fourth of radio listeners as compared with one-seventh of the nonlisteners. Why are the differences not still larger? The authors of the report suggest an explanation: "Egyptian newspapers are written primarily for urban readers . . . and thus did not explain the plebiscite in a manner understandable to the villagers. Regarding radio listeners . . . the majority of them prefer Koran readings and popular music over all other programs."[14] Thus, the availability of the media makes a great difference, but what comes over the media makes an even greater difference.

Deutschmann has reported on the effect of media exposure in a mountain village in Colombia.[15] He developed a scale of media exposure so that persons who used several media or used them often could be distinguished numerically from those who had little contact with the media. Table 8 gives some of the comparisons he was able to make of persons of high media exposure with those of low media exposure.

We are not arguing, of course, that media exposure is necessarily the only reason why some villagers have more information than others. Education is very likely to make a difference. People "learn to learn," and therefore seek out the media. People who are "achievers," who are more anxious to learn, may also be more likely to seek out the media, and therefore personality and norms must make a difference. But Deutschmann did a very interesting thing in trying to determine what effects could be attributed to the mass media, and which to education or other. He eliminated all literate and educated people from his sample, and then divided the remain-

TABLE 8. Persons of High and Low Media Exposure in an Andean Village Compared on Knowledge, Attitudes, and Behavior Related to Economic and Social Development

	High Media Exposure (N = 24)	Low Media Exposure (N = 26)
Use hospital for childbirth	75%	35%
Use midwife for childbirth	25	27
Inapplicable		38
Want sons to follow occupation other than farming	59	19
Want sons to follow farming	33	39
Inapplicable	8	42
High political knowledge	62	4
Some political knowledge	25	19
No political knowledge	13	77
Had early knowledge of six farm innovations	54	44
Adopted early:		
a) Vaccination of chickens for cholera	17	11
b) New varieties of seed potatoes	37	33
c) Fungicide	63	28
d) Food supplement for livestock and poultry	66	44
e) Spray guns	60	44
f) Chemical fertilizer	69	44
Mean number of practices adopted	4.26	3.69

Source: Paul J. Deutschmann, "The Mass Media in an Underdeveloped Village," *Journalism Quarterly, 40* (1963), 27–35.

TABLE 9. Adoption of New Practice, Related to Mass Media Exposure,
among Unschooled and/or Illiterate Persons in an Andean Village

	High Media Exposure	Low Media Exposure
High adoption (4 or more new practices)	71%	38%
Low adoption (3 or fewer new practices)	29	62

Source: Paul J. Deutschmann, "The Mass Media in an Underdeveloped Village," *Journalism Quarterly, 40* (1963), 27–35.

ing people into high and low media exposure groups. These people could use radio and films, of course, and could sometimes have newspapers or other periodicals read to them. When he compared the high and low media exposure groups among the illiterates, on the basis of how many new agricultural practices they had adopted, he got the results reported in Table 9.

Thus it seems that the mass media do make a substantial difference in bridging the information gap within a developing country.

Devices to extend personal communication

Not only are the mass media scarce outside the cities of underdeveloped countries; there is also a scarcity of the facilities that make it possible for persons to talk to any except those close around them. Travel is more difficult than in highly developed countries. Many villages in Asia and Africa have no roads to connect them to other settlements, and although some of these villages are reached by occasional buses or hardy automobiles, the vehicles have to ride over the open field rather than the highway. The opening of a road from a village to a city is therefore a highly significant event. But roads or no roads, villagers in traditional society seldom go far from home and seldom see visitors.

Nor is there a very efficient postal service in the villages, or many telegrams sent, or telephones available. Table 10 compares post, telegraph, and telephone in some developing countries with the corresponding facilities in several countries that are further developed.

This table should be compared with Table 7. It will be seen that about the same degree of underdevelopment exists in domestic as in foreign post and telegraph.

TABLE 10. Number of Pieces of Domestic Mail and of Domestic Telegrams
per Year per Capita, and Number of Telephones per
1,000 Persons, in Selected Countries

Country	Pieces of Mail	Telegrams	Telephones
India	8.1	.07	1
Nigeria	2.6		1
Indonesia	2.1	.07	1
Thailand		.09	3
Egypt	8.7	.14	9
Turkey	7.9	.32	9
Morocco	2.6	.03	11
Chile	13.0	.88	26
Poland	29.8	.32	32
France	166.7	.26	101
United Kingdom	190.6	.25	161
Norway	109.0	.93	214

Source: *United Nations Statistical Yearbook,* 1962.

It might be thought that in the absence of adequate mass communication, the more traditional means of communication would
take over to bridge the urban-rural information gap. And so far as
possible, this does happen. Meetings are held by government officials and political spokesmen. Folk plays, puppets, singers are as
popular as ever. Bazaars and markets still provide excuse for exchange of information along with exchange of money or goods.
The communication "grapevine" still flourishes. But most of these
are slow or limited channels. The "grapevine" is sometimes very
swift, but, as Pye says, it is limited in what it can carry. Word of
a great event—Gandhi's death, the fighting in the Himalayas—news
like this can be carried effectively by grapevine. But interpretive
material, explanatory and technical material, persuasive material
—these are hopelessly distorted, if carried at all, by the grapevine.

Traditional means of communication make it hard even for one
village to talk to its neighboring villages. In some respects, governmental and political connections forge a stronger communication
link between villages and the seat of government than between
villages. But the link to the center is tenuous at best, and therefore
if village communication is traditional communication, and if
roads, telephones, good postal service, and other extenders are

not available, then the country is not very likely to move its villages out of their isolation and their traditionalism.

The spread of development information

Most information programs in national development are a combination of mass media and personal advice and persuasion. The mass media impact inevitably lessens, farther from the cities, as mass media become less readily available. Most developing countries try to make up for this diminution of impact by making special use of mass communication—for example, printing posters, wall newspapers, and similar documents full of development information—by planning radio programs around rural discussion groups or programs aimed at local problems; or by making films of development topics for traveling film vans or other exhibitors. More important, they try to hire and train skilled field representatives in such fields as health, agriculture, and community development, to talk directly to the people. Many countries have done remarkable things of this kind. But there are almost always too few field representatives for the number of rural people that must be talked to, and many of the representatives are not well enough trained. The special uses of mass communication tend to be too little and too scattered. The chains are often very long ones, and so the posters don't get beyond the district level, or the supply doesn't go around, or the *particular* information needs of a village aren't met by a *general* poster. The film vans don't come often enough to the more distant places. Many villages have no radio. And so, despite the best efforts of a development ministry or commission, the level of information on national development, like news and other information, falls off away from the cities. Nothing like an even diffusion can be hoped for until the mass media, the schools, and other channels of communication are more evenly diffused.

This is the import of Rao's observations, Damle's, Lerner's, and many others. These people have cited examples of how the national developmental effort, and the specific parts of that effort directed toward village health, agriculture, and community development, have failed to reach the villages far removed from the cities, and how hard it is, in the absence of multiple channels, for a villager to check and supplement what gets to him.

What this means to a developing country

It is hard to summarize what we have just written except in discouraging terms. The news from developing countries is likely to be scant unless the country is in trouble—for example, with war, revolution, or disaster. The flow of informational materials into developing countries is likely to be clogged by the shortage of currency, by resulting import restrictions, and by tariffs. The general flow of persons and messages into developing countries is likely to be much less than into highly developed ones. Within a developing country, the flow and supply of information drop off sharply as one goes from the cities toward the villages. Thus the flow of information is least where information is *already* least, and where attitudes and behaviors are most in need of change—where change is likely to be threatening and most likely to be resisted.

THE TRANSITION TO MODERN COMMUNICATION

When a society begins to modernize, one of the first signs of the development is the lengthening out of communication channels.

In a completely traditional and illiterate society, the effective environment extends about as far as one can see, although it does include folk wisdom and religious beliefs handed down from parent to child, or priest to believer. Occasionally a traveler, a minstrel, or a message comes with words about the land beyond the horizon. Occasionally, an adventurous young man is stimulated to find out for himself what lies beyond that horizon. But for the most part, the traditional village lives on in its ancient life patterns and its restricted horizons—until "development" begins. Then government, roads, schools, literacy, and mass media invade the privacy of the village and invite the villager into a larger world.

With that larger world comes a profound psychological change. The traditional villager has lived in a world that he could encompass with his feet and his senses. Now he is shown a world that he has to depend on others to tell him about. He has lived in a stream of information about dangers and opportunities that were geo-graphically, physically local. Now he is presented a stream of in-formation in which he recognizes *nonlocal* events as dangers and opportunities. It must be a strange experience indeed to be brought into a world in which the blockade of a distant island, fighting on high mountains near the heart of Asia, or stern words spoken by the ambassador of one foreign nation to the ambassador of another foreign nation in a glass-walled building on the banks of the East River in New York would come to be regarded as dangers to an individual in a village; and in which a man in orbit around the earth, the discovery of invisible bacterial life in a foreign labora-tory, or the finding of a thing called a "DNA code," supposed to govern one's physical inheritance from his parents, should be inter-preted as an opportunity. These changes amount to a redefinition of "localness." Many things that are physically local are now seen to be trivial, and many things that are physically distant are seen to be local in their import. Fighting in the Himalayas had a local meaning to villagers in the heart of India. Discovery of a treatment for the yaws had a local meaning to villagers in the heart of Africa.

More than anything else, it is the coming of the mass media that makes this difference. When radio receivers become available in villages or small towns, they carry chiefly nonlocal news. When newspapers come in, they carry a high proportion of national and international news and editorials, and have relatively little cover-age below the regional metropolis or the state capital. Look, for example, at Table 11, with its analysis of the content of three dailies in the regional metropolis of Nagpur, India.*

Wherever these three papers go, in the villages and small towns

---

* These proportions are not greatly different from those of newspapers in coun-tries that are further along in economic development. For example, the 21 daily newspapers of the state of Oregon, during one month in 1957, carried 32.9 per cent local news, 29.0 per cent state news, 30.0 per cent national news, and 8.1 per cent foreign news (Schramm, "Newspapers of a State as a News Network"). Oddly enough, there is more truly local—e.g., village and small-town—news in the Oregon papers because smaller towns can support newspapers in a more advanced economy, and the news-gathering mechanism is better developed. For other studies of newspaper news content, see Kayser; International Press Institute, *The Flow of the News*; and Schramm, *One Day in the World's Press*.

TABLE 11. News and Editorial Content of Three Nagpur
Dailies, in October 1961

	News (percentage)			Editorials (number)		
	Inter-national	National	Regional	Inter-national	National	Regional
Nagpur Times (English)	24.8%	56.3%	18.9%	10	12	8
Nava Bharat (Hindi)	14.5	68.0	17.5	7	15	8
Maharashtra (Marathi)	14.3	63.3	22.4	8	20	2

Source: K. E. Eapen, "Content Analysis of Three Nagpur Dailies," *The Hislop Journalist,* 2 (1962), 43–44.

around Nagpur, they are obviously carrying a great deal of information from far away, and are commenting on faraway events which have now come to be of interest to the people of the Nagpur region.

We have been talking about news and public affairs only as one illustration of what happens to information generally as a country develops. Not only the news from New York or Moscow, but also the agricultural methods in distant countries, the scientific developments in faraway laboratories, the arts and ideas in distant centers, books and broadcasts from foreign places—all these, too, become of interest and importance to the newly developing country. And at the present pace of development, this change occurs almost suddenly.

Therefore, in a developing country the channels of information are enormously lengthened in a very short time. To the old connections of neighbor to neighbor, watchman or council to citizen, parent to child, or direct observation—to these must be added channels that reach far beyond direct experience and often to the other side of the world. Unfortunately, a certain amount of inefficiency always accompanies *new* channels, and *long* channels.

The loss along the channel

The longer the channel, the less likely that the original information will get through it. This is true whether the channel is in a highly developed or a less-developed society. It is easier to demonstrate in a well-developed society, because it has been more often measured there. Let us take, for example, what happens to wire news copy as it passes from the main office of a news agency to the readers of daily newspapers.

The news flow recorded in Figure 3 was measured during a five-day period in 1953. The results, therefore, are not precisely applicable to any other news agency, any other country, any other newspapers, or any other time. But the results are representative enough to give us an idea how much information content falls out as it passes through a long channel with many gatekeepers. The answer, in this case, is that about 98 per cent* of all the news copy that comes into the national office of a news agency may fall out by the time it has gone past the bureau manager who makes up the trunk wire, the state bureau manager who makes up the state wire, the news editor who makes up the paper, and the reader who decides which stories to read.

Now suppose that we lengthen the channel. Suppose, for example, we begin in India, China, Nigeria, or the UAR, with the hundreds of news events that happen in those countries every day. What proportion of those items are likely to pass the gatekeepers and get even as far as the main office of the news agency?

Suppose we lengthen the channel at the other end. Let us imagine that the flow of wire news is coming to a rural newspaper in a developing country. This will probably be a small newspaper, because of scarcity of readers, advertising support, and newsprint; therefore, it will publish even a smaller proportion of the news available to it. But its readers will have perhaps more reason to read the newspaper thoroughly and more reason to tell others what they have read. How many items in the paper will be passed on by word of mouth? Certainly the loss will be very great, and the accuracy less than perfect.

The flow of *news* is easier to count and there have been more

---

* Assuming that 120,000 words of copy were available in the main office, and that the average reader read perhaps 2,000 of these. (S. C. Cutlip, "Content and Flow of AP News—from Trunk to TTS to Reader," *Journalism Quarterly,* *31* (1954), 434–46.)

An estimated 100,000 to 125,000 words of news copy flows into the AP from various sources, each news cycle. The exact amount of copy is not known.

News flows into the AP, then goes

From this copy, the AP editors select and transmit about 283 items totaling nearly 57,000 words. This volume of news rolls across the United States each news cycle, on the several AP wires.

from AP Bureaus to trunk wires

From this mass of news, Wisconsin's AP Bureau selects about 77 items and 13,352 words for retransmission to nonmetropolitan Wisconsin dailies. This is about 27 per cent of items, 24 per cent of words, received on the trunk wires. To these, the Bureau adds about 45 stories and 6,000 words of Wisconsin news. To the state wire, therefore, it sent 122 items, totaling 19,423 words.

from trunk wires to state TTS wire

From the state wire, four typical Wisconsin dailies select and use about 74 items and 12,848 words. This is about 61 per cent of items, 66 per cent of words available on the state wire.

from state TTS wire to daily newspapers

The *Continuing Study of Newspaper Readership* and other readership studies show that the average reader reads a fourth to a fifth of the stories printed in his paper. Of the total number of stories reprinted from the state wire, he would therefore read about 15 stories, or about 2,800 words. Of the 283 items that started out on the trunk wire, he would probably read about nine.

from newspapers to readers

FIGURE 3. Flow of Associated Press news from agency home offices to four Wisconsin nonmetropolitan daily newspapers. Source: S. C. Cutlip, "Content and Flow of AP News," *Journalism Quarterly, 31* (1954), 434–46.

studies of it than of other kinds of information. But there is the same kind of loss in the flow of scientific, economic, political, and community development information to the people of a village; and even a higher loss in representing the needs, wishes, and difficulties of a village to the governmental leaders. Anyone who has observed the flow of development information from the state capital or another distant source to the villages will recognize in Figure 3 what he, too, has seen; the gradual depletion of the flow as it moves farther from the source. The dissemination of development information is aptly compared to irrigation: the need is to assure an adequate flow at the end of the channel despite the amounts that seep out en route through the desert. Therefore, long channels reduce the already short supply.

Another problem with long channels is that information, if it is to be applied locally to agriculture, community development, political participation, and the like, must be in a form to be *used* locally. Local needs differ sharply in types of farming, seasons, customs, stage of development, degree of acceptance, and sometimes language. Therefore, it becomes important not only to lose as little as possible of the information, but also to translate and adapt it for local use, and to complement it by information which can be carried through other channels, many of which can be shorter and more specifically directed to the target. This brings us to mention "gatekeepers" and "multiple channels."

Gatekeepers

The longer the information channel, the more points along the channel at which someone will have the right to say whether the message shall be received and retransmitted, and whether it shall be retransmitted in the same form or with changes. The Viennese psychologist Kurt Lewin was perhaps the first observer to point out the existence of these "gates" and "gatekeepers."[16] He perceived that all along an information channel are points at which "in" or "out" decisions have to be made, and therefore the power to operate these gates and the rules or personalities that govern their operation become crucial in the flow of information.

Gatekeepers are found in interpersonal channels as well as in mass media channels. Any person along an interpersonal channel can decide whether or not to repeat, or in what form to repeat, a message that comes to him. There have been many studies of what happens to rumors being passed by interpersonal chains.[17] These messages are often transformed by the particular interests and knowledge of the person at the gate. When the channel is long enough, the message that comes out at the end of it often bears little resemblance to the one that started.

But consider what power gatekeepers have in mass media channels. Consider, for example, the channels that carry news around the world. The first gatekeeper is the person who sees the news happen. He sees it selectively; notices some things, not others; reports some parts of the event, not others. A second gatekeeper is the reporter who talks to the "news source." As a matter of fact, the reporter may have to talk to a number of news sources; but in any case he has to decide which facts to pass along the chain, what to write, what shape and color and importance to give the event. He gives his story to his editor, who must decide how to edit the story, whether to cut or add or change. Then he has to decide whether the story is worth showing to the wire news service. If he decides it is, then someone at the news service must decide whether it is one of the few stories which, out of many hundreds, will be picked up and telegraphed to other towns. Someone else will decide whether it is worth sending overseas, and if so, in what form and how long it should be. If it does indeed go overseas, then it will probably come to the very big gate where two news agencies exchange copy; and here again the second news agency must decide whether to pass it along, whether to cut or rewrite. There is always more news than can be sent on. If the story goes on, it comes to still more gates: the national news wire, the regional wires, ultimately the newspapers or broadcasting stations where news editors must decide which items to print or read over the air, and how much to cut and to rewrite. It is hardly surprising, therefore, that of many thousands of items that start along the world's news chains, only a few dozen may finally reach readers or listeners in any given country, and that at the end of the chain they will be briefer and sometimes altered.

In a developing country, the chains of information from the leaders to the people and back, and among the people, are particularly dependent on gatekeepers, not only because they are long and seldom supplemented or checked upon by parallel channels (as we shall have occasion to observe in the next few pages), but also because of the need to adapt the information for local use. The earlier the stage of development, the more specific the local needs will be. Therefore, the more responsibility will rest on the community worker, the agricultural adviser, the literate villager who reports to others on what the newspaper says, the elected representative who speaks for the people to higher levels of government and explains government actions to the people, the regional newspaper that selects wire news for local use and is in position to tell the people how the development program is going, the reporter or correspondent who is in position to report to the government on how the program is going and what it needs, the "influential" villager who is asked for advice—these and many other gatekeepers. But in a new country expert gatekeepers are usually in short supply. The agricultural, health, and community development organizations are not yet adequately built. There are few local radio stations or local newspapers, and the news-gathering services are not very local in nature. The "middlemen" who help to make new knowledge usable to the people of a highly developed country are scarce in new countries. And therefore information must get along as best it can. Highly developed countries have found that their store of scientific and technical knowledge was of very little use to the nonscientist until expert middlemen were developed to explain or apply this knowledge. Furthermore, the knowledge was neither as much as needed nor in a form for best application until these middlemen reported back to the laboratories on how the knowledge worked in the field, and what new problems demanded answers. Thus, biological and physical sciences grew swiftly after skilled appliers like physicians, pharmacists, and engineers became available, and only then did medical and engineering knowledge begin to realize their real potential for usefulness. Similarly, the development of skilled explainers, such as writers about science, agricultural agents, and health extension and social service workers, made a profound difference in how well the new knowledge was understood and what use the people were prepared to make of it.

The scarcity of appliers like physicians and engineers in the developing countries is a matter these countries have long been trying to do something about. The importance of skilled informational middlemen is perhaps less well realized. Yet where the channels of information are thin and few, it becomes all the more important to make the message clear and convincing. Where people have had little technical education, it becomes all the more important to explain technology in terms the people know. Where change is called for, it is all the more important for the writer or speaker or adviser to be able to empathize with the people who are asked to change.

The usefulness of multiple channels

The scarcity of skilled gatekeepers is related to the scarcity of multiple channels for reaching the people of a developing society.

One reason why information flows faster in a country at a relatively advanced stage of development is that more channels are available. There are more radios, more copies of newspapers, and so forth. But there are also more *kinds* of channels. That is, the same person will have radio, newspaper and other sources of information. This is a matter of some importance.

In the early spring of 1963, 3,168 persons in 198 villages in all parts of India were interviewed to find out whether they knew about the Chinese-Indian fighting in the Himalayas, and, if so, how they had received the information.[18] The survey was conducted several months after the events on the northern borders. By that time, 83 per cent of the villagers had heard the news. Of those who had heard, approximately 40 per cent had received their information from the mass media, and 60 per cent from individuals —friends, family, shopkeepers, and the like.

We can put these figures in perspective by comparing them with a study of news reception in a society that is economically more highly developed.[19] When the circulation of three important news stories was measured in three American cities and towns, it was found that 93 per cent of the people had heard the news within 24 hours. This indicates somewhat faster circulation, especially since none of the three stories equaled in importance the events in India. Of the 93 per cent who had heard the news, 88 per cent had received it through mass media (as compared with 40 per cent in the Indian villages). These persons were fairly evenly divided among those persons who had heard the story on television (37 per cent), radio (27 per cent), and newspaper (24 per cent). Among the Indian villagers 22 per cent had first heard the news from radio, 17 per cent from newspapers, and 1 per cent from posters.

Thus, the more highly developed society has at least three strong media channels to bring it news, and these reach most or all of the people.[20] The village society, on the other hand, has only two, and these reach perhaps less than half of the people.

If they want additional details on news, or want to check up on what they have heard, people in a more highly developed society can easily turn to another medium. If they want more details on a news story heard on the radio, they can turn to the newspaper. If they want pictorial coverage of the news event, they can turn to television. But the majority of the people in a developing village are likely to have no secondary source except other people.

This means that, not only is there less likelihood of reaching any person in the first place, but also less opportunity for a person to check up on what has been heard about the new agricultural program, where the clinic is to be, how the fertilizer is to be obtained or used, what the new tax plan is all about, or any other kind of development information likely to be circulated. One possible consequence is misunderstanding. Rao has described another consequence.[21] He found in his village study that when additional information was available to support, confirm, or clarify suggested changes, then favorable action was much more likely to take place.

When supplementary information was not available, the suggestions for change were typically received with suspicion and often resisted.

When multiple channels are available, then it is much easier to furnish a *local* service, discover and meet local needs, and direct information to them. Increasingly, as a country develops, local newspapers, local radio stations, local production of leaflets, and the like come into existence. In a newly developing society, however, these are scarce. Demands on the budget require that the radio serve as large an area as possible. A village, even a small town, cannot support a newspaper: regional support is necessary. When investment capital is hard to come by, multiple channels look like an unnecessary luxury.

This is an unfortunate fact of life in the early stages of economic and social development. Information would flow more freely if it could travel multiple channels. It would be received more accurately and be more effective. If local media could supplement regional and national media, they could play the part of middlemen, interpreting the information and fitting it to local conditions and needs. The coming into existence of these multiple and local channels is therefore one sign that the transition to modern communication is well on the way. But during at least the early part of transition, the lack of multiple channels, the problems of new and long channels and consequent information loss, and the scarcity of skilled gatekeepers and local media must be added to the other problems of information flow we have noted in this section.

3. How the Mass Media Are Distributed in the World

THE IMPORTANCE OF MASS COMMUNICATION

We have been speaking of the transition to modern communication as though it were a certainty. And, indeed, it is a certainty, barring some unforeseen event that would reverse the direction of economic and social development. The question we are considering in these pages is not *whether* the mass media will ultimately come into wide use in the developing countries as channels of information and education, but rather whether their introduction should be *hurried* so that they can do more than they are doing at present to contribute to national development.

The mass media have a particular importance at this point in history. They are the great multipliers. Just as the machines of the Industrial Revolution are able to multiply human power with other kinds of energy, so are the communicating machines of the Communication Revolution able to multiply human messages to a degree previously unheard of. We saw evidence in Chapter 2 that the presence of mass media makes a significant difference in the level of information *even among people who are unable to read the printed media and do not have access to the electronic media.* The fortuitous fact about the relation of information to national development is that mass communication should be available and well developed, and its use relatively well understood, when so many new countries are trying to communicate so much so quickly to so many people.

Mass communication, throughout its entire history, has been effective in combating privilege. The significance of the development of printing in the fifteenth century was not only to swing the balance from the long centuries of spoken firsthand communication toward visual and secondhand communication on a grand scale, but, more important, to extend learning beyond a privileged handful. Almost at once, the printed media became tools of political and social change. The revolutions in Europe and North America would have been most unlikely without the printed media. The development of public schools would have been most unlikely, if not impossible, without the printed media. In the nineteenth century, new developments in mass communication reached over the heads of the specially privileged and the specially educated to offer information and education to the great masses of men. Political democracy, economic opportunity, free public education, the Industrial Revolution, and mass communication were all woven together to make a great change in human life and society on several continents. Now the new electronic developments in communication have swung the balance back toward communication in which one can see and hear the communicator. They have given the developing countries potential channels of information with which to reach fantastically large audiences, to communicate with underprivileged masses despite the literacy barrier, to teach difficult skills by "showing how" they are done, to speak almost with the effectiveness of face-to-face communication.

It may well be that mass communication (and the interpersonal communication we have learned to combine with it) are about to play a key part in the greatest social revolution of all time—the economic and social uplift of two-thirds of the world's people. We are not implying that mass communication can do it alone. Without determined national leadership, adequate population and resources, and sources of capital, the most efficient communication system in the world could not bring about economic development. But this at least we can say with confidence: if the mass media or some equally potent and rapid means of information were not available, it would be utterly impossible to think of national economic and social development in terms of the timetables that are being attached to such development today.

Let us therefore see how widely available the mass media are for such use in the developing countries. Where are the facilities

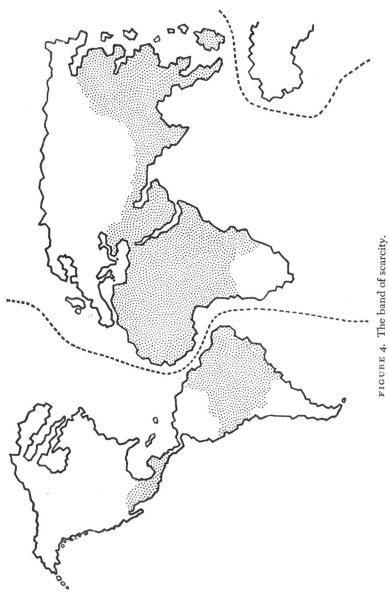

FIGURE 4. The band of scarcity.

adequate, and where are they in short supply, for the battle of development? What is the rate of growth of these media, and what are the conditions under which they grow or lag?

THE HAVES AND HAVE-NOTS

Let us not harbor any delusion that the mass media are alike in all the underdeveloped countries. Quite the contrary: there is a great and sometimes astonishing variety. The media systems are as different from each other as the countries themselves. For example, in seven African countries there is no daily press except roneotyped bulletins from a government information service, and in 15 African countries there are no daily newspapers of any kind.[1] On the other hand, throughout Latin America the press is well developed in both large and small cities. Despite lagging national economies, a highly sophisticated daily press has emerged—one example out of many is Chile. In some underdeveloped countries—Mauritania, for example—it is necessary because of lack of printing facilities to have such periodicals as exist printed outside the country. In other underdeveloped countries, like India, the printing industry is highly developed and equipped to publish in a number of languages and a variety of technical subject matters. In some countries the whole broadcasting operation depends on an ancient transmitter held together only by loving care and constant maintenance. In some almost equally underdeveloped countries, the radio stations are shining with new equipment. The writer has been in a country where the breakdown of a single projector, and the difficulty of getting someone to repair it, eliminated for months a large part of the total capability of the country for showing educational films, and in another underdeveloped country where one educational center had been given a quarter-million dollars' worth of audiovisual equipment.

Thus there is no single pattern. But as one moves from country to country one becomes aware of a condition that is more often the rule than the exception in developing countries. This is the condition of scarcity.

Look at Figure 4. Begin at the southern border of the United States, and let your eyes follow down Latin America as far as the southern border of Brazil. Then look eastward over the whole enormous mass of Africa. Let your eyes sweep over the Arab Crescent, and across all South and Southeast Asia, where nearly one and one-half billion people live in the area from Iran to the eastern tip of Indonesia. This, with exceptions here and there, is the band of scarcity—a band that circles the earth, including most of the illiterates, almost all the underdeveloped countries, and most of the countries where communication systems also are underdeveloped.

Unesco has suggested a yardstick by which to measure the sufficiency or insufficiency of mass communication facilities in the developing countries. As an "immediate target," the organization says, every country should aim to provide for every 100 of its inhabitants ten copies of daily newspapers, five radio receivers, two cinema seats, and two television receivers. In a report to the United Nations, Unesco said:

As many as 100 states and territories in Africa, Asia, and Latin America fall below this very low "minimum" level in all four of the mass media. These countries have a combined population of 1,910 millions, or 66 per cent of the world total. An additional 19 countries, representing 2 per cent of the world population, fall below the "Unesco minimum" in respect of three of the media. In short, nearly 70 percent of the world's peoples lack the barest means of being informed of developments at home, let alone in other countries.

In point of fact, the actual situation is even worse because the above criteria do not take into account the distribution of facilities within countries. In many underdeveloped countries, over 60 per cent of the population live in rural districts, whereas the facilities for information are concentrated in a relatively few urban areas. Consequently, the above very general analysis does not fully reflect the dearth of facilities in the rural areas of most underdeveloped countries, and even of most semideveloped countries which otherwise stand above the "Unesco minimum" level.

Another striking fact is that some 40 sovereign states[2] in the underdeveloped regions have no national news agencies and must rely for much of their domestic news on the five world agencies—Associated Press and United Press International (U.S.), Reuters (British Commonwealth), Agence France Presse (France), and Tass (USSR). Moreover, news about these countries is sent abroad largely through the world agencies—that is, through services which are not their own.

The above evaluation of development of the mass media in some 120 countries corresponds very closely with the United Nations designation of countries which are generally underdeveloped. With due regard for the limitation of the method of classification used, the United Nations considers that a country is underdeveloped if the average per capita income is less than $300 annually. One hundred and one countries are found to be below this income level and an additional 16 countries fall within the $300 to $400 range. The countries in these two groups are, with few exceptions, those which fall below the "Unesco minimum" for information facilities or which stand only slightly above that level.[3]

If Unesco's minimum standards were achieved, it would mean that approximately one out of every two families would have a daily newspaper, and one out of every four families, a radio receiver. There would be one television set and one cinema seat for every ten families. Not too much to ask. The newspaper minimum is almost exactly the present world average; the other two minima are considerably *below* the world average. Yet at least 100 states and territories, representing two-thirds of the world's people, fall below even those standards. Table 12 sums up progress toward "Unesco minima" in the great regions of the world.

TABLE 12. Numbers of Daily Newspaper Copies, Radio Receivers, Cinema Seats, and Television Receivers per 100 Persons in Regions of the World, 1961

	Copies of Daily Newspapers	Radio Receivers	Cinema Seats	Television Receivers
The world	9.8	13.2	2.3	3.8
Africa	1.2	2.3	0.6	0.07
North America	25.0	73.0	5.5	23.4
South America	8.0	11.0	3.4	2.0
Asia	4.0	2.1	0.6	0.6
Europe	23.0	21.8	5.4	7.4
Oceania	29.0	20.6	7.7	8.8
USSR	18.1	20.5	5.6	3.0
Three mostly underdeveloped regions (with two-thirds of the world's people)	3.8	2.7	0.8	0.6
Four mostly developed regions (with one-third of the world's people)	22.7	35.8	5.5	10.7

Source: Calculated from Unesco, *World Communications* (Paris, 1964).

This table separates the haves from the have-nots in a most dramatic way. Look at the figures on Africa for a moment. That great continent has less than one-sixth of the world's per capita average newspaper circulation, a little over one-sixth the world per capita average on radio receivers, one-fourth the world average on cinema seats, one-sixtieth the world average on television sets. The people of Africa have, on the average, one-twentieth as many daily newspaper copies per 100 persons as do the people of North America, one-thirty-fifth as many radios per 100 persons, one-five-hundredth as many television sets in proportion to the population. Asia is only slightly better off. On the other hand, it is clear that South America is relatively in better position compared with the more highly developed continents—in fact, it is actually over the Unesco minima in both radio receivers and cinema seats. This last table represents what we might call the *receiving network*. We can get some measure of the *sending*, or *propagating*, network from Table 13.

This table also, in its own way, separates the haves from the have-nots. Two-thirds of the world's people have but one-third of the daily newspapers (and much less than one-third of the circulation); they have one-fourth of the world's radio transmitters,

TABLE 13. Number of Daily Newspapers, Radio Transmitters, Long Films Produced per Year, and Number of Television Transmitters, in Regions of the World, 1961

	Daily Newspapers	Radio Transmitters	Long Films Made	Television Transmitters
Africa	220	400	43	25
North America	2,200	5,700	306	759
South America	750	1,900	59	87
Asia	1,270	1,220	1,618	258
Europe	2,980	2,820	1,030	1,406
Oceania	110	250	1	19
USSR	460	410	137	173
Three mostly underdeveloped regions (with two-thirds of the world's people)	2,240	3,520	1,720	370
Four mostly developed regions (with one-third of the world's people)	5,750	9,180	1,474	2,357

Source: Calculated from Unesco, *World Communications* (Paris, 1964).

TABLE 14. Growth in Per Cent, 1950–61, of Press, Radio,
and Film in Major Regions
Facilities per 100 persons

	Newspaper Copies	Radio Receivers	Cinema Seats
Africa	30%	229%	20%
North America	−13	67	
South America	33	72	3
Asia	33	100	100
Europe	−5	133	10
Oceania	−3	1	
USSR	55	230	

Source: Calculated from Unesco, *World Communications*, 1964 and former editions. Figures for cinema seats in North America, Oceania, and the USSR were not available.

and 12 per cent of the world's television transmitters. Only in the field of film making, thanks largely to the highly productive studios of India and Japan, do the three less-developed continents compare well with the other regions.°

Another way to measure the world's supply of mass media is to ask how fast the supply is growing. Because of the existence of 1950 figures, we have a 12-year yardstick on which to measure growth in the media. In Table 14 are such growth figures for news-

---

° The table in Appendix A describes numerically the communication development of all the African, Asian, and Latin American countries. Looking at this, it is easy to see the exceptions on those continents to the general rule of underdeveloped communication systems. Latin America is obviously somewhat further along than the other two regions, both in literacy and in the facilities of mass communication. The countries in the southern part of South America—Argentina, Uruguay, Chile—can hardly be said to be underdeveloped in communication. In Middle America, countries like Costa Rica, Mexico, and Cuba are somewhat ahead of their neighbors. In Africa, the southernmost countries and the northern tier of countries are slightly in advance, so far as communication development goes, of the sub-Sahara tropical countries. In the Middle East, Israel and Lebanon have developed further than the countries around them. In Asia proper, Japan, of course, is a highly literate country with a well-developed communication system. Hong Kong, Singapore, China (Taiwan), and the Federation of Malaya have also developed their mass media, in one way or another, somewhat faster than their neighbors; and the high literacy in countries like Burma, Thailand, and the Philippines is promising for the future. It is tempting to develop these differences in greater detail. But it is clear that the striking and important differences are not among the developing countries, but rather between the developed and the developing.

TABLE 15. Growth in Per Cent, 1950–62, of Numbers of Daily
            Newspapers and Radio Transmitters in
            Major Regions of the World

	Daily Newspapers	*Radio Transmitters*
Africa	20%	156%
North America	5	58
South America	25	140
Asia	35	180
Europe	25	355
Oceania	10	25
USSR	16	310

Source: Calculated from Unesco, *World Communications,* 1964 and former editions.

paper circulation, radio receivers, and cinema seats. (Because
television is so recent, growth rates are unreliable for the newer
countries.) Table 15 shows comparable figures for some of the
propagating networks.

It is apparent that radio has been growing much faster than
newspapers, and that its rate of growth in Africa is quite phenom-
enal. We must remember, however, that Africa in 1950 had less
than one receiver, on the average, per 100 persons. It is interesting also to note that newspaper circulation in three of the highly
developed regions has actually fallen, relative to the population,
in the last dozen years.

Here the impressive rate of growth of radio facilities stands out
from the rest of the table. Africa, Asia, and South America all are
developing their radio facilities at an average of 10 per cent or
more annually. Asia had only 440 radio transmitters (including
Japan's) in 1950, and Africa had only 140. Now Asia has 1,220,
and Africa 400.

We can sum up in the following way what these tables have to
tell us about the distribution of mass communication throughout
the world.

1. In every respect except film making, Latin America is somewhat further developed in communication than either Asia or
Africa. This is most notably true of radio and television, but also
holds in the case of newspapers: per capita circulation in South

America is twice what it is in Asia, and six times as much as in Africa. The busy Asian studios outproduce those of South America, but the annual attendance per person is greater in South America than in either Asia or Africa.

2. The underdeveloped regions of the world are moving along impressively toward meeting the Unesco minima in radio. The rate of growth in radio will take both Asia and Africa over the Unesco standards within a relatively few years. South America has already passed the minimum. It seems apparent that the less-developed lands are planning to depend chiefly on radio to reach their scattered and largely illiterate populations.[4]

3. The underdeveloped regions are lagging in newspaper development. This is probably related to the development of literacy and education; and when the growth is sufficient in those two areas, we can expect faster growth in newspaper circulation.

4. But all these differences are overshadowed by the great overall difference between the parts of the world where economic development is far along and the parts where it is not. It is the same order of difference we have noted earlier, in comparisons of life expectancy, productivity, industrialization, income, and the like, and here the discrepancies are fully as spectacular as the earlier ones. In every respect, the peoples of Africa, Asia, and Latin America are have-not people in mass communication. Latin America does very well in newspapers and radio, it is true, but is still below well-developed regions, and it lags, despite its widely used common languages, in forming news agencies. The band of scarcity is no illusion. This is what Unesco was talking about when it spoke of "a dearth of facilities over wide regions of the globe [which] prevents hundreds of millions of people from effectively enjoying freedom of information."[5]

THE MEDIA IN THE DEVELOPING COUNTRIES

Not all the differences between mass communication in the developing and the highly developed countries are quantitative ones.

One of the first things one notices about mass communication in underdeveloped countries is how the media cluster in the cities.

To some extent, of course, this is true everywhere. In highly developed as well as underdeveloped countries, the newspapers, broadcasting stations, and film theaters tend to be where the concentrations of people are. But in highly developed countries, the majority of people live in urban settings; in a typical underdeveloped country 80 per cent of the people live in rural settings. Therefore, if the media concentrate on urban centers in developing countries they are really concentrating on a *minority* of the people.

This is notably the case with newspapers. Consider a few examples. In Thailand, a country of 25 million, all the daily newspapers are published in the capital city. In neighboring Burma, almost all the newspapers are published in the capital, and such provincial papers as exist have minuscule circulations. Newspaper circulation in the Ivory Coast is almost entirely in or very near Abidjan. Three of Ghana's four dailies are published in Accra. Of the UAR's 37 dailies, all but four are published in Cairo or Alexandria. Only in Latin America, among the developing regions, is the provincial and smaller city press comparatively well developed.

To a lesser extent, radio and films also cluster in the cities. One would expect to find the studios and transmitters in the cities, of course, but one might hope to find in the rural regions a larger proportion of the radio receivers (inasmuch as radio can cover great distances) and a larger proportion of the film attendance (inasmuch as films, like radio, can jump the literacy barrier). But actually only a little more than one in ten of India's radio receivers, to take one example, are in the villages, where the rural four-fifths of India's people live, and the bulk of cinema attendance is likewise in the cities. It is spectacular in many developing countries to see the signs of the media all but vanish at the borders of the cities. One can read the morning papers in his hotel, see the young people stroll past his window carrying transistor radios, see the advertisement for the current movie across the street; then drive out of the city to spend the day in the villages, and probably see not a single newspaper, radio receiver, or film theater all day.

Why should this be? One reason is the inordinate difficulty of circulation. The newspapers have to combat inadequate roads,

washouts in the rainy season, inadequate postal services. Radio
and films face a lack of electricity in the villages, and lack of technically trained personnel outside the cities to repair receivers or
operate film showings. In more than one country, a well-meant plan
to extend the coverage of radio has failed simply because there
was no one to recharge or replace a battery in an otherwise oper-
able receiving set.

Literacy too drops off at the edge of the cities. In the cities there
are concentrations of literates, even though the overall percentage
may not be very high. But a village may have no more than one or
two persons able and willing to read a newspaper. Serving such
minuscule audiences makes an obviously difficult circulation problem.

Money for mass media is harder to come by in subsistence economies and in the village. A workman in California with what he
earns from one hour's labor can buy 50 copies of a 40-page newspaper, if he wants to—2,000 pages. In Indonesia, one hour's labor
will buy seven copies of a four-page paper—28 pages.[6] A villager
in Burma or Malaya will be investing a sizable part of his annual
cash income if he subscribes to a magazine. By the same token, a
radio is a major purchase in a village. If Unesco's long-pursued
goal of a five-dollar radio could be realized, it would make a considerable difference in the circulation of radio in the rural regions
of developing countries.

Still another reason for impeded circulation is the language
problem. The existence of Spanish (and in Brazil, Portuguese) as
lingua franca may be one of the key reasons why the press has
developed faster and more fully in Latin America than in Africa
or Asia. Some of the language problems facing the media in Africa
and Asia are fantastic. India is the classical example: 14 states
with their own languages, 72 different languages spoken by at
least 100,000 persons each, a national radio system that can hardly
ever broadcast nationally, national wire news services that must
be translated for each of the vernacular newspapers, government
agricultural and community development information that must
be either decentralized or translated at each state or district level.

Yet India is not unique in this respect. Most of the Asian countries have to deal with several languages, and Africa is a veritable crazy quilt of languages. Thus, Nigeria has to broadcast to its own people in Hausa, Ibo, Yoruba, English, and 11 other local languages. Ghana must broadcast to its people in Akan, Hausa, Dagbani, Ga, Ewe, English, and French.

All these things make for small audiences. In all of Guinea, for example, there is but one daily; its circulation is 600. Mali has three dailies, with a total circulation of 3,000. Even in India, with its 440 million people and its enormous cities, the largest newspaper circulation is not far over 100,000.

Low circulations make for financial difficulties. When theaters are few and admission small, a developing country finds it hard to make films. In some South Asian countries, exhibitors calculate that films must run six or seven weeks at each theater in order to make a profit. Newspapers in developing countries often face a cruel financial struggle. The Unesco conferences on development of the mass media reported that only a small percentage of the papers were in sound financial position. The ones doing best were, for the most part, those that "had access to credit from the outset, the initial investment having been made by governments or foreign interests."[7] In many countries of Africa the foreign-owned press, usually in English or French, is well financed, well equipped, and prosperous; but the vernacular press, locally owned, is struggling for its financial life. In a country like India, most of the large and prosperous papers are in the English language, and the vernacular papers are usually less large and less prosperous.

It is true that in many of the developing countries today one can start a newspaper for a few thousand dollars, as it was possible to do a century ago in some of the highly developed countries. But before we permit ourselves to become sentimental about this, we should take note of a remarkable analysis by A. R. Bhat, president of the Indian Language Newspaper Association, of the financial problems of a small daily in a developing country.[8]

It *is* possible to start such a daily (meaning a daily published in one of the Indian languages, aimed at an expected circulation of 5,000 to 10,000, in a "town" of perhaps 100,000), says Mr. Bhat, for somewhere between $7,500 and $15,000. But that only begins to solve the problems.

The English-language newspapers with prestige receive a major share of government and private advertising budgets. The remainder of the advertising money goes first to Indian-language papers in the great cities and state capitals. Only a small amount trickles down to the Indian-language papers trying to serve the smaller cities. Because of this, the smaller papers have to charge higher advertising rates in an effort to survive. This makes their advertising still less attractive to purchasers.

Newsprint costs more outside the great cities. Because of shortages of capital and foreign exchange, the smaller papers often have trouble making long-term agreements for purchase of newsprint, and therefore may have to pay premiums on prices that are already higher than their city competition pays.

News agency costs are proportionally higher on a small daily, and, if it is a local-language daily, the cost of translation must be added to the fee for the wire service. But if there is no wire news, the paper is not doing the job it should do, and is less attractive to subscribers.

Furthermore, in some countries even the wastepaper value of a newspaper is something that purchasers or subscribers take into account. They can subtract from the price of the paper the money they receive from selling the used copy. This, too, makes life harder for the smaller paper. The less advertising it has, the fewer pages it can print, and the less it will be worth as wastepaper to the subscribers.

Mr. Bhat estimates that it takes at least three years for a small vernacular paper to begin to make ends meet. During that time, the publisher must be prepared to take losses at least equivalent to the initial capital he has invested. He finds it hard to borrow, because commercial banks do not normally grant installment loans or accept machinery and other fixed assets as security.

But suppose the paper does get its head above water. Suppose it is so successful that its circulation, after three years, rises above

10,000. This is too many papers for a flat-bed and cylinder press; another press is needed. The paper faces a staggering outlay of capital if it is to grow larger—$40,000 or so for a rotary press.

Thus, although a new paper can be started inexpensively, it finds it hard to keep going and hard to grow.

Something of a phenomenon, in view of the cost problems, is the introduction of television into so many developing countries. Television is the most costly of the media to capitalize, and it requires perhaps a wider diversity of skills than any other medium. Its receiving sets are expensive, compared with radio, and repairs are more difficult and costly. Some new nations have introduced television chiefly as an aid to their educational systems; others, apparently, because television has prestige. We do not mean to imply that the introduction of television may not be economically desirable; indeed, later on we shall point out situations in which it may save money as well as contribute to the speed of development. But in many places it contrasts oddly with the communication shortages one sees on every hand: shortages in machinery and technical personnel, raw film, newsprint, trained management and editorial personnel, and research.

Yet, despite the shortages, the machinery runs. Communication flows. One reason why the system works better than might be expected is that the common and traditional channels of communication are pressed into use to extend the new media. Not every country has a communication device so spectacular as the Yoruba talking drums, and yet almost every developing country has the custom of reading the newspaper to illiterates—in the coffee house, the village square, the schoolhouse, or any other place where people congregate. Institutions like the bazaar, where for centuries people have exchanged information, now serve to carry information first planted by the mass media. Where the mass media cannot readily reach, the puppet shows, storytellers, poets, ballad singers, and dramatic groups carry some of the same information and persuasion. Radio listening and discussion groups are formed around some of the radio receivers. Leaders of many of these countries have learned to use very large public meetings with great skill, and, indeed, the crowd at a meeting may be more numerous than the readers of the local newspaper, or the listeners to a speech on the radio. Thus we must not think of the media in a developing country as standing by themselves. They fit into the larger communication system of the country; and the drums, the bazaars, the meetings, and the ballad singers all help to carry the word.

It may be that the media are proportionally more visible when they are still new and small. We sometimes forget how the mass media must appear to the people of a developing country, and only when we are in a village and hear the shouts of joy at the appearance of the cinema van do we realize that a movie to these people is not what a movie is in a highly developed culture. The mass media come to the traditional villages of the world with a freshness they have long ceased to carry in highly developed cultures. Motion pictures open a bag of wonders. Radio serves as a bridge, as Hortense Powdermaker says, between the tribal and the modern world.[9] Print, when one learns to read, is not only a source of much pleasure, but also a source of understanding of many problems in the modern world. Even beyond that, to quote Miss Powdermaker again, "Literacy is not just learning how to read but is concerned with comprehending a form of reality beyond immediate experience."[10] Print, therefore, is a liberating, a revolutionary experience; it helps free an individual from his group, his social customs, his routine.[11] In societies that developed earlier, the chief function of the printed media has indeed been to introduce the reader to a new and secondary level of reality. The reader learned this from print, and therefore was not so bowled over by the audiovisual media. But the citizens of the developing countries, for the most part, are meeting radio and film before they are exposed to print, and therefore we can reasonably expect that both these media will have an importance and a vividness for such countries that they have never had in a country where printed media were highly developed before the audiovisual ones appeared. Although we have scant information about the way in which rural people in the underdeveloped countries listen to and view these new media, still there is little doubt that the media are perceived differently by persons more accustomed to them, and this gives rise to some misunderstandings and failures to communicate. But the potency of the media, especially for people who are changing and are looking for guidance and reinforcement, is not in doubt. There is little question of the power they are able to impart, for example, to the man who owns the first radio in a village, or is first to receive a newspaper. The first radio is a marvel. The first film is a miracle. The newspaper is more wonderful before it becomes generally available. Therefore, we should be unjustified if we equated effect completely with the size of the medium.

And yet, one comes away from a developing country worrying that the media numbers are so small, the coverage is inadequate, the rural targets are not being reached, the media are not being integrated fully enough with interpersonal organizations and communications. This is true, as we have said, in some places and some media more than others. In Asia, although there is usually too little chance to see films, there is a remarkable amount of film making. In Latin America, the press is well developed, and radio coverage is more extensive than in either Asia or Africa. But there is still not enough development of the media, not enough integration with the interpersonal channels, not skillful enough or general enough use to let mass communication do the job it is capable of doing. The question is, how can we raise these quantities until they reach the size of a "critical mass" which will set off the necessary chain reaction among the other components of development?

AUXILIARY SERVICES

How fast the mass media grow depends in part on how fast certain related elements of society grow. For example, the printed media are limited by the growth of literacy and the availability of newsprint. Where electrical mains are available in a country, there it is far easier to install radio transmitters and receivers, film projectors, and printing machinery. Growth rates of all the media are immensely stimulated by the spread of public education, and slowed by the lack of it. The mass media, like other parts of society, cannot develop far in advance of other social developments that are related to them and support them. Therefore, let us take electrification, newsprint, literacy, and public education as examples of the materials, services, and skills which are supportive of mass media, and inquire about their rate of growth.

Electrification

The pace of electrification may be indicated by the record of India between 1951 and 1961, presented in Table 16.

Thus it will be seen that the larger cities receive electricity first, and then the lines crawl slowly among and to the villages. Between 1956 and 1961, the mileage of high-voltage transmission lines in India more than doubled. And still electricity reaches less than 3 per cent of India's villages!

Where electricity is most needed to speed the development of mass media, there it is least available. The villages and the smaller towns are less likely than the cities to have it. The developing regions have less of it than the regions where development is already far along. North America, in 1961, produced 3,744 kilowatt hours of electricity per capita; Europe, Oceania, and the Soviet Union, about half that much. But South America produced 364, Africa 165, and Asia (without Japan) only 69 kilowatt hours per year.[12] This dramatizes the need for battery-powered transistor radios, if broadcasting is to be extended rapidly in Africa and Asia.

Newsprint

If the world's present supply of newsprint were divided evenly among all the people in the world, each person would receive about ten pounds a year. This is little enough. Newsprint is the physical

TABLE 16. Towns and Villages Electrified in India, by Size, 1951–61

Population Range	Total Number, Census of 1961	Number Electrified (March)		
		1951	1956	1961
Over 100,000	73	49	73	73
50,000 to 100,000	111	88	111	111
20,000 to 50,000	401	240	366	399
10,000 to 20,000	856	260	350	756
5,000 to 10,000	3,101	258	1,200	1,800
Less than 5,000	556,565	2,792	5,300	15,861

Source: Government of India Planning Commission, *Third Five-Year Plan* (New Delhi, 1960), p. 188.

material of newspapers. Ten pounds of it is enough to print perhaps three copies of the large Sunday edition of the *New York Times,* or one copy per week for a year of the smaller newspapers which are more typical throughout the world. If it were divided evenly in the world, each family of six would be entitled to about enough paper to print a four-page daily newspaper.

But, of course, the supply is not divided evenly. An individual in North America averages about 60 pounds of newsprint per year, whereas one in Africa averages about two ounces, and one in Asia three. For Asia or Africa, therefore, this averages out to not much more than one newspaper a year per person. Of course, newspapers aren't distributed that way: one person gets a daily or weekly paper, and many other persons get no papers. But the unevenness of distribution between the developed and the underdeveloped regions is striking.

About 85 per cent of the world's total consumption of newsprint is in the three regions that are most developed, whereas only 15 per cent of it is in Africa, Asia, and Latin America, where the great majority of the world's people live. Per person, about 46 times as much newsprint goes to North America as to Africa, about 31 times as much as to Asia.

Between 1948 and 1960 the world supply of newsprint has nearly doubled—7.5 million metric tons to nearly 14 million. In the same period the production of paper other than newsprint has almost exactly doubled. A sample of developing countries shows that their use of newsprint has in many cases increased considerably in 10 or 12 years, as Table 17 shows. These are not unencouraging rates of growth, and yet the increase must be far greater before Asia and Africa can approach Unesco minima for newspaper circulation. When Asian and African newspapermen meet to talk about their problems, newsprint is always high on the list.

A recent study has in fact shown that the spread of literacy, in addition to growth in population and per capita income, is likely to bring about a huge increase in demand for printing paper. The report[13] notes that in countries with a very high rate of illiteracy, an increase of 1 per cent of literacy is likely to have the same im-

TABLE 17. Consumption of Newsprint in 12 Developing Countries, 1946–50 and 1961

	Average, 1946–50 Kilograms per Person	1961	Increase of Consumption per Capita
Brazil	1.6	2.9	81%
Burma	0.1	0.6	500
Colombia	1.3	2.6	100
El Salvador	1.0	2.1	110
Ghana	0.1	0.5	400
Guatemala	0.6	0.9	50
India	0.1	0.3	200
Indonesia	0.1	0.2	100
Iran	0.1	0.4	300
Nigeria	0.05	0.2	300
Thailand	0.2	0.9	350
UAR	0.7	1.9	171

Source: *United Nations Statistical Yearbook, 1962.*

pact on demand for printing paper as an increase of 5 per cent in per capita income. The report then applies this finding to the situation that is likely to develop in Africa and Asia. In 1955, consumption of printing and writing in these two regions totaled 732,000 metric tons. Assuming an annual rate of growth of even as little as 1.6 per cent in population and only 2 per cent in per capita income, combined with a two-thirds reduction of illiteracy between now and 1975, demand in that year would amount to some 4,400,-000 tons—about six times the 1955 figure!

Literacy

About 90 per cent of all the adult illiterates in the world—estimated conservatively at 700 millions—live within the area we have called the band of scarcity. In 97 per cent of all the countries of Africa and 70 per cent of all the countries of Asia, less than half of the people are literate. Where the mass media are most needed is where the literacy base of media growth is lowest.

There are no world-wide comparable figures on literacy that would let us measure the rate of growth as we have measured the growth in newsprint and electricity. The figures available to us indicate that literacy is growing, illiteracy is on the wane, throughout the developing regions. The order of growth may be suggested by India, which has gone from 16 to 24 per cent adult literacy in ten years, despite its great growth in population.[14] Mainland China, another country with rapid population growth, claims a gain in literacy considerably greater than its population increase.[15] Some of the new nations of Africa have shown very respectable advances in literacy, but many of them started very low. When Libya, for example, came to independence, fewer than 5,000 of its people had been to school even for as much as five years, and there were only 14 university graduates in the country.[16]

In general, it appears that the rate of increase in literacy is running somewhat, but not greatly, above what would be expected on the basis of school activity alone. If we have to wait until the public schools have solved the developing nations' literacy problem, then a large part of the present adult generation will never be able to use the printed media, and the growth of these media will be slow indeed for the next generation.

Schooling

Public education is both a leading channel of information to the people and a chief support of the mass media. Schools build literacy. They instill the kinds of interests and needs that require mass media. They make for technical skills and higher incomes; a greater percentage of educated people can afford the mass media. And schools are distributed as unevenly in the world as the other elements we have been looking at.

Median enrollment ratios in 1950/54 were: in Australia and New Zealand, 88 per cent; in Europe and the USSR, 72 per cent; in North and Central America, 70 per cent. But in South America, only 51 per cent were enrolled, in Asia 44 per cent, and in Africa 27 per cent.[17] In that same year, only about one out of four boys and girls who entered schools in underdeveloped countries got as far as the fifth grade.[18] Around 1960, out of each 100,000 persons of all ages in the United States, 1,046 graduated from secondary school in a given year. In Japan the comparable figure was 1,002. But in Iraq, only 84 graduated; in Brazil, 32; in Ghana, 58; and in Haiti, 8.

In part, the reason for this difference is the lack of tradition for broad public education, in part the lack of facilities for education, and in part the lack of money for facilities and teachers. The countries of Asia and Africa in 1958 spent an average of about 2.5 per cent of their national income on education. The countries of Latin America averaged about 2.1 per cent. In this same year, the countries of Europe averaged 3.2 per cent of their national income on education; the countries of North America, about 4.3 per cent; and the Soviet Union about 6.8 per cent.[19] It must be remembered, of course, that the highly developed countries are spending a percentage of a much larger national income. For example, 3.1 per cent of national income that Sweden spent on education in 1958 meant about $35 for every man, woman, and child in the country; the 4.1 per cent that Great Britain spent was the equivalent of about $41 for every person; but Egypt's 3.9 per cent was only about $5 per person, Paraguay's 1.7 per cent added up to less than $2 per person, and India's 1.7 per cent and Nigeria's 1.9 per cent were less than $1.50 per person.

So where the underdeveloped countries are, there we find fewer people in school, fewer schools, and far less money being put into education.

In the last decade, despite these discouraging figures on support, there has been a great increase in schools and school attendance. This, of course, has been going on a long time. In 17 countries of Africa, the median primary enrollment ratio more than doubled between 1934 and 1953; in 11 countries of Asia it grew 80 per cent; in 10 countries of Latin America, 30 per cent. Table 18 presents some figures on what happened to educational enrollments in eight African countries in the seven years between 1953 and 1960. To see what figures like these mean, let us focus on *one* African country. This was the order of educational growth in Kenya between 1951 and 1961:

	1951	*1960*	*1961*
Schools	2,860	5,024	5,662
Pupils	260,279	726,892	830,191
Students in teacher training colleges	1,156	4,089	3,897

TABLE 18. Ratio of School Enrollment to Total Population and Increase in Enrollment in Eight African Countries, 1953 and 1960

	Ratio of School Enrollment to Total Population		Percentage Increase in School Enrollment 1953 to 1960	
	1953	1960	Primary	Secondary
Ethiopia	0.5%	0.9%	115%	208%
Ghana	10.8	13.5	28	69
Guinea	1.1	3.4	310	388
Ivory Coast	2.0	7.7	416	293
Nigeria	3.7	8.8	166	304
Senegal	2.7	4.2	131	119
Uganda	5.7	8.6	85	141
Upper Volta	0.8	1.7	133	175

Source: Unesco, *World Survey of Education.*

We must remember, however, that education has a slow payoff. Not until the next generation comes into productive adulthood will the full impact of the present educational growth be felt on the mass media.

We can sum up very briefly. The less-developed countries have less-developed mass communication systems also, and less development in the services that support the growth of mass communication. Their systems are underfinanced and underequipped, and as a result the flow of information is much less than it could be. However, there is an encouraging rate of growth throughout the developing regions, both in the mass media and in their supporting services. The question is whether it is fast enough for countries in a hurry.

Perhaps the best way to evaluate these growth rates is to calculate how long it would take the underdeveloped countries on two of the less-developed continents to reach the Unesco minima—ten copies of daily newspapers, five radio receivers, two cinema seats for every 100 persons—at their 1950–62 average rate of growth. This we have calculated,* using 1962 figures as a baseline and taking

---

* This estimate has been made by using the same formula as for compound interest, $A = P(1 + r)^n$, in which A is the amount to be attained at a given future time, P is the present amount, r is the rate of growth compounded annually, and n is the number of years.

the average annual growth rate through the period as the angle of projection. If they continue to grow at this rate, it then follows that

—To reach the standard of ten copies of daily newspapers for each 100 persons would take Africa until 2035, Asia until 1992;

—To reach the standard of five radio receivers for each 100 persons would take Africa until 1968, Asia until 1970;

—To reach the standard of two cinema seats for each 100 persons would take Africa until 2042, Asia until 1981.

Is that too long? Certainly it seems an inordinately long time for Africa and Asia, at least, to wait. Of course, in making the estimate we have assumed a steady rate of growth. This may not prove to be the case. It may well be that at a certain point in the growth of literacy and education, the circulation of newspapers will rise faster, or that, at a certain point in the progress of electrification, there will be a swifter growth of cinemas. It may also be that a decrease in the rate of population growth will occur and make the per capita figures look better. This we can hope for. But the picture points to the importance of radio in the decade ahead, and calls for increased efforts to speed the growth of the other media and their supporting services. Countries in a hurry can hardly be expected to be satisfied that—at the 1950–62 rate of development—Asia would not reach Unesco minima for daily newspaper circulation until nearly the end of the century, and Africa not for 70 years!

4. What Mass Communication Can Do, and What It Can *Help* to Do, in National Development

HOW SOCIAL CHANGE OCCURS

Increasing the number of radios, newspapers, and cinemas will not necessarily bring about a corresponding increase in the rate of social change. Merely multiplying messages and channels is not enough. For instance, several countries have found that adding a farm radio program has not by itself appeared to accomplish much in the adoption of new practices.[1] Yet, a question-and-answer program on farm practices in Jordan has proved to be very useful, and the combination of radio broadcasts with group discussion in rural forums has been very helpful in bringing about change.[2] Radio has not generally proved useful in literacy training, but in schools it has been highly useful.[3] It is obvious from examples like these that there are some tasks the mass media can and some they can't do and some they can do better than others, and that *how* they are used has much to do with their effectiveness. Therefore, we shall need to look at some of the evidence on how the mass media may be used effectively in the service of national development.

In the service of national development, the mass media are agents of social change. The specific kind of social change they are expected to help accomplish is the transition to new customs and practices and, in some cases, to different social relationships. Behind such changes in behavior must necessarily lie substantial changes in attitudes, beliefs, skills, and social norms.

How do changes like these occur? They may come about slowly, in the ordinary course of history, by continuing contact with another culture that leads to the borrowing of customs and beliefs. They may come about more quickly (although perhaps less permanently) by force—for example, when a conqueror or ruler *imposes* new patterns of behavior. The kind of change most developing countries are seeking today is neither of these. It is intended to be faster than the measured rhythm of historical change, less violent than the process of enforced change. It aims at a voluntary development in which many people will participate, and the better informed will assist the less. In place of force, it prefers persuasion and the provision of opportunity; in place of the usual rhythm of acculturation, a heightened flow of information.

Basically the mechanism of such a change is simple. First, the populace must become aware of a need which is not satisfied by present customs and behavior. Second, they must invent or borrow behavior that comes closer to meeting the need. A nation that wants to accelerate this process, as all developing nations do today, will try to make its people more widely and quickly aware of needs and of the opportunities for meeting them, will facilitate the decision process, and will help the people put the new practices smoothly and swiftly into effect.

Superficially, therefore, the process is simple. Actually, it is far from that.

Cultural linkage

One reason why it is not simple is that any custom or practice that is to be replaced or introduced will be closely linked with other customs and beliefs. Social organization is an interrelated whole; a change in any part of it will be felt in other parts, and a change in any aspects of man's behavior will be reflected in other aspects of his behavior. Therefore, when we think of social change we must think of it in terms of the change it will bring about in the *whole society* and the *whole man.*

Take a few examples. Among many people, as Margaret Mead points out eloquently, health is the expression of harmony with the universe.[4] Indeed, in many parts of the world man is thought of as continuous with his environment; his environment must be healthy in order for him to be healthy, and his acts will affect the health of his total environment. Therefore, a change in health practices may

well require even a change in religion if it is to be accepted. Such
an apparently simple matter as killing insect pests may bring down
a whole village on a resident because by adopting such a practice
he violates a prohibition against taking life. Such an apparently
routine matter as going for medical treatment may require an individual to decide whether it is more dangerous to forgo treatment
or to leave his own land, to which he has a magical relationship.
Amputation may require not merely learning to use the remaining
limbs more efficiently, but also a change in belief concerning the
sacredness of the missing limb. A physician's willingness to attend
dying patients may lead the people to lose their faith in him, as Dr.
Albert Schweitzer discovered at one time early in his African experience. The native medicine men refused to risk their reputations
on patients who might die; Dr. Schweitzer's action was not interpreted as humaneness but as lack of ability, and many natives
avoided his hospital because it was a place "where people went to
die."

As Dr. Raymond Fosdick said in summing up the Rockefeller
Foundation's world-wide experience with raising the standards of
medical care, public health is thus "an integral part of the social
process."

In economic and social development, change often begins with
agriculture. In this area cultural linkage is particularly strong. The
agriculture of the Egyptians, to take one example from a leading
scholar on Egyptian rural reconstruction, "is a highly integrated
way of life that is deeply rooted in centuries of tradition. It involves
personal emotional expression, family ties, religious sentiment, social intercourse, and firmly established habits of behavior."[5] To the
agricultural expert, as Mead says, "the large amount of time and
human energy spent in ritual, magic, and other religious practices
seems to be wasted. . . . But to the native, they give him faith in
his work, saving him from the anxieties which so often attend the
work of the cultivator. . . . [In many traditional cultures, agricul-
ture] is a total pattern of life rather than a means of earning a living. . . . Religion and agriculture are not compartmentalized."[6]
Practically, this means that any agricultural innovation that is rec-

ommended must be considered not only in terms of its expected productivity, but also in terms of what it would do to other parts of the cultivator's life and in terms of the beliefs and values, if any, that might lead him to resist it.

The experience of industrialized countries often furnishes little basis for understanding the resistance to change which is found in more traditional cultures. One example of this is the Western impatience over "featherbedding"—the employment of unnecessary workers—which is common especially in Asia. Behind this custom, of course, is the traditional sacredness of family ties. An employer is obligated to give jobs to his relatives, and he usually does not fire them (even when they are incompetent) any more than he would expel a misbehaving son from the family. The authority structure of the business often follows family lines, and if a more orthodox structure is imposed, neither the employer nor the employee is likely to know how to behave in a foreman-worker relationship. Consultants from industrialized countries have reported their puzzlement over the results of changing industries to a Western pattern of organization, when persons for whom "honesty was a matter of family policy acted with dishonesty in terms of the industrialized organization the validity of which as a unit they did not recognize."[7] This is not to say that industries should not be modernized—merely that such a change involves much more than revising the table of organization.

On the other hand, when a change is introduced in such a way as to take advantage of, rather than tear, cultural links, then the results may be good and far-reaching. An example of this is what happened when the first wagon was introduced to the Papago Indians.[8] Almost at once, the wagon became important in meeting long-standing needs of the community. It was used for hauling water, which had long been in short supply. The large pottery *ollas* made by the women were found to be broken too easily in the wagon, and they were soon replaced by wooden barrels and later by metal casks. This freed the women for other useful work. Soon one of the men learned the skill of working iron by heating and pounding it, so that he could shoe horses and repair the metal parts of the wagon. In order to use the wagon for hauling between the winter and the summer villages it became necessary to construct a road. This led to the development of some engineering skill, and a new form of group labor. With a few roads available, they began to use the wagon for trading journeys, and the village entered into a cash economy by cutting wood and raising extra corn and wheat for sale. And the use of the wagon as a common resource of the community led to wider cooperation in village government. Thus one simple innovation led a village a long way down the road toward modernizing.

The practical import of cultural linkage is, therefore, that any item of social change must be considered on a very broad basis, in order to anticipate the secondary effects and the resistances, take advantage of relationships where possible, and smooth the transition. To be able to do that, it is necessary to know the culture well, and to understand the whole pattern of life of which the proposed change is a part. What would such a change *mean* to the people who are being asked to change: that is the pertinent question.

Group relationships

Another reason why social change is complicated is that group relationships must always be taken into account. It is individuals who must change, but these individuals live in groups, work and play in groups, enjoy many of their most cherished experiences in groups. Many of the beliefs and values they hold most strongly are group norms—commonly held, and mutually defended. It is very difficult for an individual to turn against a strong group norm, for in that case either the whole group must change or he must find a new group.

Practically this means that social change is much easier if it is not contrary to group norms. But many of the group norms in almost all traditional societies are inimical to modernization. Among such norms are the religious beliefs about fatalism and man's inability to do anything about nature, the taboos against killing living things no matter how dangerous to health and crops, the belief that hard work is demeaning, and the custom of going deeply into debt for weddings and dowries. It is impossible, in the process of moderniz-ing, to avoid some confrontations with group norms. The question is, how to confront them.

Kurt Lewin did some challenging experiments in the early 1940's on the problem of persuading people to do previously unaccepta-ble things. For example, he tried to persuade housewives, in times of meat shortage, to serve previously unpopular cuts of meat. He found that lecturing to them, or letting them read an article, ac-complished relatively little. But when he gave them a chance to discuss the problem, very often the whole group decided to try the new meat dishes. And with the social backing of their peers—the knowledge that everybody was doing it, and therefore it was an approved social norm—most of the women actually did use the new and unfamiliar cuts of meat.[9] Other scholars have tried this kind of experiment on different subject matter. For example, Levine and Butler compared the effectiveness of lecture vs. discussion in changing the behavior of supervisors in an industry. The results were almost exactly those Lewin got. Without the opportunity to talk it over and get the whole group somewhat committed to change, very little happened.[10] This is the principle behind rural radio forums—assemble a group of farmers, introduce the problem by radio, and then give the listeners a chance to talk it over and decide what to do about it.[11]

The essential ingredient in the operations we have just talked about is not the discussion. The Radio Clubs formed in England before the war of 1939–45 discussed at great length, but before long the members grew weary of discussion for discussion's sake and attendance dwindled away. The act of discussion is important, but the essential ingredient is *participation in decision making and action*. Wherever a radio forum has been successful, its discussion has been, wherever possible, preparatory to action. Recognizing this, the Canadian Farm Forum has used as its slogan, "Listen, dis-cuss, act!"

Participation in decision making is therefore a powerful device to speed and smooth social change where group norms are involved. Where it is omitted, a program runs a great risk. For example, there was a widely known project in the 1930's and 1940's to save the Navaho ranch land from eroding away because of overgrazing. In order to save the range, the size of the Navaho flocks, particularly the sheep and goats, was arbitrarily reduced. More than 100,000 goats and more than 200,000 sheep were taken from the people for nominal payments. The program was successful in reducing the flocks and ultimately in reducing the erosion on the range. But it caused bitter trouble between the government and the Navahos, and nearly paralyzed every other effort to help the tribe.[12]

Two things were chiefly wrong with the way the program was put into effect. For one thing, it was imposed from the top, and for a long time no effort was made to bring Navahos to participate in laying out the rules. In the second place, the persons who designed the program of livestock reduction had no idea what the livestock, sheep most particularly, had come to mean to the Navaho. The entire economy of the tribe was based on sheep raising. The people lived on mutton, sold wool and lambs, and from some of the wool wove rugs and blankets for use and sale. Taking away the sheep was therefore a threat to the Navaho's already precarious existence. A slow and careful beginning, bringing the Navahos themselves into the planning, might have accomplished the goal without much ill-feeling. But the direct attack on the flocks was considered by the people an attack on them. It became a source of bitterness toward the government which has lasted more than 20 years, and has been responsible for stalling or slowing every program the government sought to put into effect to help the Navahos, and for the deep suspicion with which every government overture has been received. In fact, as Spicer says, "flock reduction" has become for the Navaho a symbol with the same unpleasant antigovernment overtones as "The Long Walk"—the hated and never forgotten march the Navahos were forced to make as prisoners in 1863.[13]

The mistake with the Navaho project, as with many other development programs, was in not securing the *understanding coopera-*

tion of the people. The phrase is Dube's. Describing a project in India, he mentions the "rigid schedule . . . , the higher authorities [laying] great emphasis on completion of physical targets, the officials . . . interested in getting things done somehow . . . ," the result being a certain amount of participation by the people in work drives, but very little understanding of the purpose of these drives, and a general feeling among the people that they were being coerced. "Communication is a two-way process," he comments. "It involves *giving* as well as *receiving* information and direction. While this fact has been recognized in defining the role of the Community Development Projects as agents of communication and change, in actual practice the Projects have tended to assume the role of the giver and the village people have mostly been at the receiving end."[14]

Bringing about *understanding participation* in the decision making on social change, then, is one way in which an effective program can take account of group relationships. A second is making use of the channels of communication and influence that exist in a community where change is desired. It is axiomatic that a change-agent begins to work with leadership. Dube tells how agricultural workers in an Indian village made the mistake of working with the elected political officials, who responded enthusiastically but had no particular influence over agricultural practices. The agricultural leaders, as the visitors later found out, were entirely different people from the political officials.[15] In the village there are many levels and specialized functions of leadership, and to work efficiently in that culture these must be understood and utilized.

Furthermore, it is obvious that many kinds of social change are threatening to old social relationships and positions of authority. The extended family, for instance, is threatened when the young men go into industry or move to the city. Young, educated men tend to be impatient with the traditional leaders. Technical skills and a money economy offer the people occupational alternatives, and consequently a degree of self-determination they have not before had. As a result, new concentrations of power, new leaders, and new work groups challenge old leaders and old patterns of relationship. There is always a certain degree of social ferment connected with economic and social development.

Practically, this means that, just as one must understand the cultural linkages, so also must one understand the social relationships, if the objective is to speed and smooth social change in the culture.

Modernizing skills

Another thing that complicates social change is that changes in many instances require people to learn new skills. When development that would ordinarily take centuries is compressed into a few decades, and particularly when a society is moving into technology, as the developing countries are today, it is often difficult to teach skills soon enough. If a small factory were built in a village of Africa or Asia tomorrow, the skilled workers would not be on hand to operate it. When radios are distributed in villages, there are no technicians locally available to repair them; and if a tube or a condenser goes bad, they may rest in peace and silence forever.

Therefore, any social change in the direction of modernization requires a program in teaching the necessary skills. Some of these are general skills; for example, no society will modernize very far until a substantial proportion of the population can read and figure. Others are quite specific—for example, repairing radios and farm machinery, operating machine tools, bookkeeping, surveying, medicine, and pharmacy. Almost invariably, skills like these are in short supply when development begins, and one of the great tasks of smoothing social change is to make technical skills and technical development march at the same pace, so that technology does not wait for workers, nor skilled workers for machines and jobs.

IMPLICATIONS FOR THE MASS MEDIA

What we have just said suggests two generalizations concerning the efficient use of mass media to accomplish social change.

For one thing, it is clear that they risk being ineffective—indeed, being counterproductive—if they are used without adequate knowledge of the local culture where they are going to be received. This is true of any communication, mass or interpersonal, but it is particularly true of the mass media because they cover larger areas, operate from a distance, and get less feedback from their audiences. A village-level worker, talking to a cultivator about contour plowing, can tell at once whether he is being understood; the same village-level worker, speaking over the radio to several hundred villages, many of which he has never seen, may never know whether his listeners have understood, and certainly he will not learn in time to make a change in the talk he is broadcasting. Therefore, an efficient use of the mass media for economic and social development implies that they should be as *local* as possible. Their programs should originate no farther than necessary from their audiences, the programs should be prepared by persons who understand the cultures to which they are speaking, and means should be available for the audiences to report back to the media. (We shall say something more about this last point under the heading of "research.")

Campaign after campaign has failed, in developing countries, because the campaigners misjudged or misunderstood the local situation. In a South American country, for example, there was a major effort to introduce a new maize which seemed in every way superior to the old variety. The new maize was hardier, had more food value, produced a higher yield, and so forth, and there were high hopes that it would improve the diet and health of both humans and animals. There was only one flaw in the plans. The maize (because it was so hardy and disease-resistant) was too hard to grind by hand, and villagers did not want to haul it to the mill in town. But it proved to make excellent commercial alcohol, and thus the campaign resulted not in improving diets but in promoting alcoholism.[16] There have been cases in Africa and Asia where women have refused to make use of newly installed running water in their homes for washing clothes, because they lost the chance to visit with their friends while they washed clothes in the creek.[17] There was a village in India which rejected an opportunity to install new and inexpensive smokeless stoves, although without such stoves people had to cook on the floor of the house. Each house soon filled with smoke, which gradually filtered through the thatched roof. People had sore eyes and upper respiratory infections. But the smoky house had one great advantage which the campaigners had not known: the smoke kept down the white ants which infested the roof. Without the smoke, the ants soon ate all the thatch, and the roof had to be replaced at considerable cost.[18] These are examples of unforeseen consequences of campaigns which failed because of lack of local knowledge. Localness is not a strong attribute of the mass media, and without a local field staff the media are not likely to know such things as we have mentioned about small localities they serve.

Localness is an even more important aspect of the decision process which underlies most community change. One priceless ingredient in the change process is local example or demonstration. Ataturk used to visit as many villages as possible while he was making his sweeping changes in Turkish life. When he was preparing to forbid the fez, he would visit the villages wearing a hat.[19] In China, Margaret Mead points out, the mass education program was carried out by intellectuals who lived in the villages and learned the needs of the people and how to talk with them.[20] Many a city-born agricultural agent has succeeded in his mission only when he has taken off his shoes and gone into the rice paddy. Traditional villagers who fear change and experiment can often be convinced only by demonstration, and convincing demonstration can only come from local knowledge. A demonstration based on generalized rather than local knowledge, like one in Burma which taught the farmers to plow their rice paddies deeply and resulted in destroying the soil pan that held the water in the paddy, will have a negative influence far wider than the immediate setting.[21]

These last examples suggest a second implication for efficient use of the mass media: there are some communication tasks they can do effectively and others that they can only help to do. The mass media can only report on someone's taking off his shoes and going into a rice paddy, and if television or films are available they can show the event happening. If television had been available, Ataturk could have shown his hat to larger audiences without so much traveling; but a proclamation or exhortation, on radio or in print, would hardly have had the effect of the leader's own demonstration that he had replaced his fez with a Western-style hat. None of the media can take over the task of the community decision-making group, but they can feed the discussion, as they do, for example, when they broadcast the initial talk for a rural radio forum. To understand where this borderline lies—where the media can work effectively by themselves and where they can accomplish their goals only in support of interpersonal communication—is one of the chief things a developing country must learn for itself before it can get the most out of modern communication.

To say that there are limits to the effectiveness of the mass media in national development is not intended to be a discouraging report. There are so many communication tasks within economic and social development, and so many of them are clearly within the powers of mass communication, that if a developing country were to use its mass media merely for all the tasks which the media can do best, the system would be far overcrowded. The problem is not to find jobs for the media to do, but rather to be discriminating about the uses to which they are put.

The communication tasks behind the social changes of national development are of three kinds. In the first place, the populace must have *information* about national development: their attention must be focused on the need of change, the opportunities inviting change, the methods and means of change; and, if possible, their aspirations for themselves and their country must be raised. In the second place, there must be opportunity to participate intelligently in the *decision process*: the dialogue must be broadened to include all those who must decide to change; the leaders must have an opportunity to lead and the common people to be heard; the issues of change must be made clear, and the alternatives discussed; information must flow both up and down the hierarchy. And third, the needed *skills must be taught:* adults must be taught to read, children must be educated, farmers must learn the methods of modern farming, teachers, doctors, engineers must be trained, workers must master technical skills, people in general must learn more about how to keep themselves healthy and strong. If these three groups of communication tasks correspond to the three basic functions of communication we talked about earlier—

the watchman, decision-maker, and teacher functions—it is no accident. These are the fundamental tasks of communication within society, whether it is traditional society or modernizing society. The only difference is that when a society is in the ferment of rapid social and economic change, all the needs are intensified.

Which of these tasks can the mass media do by themselves, and which can they only help to do? On the basis of what we now know about the media in developing countries, we can say this.

The first group of tasks—the watchman, the informing functions—are well within the capability of the media to handle directly. In fact, without the media it would be impossible to handle them on any such timetable as the developing countries propose.

The second group—the decision-making functions—are, for the most part, jobs the mass media can only help to do. These require, in many cases, group decision; they require the changing of strongly held attitudes, beliefs, and social norms; and therefore, the mechanisms of interpersonal communication are the key ones. It goes without saying that the mass media can be of great help by feeding information into the discussion, by carrying the word of the leaders, and by making the issues clear. But theirs is still a supportive role.

The third group of tasks—the teaching function—can be handled directly in part, and partly in combination with interpersonal communicators. For example, the media are perhaps best used in education when they can be employed in a classroom as part of a total educational experience under the guidance of a classroom teacher; but where teachers or schools are not available, or insufficiently trained, the media can fill in. Likewise, it is very hard for radio (to take the most common example) to do the job a skilled demonstration agent would do in teaching a new agricultural skill, but once the skill is learned, radio can be of great help by supplying additional information, answering questions, reporting results, and the like.

That may make the distinction seem more straightforward than it is. Therefore, let us look in greater detail at what the media can do and what they can help to do in the three great communication tasks.

WHAT THE MASS MEDIA CAN DO

The media as watchmen

People who live in societies where the mass media are common sometimes forget how much they learn from the media. Yet for 300 years the printed book has been the strong right arm of public education. Wherever newspapers have been available, they have become the chief reporters on environment beyond the reach of one's own senses; indeed, whole generations of people have formed their ideas of the nonlocal world largely on what they have learned from newspapers (and more recently from radio, films, television, and news magazines). Everyone who has experienced motion pictures and printed fiction has noticed the extraordinarily long-lasting memory traces of those media. Scenes, characters, plots, phrases still remain vivid, sharp, and clear, a part of one's usable resources, many years after they are first read or seen. Parents note, not always approvingly, how children learn "singing commercials," slogans, vocabulary, and customs from television, without trying to, without even realizing they are learning. In other words, all our experience with the mass media illustrates how easy it is, voluntarily or involuntarily, to learn from them.[22]

Because the media have this ability to report and inform so effectively, we can say with great confidence that they can perform certain essential services for a developing country.

The mass media can widen horizons. Many people in a traditional society correctly perceive a quality of magic in the media when they first encounter them. They are magic, a wise African said to this writer, because they can "take a man up to a hill higher than any we can see on the horizon and let him look beyond." They are magic because "they can let a man see and hear where he has never been and know people he has never met." And even after the aura of magic has dissipated, still they can help people in a developing country to understand how other people live, and consequently to look at their own lives with new insight. They are a liberating force because they can break the bonds of distance and isolation and transport people from a traditional society to "The Great Society," where all eyes are on the future and the faraway

—as Pool puts it, "where every business firm must anticipate the wants of unknown clients, every politician those of unknown voters; where planning takes place for a vastly changed future; where the actions of people in quite different cultures may affect one daily."[23]

One reason why this is important for any developing country is that it helps to develop the quality of empathy. Daniel Lerner, who has written better than anyone else about this matter, considers empathy the basic and fundamental quality which the people of a developing nation must have. This, he says, is because it

enables newly mobile persons to *operate efficiently* in a changing world. Empathy, to simplify the matter, is the capacity to see oneself in the other fellow's situation. This is an indispensable skill for people moving out of traditional settings. Ability to empathize may make all the difference, for example, when the newly mobile persons are villagers who grew up knowing all the extant individuals, roles, and relationships in their environment. Outside his village or tribe, each must meet new individuals, recognize new roles, and learn new relationships involving himself. [High empathic capacity] is the predominant personal style only in modern society which is distinctively industrial, urban, literate, and *participant*. Traditional society is nonparticipant—it deploys people by kinship into communities isolated from each other and from a center; without an urban-rural division of labor, it develops few needs requiring economic interdependence; lacking the bonds of interdependence, people's horizons are limited by locale and their decisions involve other *known* people in *known* situations. Hence there is no need for . . . a national "ideology" which enables persons unknown to each other to achieve "consensus" by comparing their opinions.

But modern society is participant in that it functions by "consensus" —individuals making personal decisions on public issues must concur often enough with other individuals they do not know to make possible a stable common governance. Among the marks of this historic achievement in social organization, which we call Participant Society, are that most people go through school, read newspapers, receive cash payments in jobs they are legally free to change, buy goods for cash in an open market, vote in elections which actually decide among competing candidates, and express opinions on many matters which are not their personal business. Especially important, for the Participant Style, is the enormous proportion of people who are expected to "have opinions" on public matters—and the corollary expectation of these people that their opinions will matter.[24]

Lerners

The Passing of Traditional Society
P. 49-51

Thus the media, by bringing what is distant near and making what is strange understandable, can help to bridge the transition between traditional and modern society.

The mass media can focus attention. In modern society, much of our picture of distant environment comes from the mass media. As traditional society moves toward modernity, it too begins to depend on the mass media. Consequently, a large share of the ideas as to who is important, who is dangerous, what is interesting, and so forth necessarily derives from the media. The newspaper, radio, magazine, serving as watchmen on the hill, must decide what to report back. This act of choice—choosing whom to write about, whom to focus the camera on, whom to quote, what events to record—determines in large degree what people know and talk about.

Thus, for example, in countries where the media are common, a political candidate has little chance unless the people have become well acquainted with him through the media. Where political campaigns have been studied intensively, the general conclusion is that the media do not directly change the voting decision of any large proportion of the electorate, but do have a lot to do with what issues or individuals are talked about during the campaign.[25] By focusing attention on certain topics rather than others, they are able to make these topics play a larger part in the campaign. Many advertising campaigns also are intended to focus attention on one brand or product. This is particularly true in cases where there is little difference except brand name between competing products. In such cases, advertising has proved the power of the media to keep public attention on one brand name rather than others.[26]

This is a significant matter for the developing countries because it means that public attention can be kept on development. From time to time interest can be directed to a new custom, a new behavior, a new health or agricultural practice, a reward to be gained by modernizing, or something that needs to be changed. By directing attention to given topics or issues of this kind, the media can also control some of the topics of interpersonal communication. The leaders of a developing country would personally go, if they

could, to every small group in the country and put in their minds
a development problem or an idea or opportunity to think about
or discuss. They cannot go personally to many villages or many
groups. But they can plant ideas and topics widely through the
mass media.

The mass media can raise aspirations. The history of advertising, the success of mail-order catalogues, and the many cases in
which families have worked hard to reach a standard of life they
have seen others enjoy or to acquire an article they have only read
or heard about or seen pictures of encourages us to believe that
the mass media may be able to raise their audiences' aspirations
in developing cultures as well as in highly developed ones.

If true, this is a matter of great importance to the developing
countries. They face the need to rouse their people from fatalism
and a fear of change. They need to encourage both personal and
national aspirations. Individuals must come to desire a better life
than they have and to be willing to work for it. As citizens they
must aspire to national strength and greatness.

Both McClelland and Lerner think that the media can raise the
aspirations of developing peoples.[27] Lerner reports that when
Radio Cairo comes into a remote village, "in terms of personal
aspirations nearly everything happens." Rao has described how
the aspirations of villagers were raised by "overhearing" mass communication, so to speak. One of the motives of newly roused aspirations in the Indian villages he studied was to own a particular
kind of shirt seen in pictures. In those villages, both the tailor and
the barber had to attend nearby movies so as to be able to duplicate the styles seen therein, because people would come in with
hard-earned money to spend on a particular cut of clothing or a
particular hairdress they had noticed on the silver screen.[28] From
aspirations for a new shirt to aspirations for national greatness and
prosperity may be a long jump, but the building of national aspirations is one of the first uses that most new nations find for their
radio and press. To take one example out of many, the Soviet mass
media have for decades been full of news of national growth and
industrialization, building into the diverse people of the USSR

a sense of belonging to a powerful nation moving toward a stronger economy and a better life.

Of course, raising the aspirations of a nation is not without danger. In the villages of Egypt, Lerner says, when the government inserted radio into the community, nothing *really* changed except the people's expectations. He continues:

This is the typical situation that over the last decade has been producing the revolution of rising frustrations. The mass media have been used to stimulate people in some sense . . . by raising their levels of aspiration—for the good things of the world, for a better life. No adequate provision is made, however, for raising the levels of achievement. Thus people are encouraged to want more than they can possibly get, aspirations rapidly outrun achievements, and frustrations spread.[29]

Therefore, when a government seeks to raise the aspirations of its people, it must consider how far it can go toward satisfying those aspirations. If appetites are stimulated but not satisfied, at best the people will not rise so quickly to the bait the next time. At worst, the government may have an ugly situation on its hands. A sound policy demands that there be some correspondence between what the people are roused to want and what they are able to obtain. But the essential point is that without raising aspirations, without stimulating people to strive for a better life and for national growth, development is unlikely ever to occur.

Thus, the mass media can create a climate for development. We can sum up by saying that the mass media can contribute substantially to the amount and kinds of information available to the people of a developing country. They can widen horizons and thus help to build empathy; they can focus attention on problems and goals of development; they can raise personal and national aspirations; and all this they can do largely themselves and directly. This amounts to creating an informational "climate" in which development is stimulated. By showing modern equipment and life in economically well-developed societies, by disseminating news of development from far away, by carrying political, economic, social, and cultural reports from elsewhere in the country and the world, the media can create an intellectual climate which stimulates people to take another look at their own current practices and future perspectives.[30]

The media in the decision process

The mass media can help only indirectly to change strongly held attitudes or valued practices. Mass communication has never proved very effective in attacking attitudes, values, or social customs that are deep-set or strongly held. One reason why they are strongly held is that for a very long time they have been found rewarding. Furthermore, they are usually socially anchored in approval by family or other groups which are important to the individual; to go against such attitudes means that the individual must go against groups in which he values membership. The individual usually feels personally involved in such attitudes and customs; to change them would cause personal anguish and alienation from the life and companions he has become used to. Therefore, such positions are strongly defended.

How firmly they are defended we can judge from the studies showing that the human psyche will go to almost any length to repel an attack on strong beliefs and attitudes. People select news or broadcasts or articles that support their strong beliefs, and reject or forget what does not.[31] If they do come into contact with mass media information unfavorable to their strong beliefs, they often misread or distort it. This is wholly irrational; they are not *deliberately* distorting; their belief structure is merely acting to preserve itself. In the research literature there are case studies of whole campaigns that have failed because their meaning has been completely misread by the persons whose attitudes they were supposed to change. For example, there was a famous campaign in which cartoons of a "Mr. Biggott" were used to pour ridicule on racial prejudice. But prejudiced people interpreted these cartoons as *supporting* the idea of racial prejudice.[32] As a result, such people became more prejudiced than ever.

Direct social control over attitudes is exerted mostly by group relationships—by persons one admires or respects, or by groups one belongs to or aspires to belong to. Why this should be is not hard to understand. Any individual enjoys a large proportion of his most rewarding experiences in groups—the family group, the work group, the recreational group of close friends, the church, the club, the group of like-thinkers about politics, the community that enjoys a common culture, and so forth. In each of these groups an individual learns to play a certain role and to follow certain norms. Role and norm understandings help to make life comfortable and pleasant in the group. A member does not have constantly to review what is proper for him to do, and he can understand and predict what other group members will be doing. Therefore, the function of the group—whether it is married life and child rearing in the family group, or work in the work group, or worship in the church group—can go forward with a maximum of satisfaction and a minimum of obstacles. So each group tries to preserve its norms and roles.

Suppose now that a member of a group ceases to adhere to the norm. For example, suppose that one child in a family group decides to quit school, or one member of a church group changes his ideas about the deity, or one member of a political group finds himself in disagreement with a central tenet of the party. Then all the pressures of the group will be exerted to try to bring the deviant back into the path. If these pressures are not successful— and the individual member is not very likely to be able to change the group—the usual result is that he has to leave the group. And very few persons want to leave the groups they value.

When an individual does decide to leave a group for reasons of belief and attitude, it is usually to join another group more in accord with his new beliefs. If he leaves Party A, it is to find congenial associates in Party B, and so forth. Influences like these almost always have to be exerted personally. A new influential figure has to come into an individual's life. A new attractive group, with somewhat different norms, has to come into his experience. Or his present group must itself decide to change norms or practices.[33]

In major decisions of these kinds, therefore, the channels of interpersonal communication and influence are far more effective than the mass media. The media can be helpful, but only indirectly. Some of the indirect ways in which the media can enter into the decision process are suggested in the following pages.

The mass media can feed the interpersonal channels. The influential persons whose advice and viewpoints bulk large in the interpersonal decision process of society are typically heavy users of the mass media.[34] For example, the man who is influential with the farmers in a given area usually reads more or hears more broadcasts about farming than does the average farmer. The man whose advice about politics is respected usually makes an abnormally high use of the political media. The young woman who is regarded as an authority on which motion pictures are worth seeing usually reads much more than the average person about movies, and herself sees more movies. In fact, the information obtained from the media, though not a sole and sufficient cause, is certainly a contributing factor in the influence exerted.

This is important to developing countries because it means that it is possible through the mass media to feed the channels of interpersonal influence. When agricultural information is carried in the mass media, there is a very high chance that this same information will be picked up and repeated by the agricultural "influentials." When information on child care is carried, there is a good chance that the women whose advice on child care is important will pick the information up and repeat it. And so on.

We must add: *other things being equal.* If the influential spokesmen have no access to the media—if, for instance, they are illiterate and they have no radios—they are not likely to pick up information from the mass media. If they hold attitudes violently opposed to those expressed or implied by mass communication, they are very likely to reject or distort the mass media message. But if they are not basically opposed, if they have ready access to the media, then there is no good reason why the media should not supply information to interpersonal channels.

In some cases, mass communication is the most effective way to conduct point-to-point communication. For example, there is the problem of reaching, informing, updating community or extension workers. Some developing countries have many thousands of such workers in agriculture, health, or community development. These are typically scattered far and wide. Often there has not been time to train them adequately, and they are still in need of information and assistance. In this case, it has been found useful to use the radio—and sometimes film and print—to upgrade and update the extension workers. Sometimes it is possible to reach both the worker and the public at the same time—that is to broadcast, show a film, or produce some printed material which the extension agent can read, so to speak, over the shoulders of the villager, and which he can then help the villager to understand and apply. The same tactics have been used in assisting and upgrading teachers.

It should be noted that in certain situations the mass media can take over some of the usually interpersonal channels of leadership. The radio addresses of Winston Churchill, during the war of 1939-45, were examples of personal leadership exerted most effectively through the mass media. The leaders of many developing countries have also learned to use the radio effectively.

The mass media can confer status. It helps an individual's reputation, of course, to be endorsed or praised by a well-regarded newspaper or radio. In fact, merely to be *noticed* by the media contributes to the status of an individual.[35] This somewhat puzzling ability of the media to confer status has been described by Lazarsfeld and Merton in these words:

> The mass media bestow prestige and enhance the authority of individuals and groups by *legitimatizing their status.* Recognition by the press or radio or magazines or newsreels testifies that one has arrived, that one is important enough to have been singled out from the large anonymous masses, that one's behavior and opinions are significant enough to require public notice.[36]

In a developing country where the media are relatively scarce and the stream of names in the news is smaller, this power of the media may be even greater than it is in economically developed countries, and may provide a way to build leadership.

Most national political leaders in developing countries have long since discovered the status conferral power of the mass media, but the local leader often needs additional status. We mean not only the elected leaders, but also the community development workers, the agricultural advisers, and other people who are in an advisory or instructive capacity with the villagers. Their voices on radio, their pictures or their words in print, are real contributions to their local standing and their visibility in the community. Similarly, it is helpful to give status and visibility to certain persons or acts that deserve emulation. The Soviet and East European mass media have perhaps done the best job of this—in publicizing heroes of labor, productivity records, successful collectives, and other exemplary models for developmental activity. Undoubtedly, the whole movement of national development can be given status through attention by the mass media. This will attract people to participate in development who by their participation will give it further status, and so on through the spiral we described earlier.

The mass media can broaden the policy dialogue. In the village, the people concerned with local policy matters are close enough to talk about them face to face if they want to and if custom permits. So far as the traditional village is concerned, this is usually sufficient, because the village is usually not much interested in policy at higher levels, and the higher levels are not much interested in sharing policy with the village. But when a country begins to develop, it has an urgent need to widen the theater of political discussion and policy making. The ordinary people need to overhear the national policy debates so that they can form opinions and, at the proper time, act on their opinions. The policy makers need to understand, more clearly than before, the needs and wishes of the villages, so that they can take account of them in making their larger policies. To accomplish these things in a nation of any size, without the mass media, would be almost out of the question.[37]

As a country develops, the mass media begin to cover news, local problems, local spokesmen. The more the local press and radio develop, the better the coverage. These items are seen or heard by audiences in other parts of the country and by the national policy makers. At the same time, the media cover the national news, the national problems, and the statements and arguments of leaders as to what policies should be adopted. Thus the theater of policy discussion is widened until it begins to be as large as the nation. As this happens, during development, the conditions of national participation are set up, national empathy is encouraged, and all the requirements for developing *as a nation* are brought within reach.

The mass media can enforce social norms. Malinowski observed that in the Trobriand Islands no organized social action with respect to behavior deviation from a social norm was taken until there had been *public* announcement of the deviation. Something like this goes on in advanced civilizations also. Many social norms are inconvenient or burdensome to individuals. Therefore, some leniency is permitted in applying the norms, and many people have private knowledge of deviations from them. So long as the knowledge remains *private,* no social action is taken to punish the deviation. But once it has been revealed publicly, then people are forced to take a *public* stand for or against the norms, and the group usually acts to dispose of the violation. As Lazarsfeld and Merton say, "Publicity closes the gap between 'private attitudes' and 'public morality.' "[38]

In modern society the job of carrying the public announcements has been given, in large part, to the mass media. Their job is to make serious deviations known. If the norms are not universally known, as they are unlikely to be in a developing society, then part of the job of the media is to publicize the norms.

Thus it is possible through the media to establish in the public mind norms for development behavior, and to police deviations from those norms. In a sense, this is the other side of the status conferral coin. Just as some developing countries have conferred status on their best farmers and laborers, so also they have not hesitated to denounce laziness, inefficiency, and corruption. Once out in the open, these deviations can be socially punished, and individuals warned away from them.

The mass media can help form tastes. Within limits, people learn to like what they hear and see. This is true notably in the area of music and art. In some highly developed countries, the success of popular songs and dances depends largely on their being introduced and made familiar by the mass media. Throughout history there have been repeated instances when new music or new paintings have been rejected because they were unfamiliar, although later they have become great "classics." The particular power of the mass media is to speed up this familiarization process, and thus to have an effect on the forming of taste.

To a developing country this has a significance quite apart from the matter of "plugging" popular songs or introducing new kinds of painting. Culture is one of the best bridges between peoples. If People A like the music or the dances or the graphic art of People B, they are predisposed to like People B. If Peoples A and B like each other's art, they are predisposed to feel a bond between them and to understand each other better. Developing countries can use this powerful mechanism to build the sense of "nation-ness" many of them need so badly. If a "national" art or music or dance exists, it can be emphasized as a rallying point for all the nation's people. With or without a national art, the folk art of different parts of the country can be used to bring those subgroups psychologically closer together. Something like this is what the Soviet Union has done by publicizing the folk dances and music of the many peoples within its borders.

The mass media can affect attitudes lightly held, and slightly canalize stronger attitudes. As we have indicated, mass communication is not very effective by itself in changing attitudes that are strongly held and deeply anchored. But it is quite possible through mass communication to have some effect on positions that are not strongly defended, or on new questions concerning which there has been neither time nor information to build up strong attitudes. To take one example out of many, a famous radio play, depicting an invasion of the earth from Mars, once caused a panic in several countries. The play was very realistic; it was largely in the form of news broadcasts like the ones people habitually hear on the radio. The people who panicked were those who believed the broadcast was genuine, were too frightened to think of a way to check up on the genuineness of the news, and saw no way to defend themselves against the new and unfamiliar danger of inter-planetary war. Therefore, they ran for the hills—until they found out it was only a play (after which, in one country, they returned and burned down the radio station!).[39] This is an example of how the mass media can be extraordinarily effective in areas where not much is known and no strong attitudes or behavior patterns have been built up. It is assumed that no developing country wants to frighten its people out of their wits, but the same principle applies to other effects also: with the mass media, it is easier to win on a new battlefield than an old one.

The mass media can also be used to make a very small change, or a slight redirection in existing attitudes. For example, as adver-tisers have discovered, once people have decided that a toothbrush is a good thing, then it is relatively easy to convince them that *this* or *that kind* of toothbrush is a good thing. If people have become convinced that it is a good thing to learn to read, then it is much easier to convince them of the desirability of going to a class or listening to a broadcast or doing something else to learn to read. If a new agriculture or health practice can be presented as merely *one instance* of an old honored custom, then it is likely to be ac-cepted. If it can be presented as merely a *tiny change* in an old honored custom, then it is more likely to be accepted than if it is shown as a frontal attack on an old custom. In these ways, at least, mass communication can be used directly to change attitudes— if no strong attitudes or behavior patterns exist on the point in question, or if the change can be shown to be merely an extension or redirection of an old strong attitude.[40]

It is clear that the mass media can be of great use in the decision making that must accompany economic and social development. But their usefulness does not lie in frontal attacks on strongly held attitudes or long-valued customs. These strongly held positions are in the domain of personal influence and group norms. If changes are made in stoutly defended customs and beliefs, interpersonal communication is usually required, and group change is usually involved. In such major decisions, therefore, the mass media can help only *indirectly*. They can feed information into the channels of interpersonal influence. They can confer status and enforce norms. They can broaden the policy dialogue. They can help form tastes. Where there are no strong attitudes, or where the only change desired is a slight canalization of an existing attitude, they can be directly effective. But for the most part, in the area of entrenched belief and behavior, they can only help.

The mass media as teachers

In a cogent article prepared for the *World Radio Handbook*, Cassirer specifies some of the tasks which information can perform for the people of developing countries. For one thing, he says, it enables the individual to see himself in the context of national unity and world-wide interrelation. It creates the climate in which adoption of new technological practices and new attitudes becomes possible. It enables the citizen to play his part in the nation. But this "awareness through information" is bound to be inadequate "as long as the individual is insufficiently educated to master new skills and new knowledge."[41]

This is the skills barrier which we have mentioned before. In the process of economic and social development, it is not sufficient merely to know the need for change or even to decide for change. Before substantial amounts of change can occur, new skills must be spread throughout the population. This requires a nation-wide program of education and training. Therefore, it is of the greatest importance to developing countries that we can say confidently:

The mass media can help substantially in all types of education and training. They have proved themselves under many different conditions in and out of schools. They have proved their ability to supplement and enrich school work. Where teachers and schools are scarce, they have proved able to carry a very large part of the instructional task themselves. They have proved to be of great help in adult education and literacy training. And they have been very helpful in training for industry and technical services, and for the in-service training of teachers.

These facts are important because, as we know, teachers and schools *are* scarce, and many of the available teachers are trained for yesterday's rather than today's teaching job. Technical skills *are* in short supply. There *are* 70 million illiterate adults in the world. Throughout the developing regions there *are* great needs for learning new agricultural skills and practices.

There is no longer any doubt of the potency of the media as teachers. Textbooks, of course, have long ago proved what they could do. Radio and film in many lands have proved helpful in adult education and schoolrooms. Now the evidence comes in on the newer devices. For example, out of 393 experimental comparisons of classes taught chiefly by television with classes taught by conventional classroom methods, there was no difference (in what the pupils could do in the final examination) in the case of 65 per cent of all the comparisons; in 21 per cent of the cases, the television class wrote significantly better examinations than the conventional class, and in only 14 per cent was the conventional class superior.[42] The early reports from programmed instruction are also very encouraging. In almost all cases, programs have been able to make a contribution to the effectiveness of a class. Students have been able to learn faster, and in certain specialized forms of training—such as, for example, computer operation and electronics —programs have been able to relieve the teacher of much of the burden of teaching details and drill.[43] These research results are chiefly from countries that are well developed economically, but research on teaching media is now beginning to come from developing countries, and first results are very encouraging. Some of them will be mentioned in the following section.

Throughout the education world there is a great deal of discussion of "the new educational media." To make it clear what these are, let us classify the media (as teaching devices) in four generations,[44] thus:

First-generation media—charts, maps, graphs, written materials, exhibits, models, chalkboards, demonstrations, dramatizations, and the like. Many of these are as old as teaching, and all of them far antedate mass communication. This generation of educational media is distinguished from the others in that it requires no machine or electronic device. Needless to say, all these media are available to, although not always in good supply in, developing countries.

Second-generation media—printed textbooks, workbooks, and tests. These depend on introducing a machine (the printing press) into the communication process to duplicate quickly and inexpensively man's writing and drawing. For over 300 years these second-generation media have been used extensively for education. Now certain newer printing methods, such as phototypesetting and off-set printing, are making them more easily usable in less-industrialized countries. These media are well known to all developing countries, and are produced in the majority of them. Supply and quality, however, leave much to be desired.

Third-generation media—photographs, slides, strip films, silent motion pictures, recordings, motion pictures, radio, and television. This generation of media depends on introducing a machine into the communication process to see and listen, or see or listen, for man. The oldest of these media is a little over 100 years old; the newest, about 35. Their technology is well known to developing countries. Films and radio are available in almost all developing countries, and television in some developing countries. Projectors and teaching films are scarce in many countries; radio is used much less than it could be for education, and instructional television is beyond the experimental stage in only a few developing countries. It should be noted that such dramatic new "educational media" as the communication satellite are merely devices to extend the range of these third-generation media.

Fourth-generation media—programmed instruction, language laboratories, electronic digital computers, used in the tutorial process and in the swift retrieval of information. This generation of media is very new, and depends in each case on communication between man and machine. Programmed instruction, which "automates" the tutorial process, is now beginning to be tried in developing countries. Language laboratories, which permit a student to practice language skills with an expert example, are likewise just beginning to come into use. The use of computers for the educational purposes indicated is still seen mostly in the industrialized countries.

Which ones are the "new" media depends somewhat on where one answers the question. In the highly developed countries, the new educational media are television, programmed instruction, and language laboratories, with the educational uses of computers beginning to come on the stage. In developing countries, for the most part, the "new educational media" are everything beyond the second generation of media; and even the printed materials of the second generation are in short supply.

But the new media, however defined, represent the great hope of the developing countries for supplying education at the rate and of the quality required.

We have said that the media can *help* in education and training, and have thus distinguished what they can do in these fields from what they can do in imparting information. In other words, we have said that the media can do the watchman's and reporter's job unaided, but that they can only *help* the teacher. This is because education and training are more than the transmission of information. They require a purposeful growth, a learning of skills, a systematic building of knowledge, a preparation for action. This is accomplished best when there is an interpersonal link in the process—a teacher to work with the pupil, a discussion group to help decide what new techniques and customs a community shall absorb into its life, or at least a monitor to coordinate some of the studying and provide or get help for the student when he needs it. In a secondary school science class, a teacher *and* a television lesson or film will be probably more effective than either alone. In literacy training, a monitor or teacher has proved necessary at the student end of a broadcast. In industrial training, films can greatly speed up learning, but ordinarily cannot do the whole job. In community adult education, discussion groups and local field staffs have contributed greatly to the effectiveness of radio. *Two-way* communication is needed somewhere in the process—someone to guide, react, answer questions, discuss. The *combination* of mass media and interpersonal instruction—expert instruction from the media and two-way interaction with a teacher—are thus extraordinarily powerful.

This implies, of course, that there *are* teachers, monitors, technical instructors, and field staffs to cooperate in the teaching process. When they are not available, or not able to teach a certain topic, then the media can and do carry a greater share of the responsibility. We do not know the limits of what the media can do in a developing situation where there is hunger for education but a dearth of teachers, monitors, and field workers. We do know that it is extraordinarily hard to learn from the media to read and write, without a teacher or monitor present. We do know that a discussion helps in community adult education because, as Cassirer says, a man will "assimilate into his own life only what has been endorsed by those whom he traditionally respects."[45] But countless men have read law and learned mathematics by themselves from books. Men have learned engineering, electronics, radio repairing, and such skills by correspondence lessons. In Chicago, the entire curriculum of a junior college is offered by television and studied quite successfully by hundreds of students who have no other contact with the college except at examination time or when they send in written assignments or ask questions. It may well be that in the atmosphere of need in a developing country, the media can carry a much larger share of the teaching load than they have been asked to carry in economically better developed countries.[46] We now need more field trials in developing regions to tell us just how far we can rely on them.

But this at least we do know: the mass media can be of great help in all forms of teaching, adult education, and skills training; that where teachers, trainers, monitors are scarce, the media can carry a proportionally greater share of the instruction; and that once the basic skills have been learned, the media can provide further opportunities to learn. For example, once the basic steps have been taken into modern agriculture, radio and print can provide a flow of helpful information on practical farming. Once a man has learned the basic skills and understandings of electronics, he can learn more by reading. Once a man has learned to learn, he finds it easier to learn without supervision or direct assistance.

5. The Mass Media in the Great Campaigns

Chapter 5 means in practical terms that there are some development tasks in which the mass media can be of more direct help than in others, and that whoever uses mass communication to help bring about social change had better know the culture he is trying to alter. In countries where people have had the most experience in using the media for economic and social development there is, however, less talk of "media" than of "campaigns" or "systems."

This is because it is recognized that the great battles of development are continuing ones, and the results come less from the impact of single messages or single media than from a succession of impacts of related messages and reinforcing channels. Campaigns to modernize some part of a society will almost invariably make use of face-to-face communication as well as the media. Whenever possible, they will use more than one mass media channel to an audience. As the campaign goes on, the nature of the messages will change, and they will require different channels or combinations of channels. For example, early in a campaign a medium like radio may be most useful in making the people aware of needs and opportunities; later in the campaign, the emphasis may have to be on face-to-face demonstration or discussion, to help the people come to a decision on a proposed change. Thus, the planners of development campaigns find themselves thinking of communication *systems* rather than media. What *combination* of messages and channels, in what *order*, will be of most help in bringing about the changes that need to occur? This is the planner's question.

Professor René Dumont, of the French Institut National Agronomique, studied the agricultural needs of French Africa and decided that the primary channel for communicating the messages of change to the rural population in that part of the world should be the public schools rather than the media or the field workers. And not the public schools as they now exist, but a radically different kind of school to replace the kind which is now, he says, "a major brake on agricultural development." Professor Dumont continues:

The African school, especially because of caste privileges, is now considered as a source of culture, it is true; but it is regarded even more as a means of access to the "paradise" of government and administration. Many Africans, when they come to France, are astounded to see whites having the social status of peasants and workers and themselves manipulating the pitchfork and the plough. They had been apt to imagine the whites as all being on the pattern of colonial administrators, that is, free of servile tasks, the idea being that education ought to enable the Africans, too, to rid themselves of the disgrace of manual work.[1]

He proposes therefore a new educational institution, designed as transition to a truly African system. This is a rural school for village boys between the ages of 10 and 14, who have been unable to go to a traditional school. Very few, if any, of these students would have a chance to go on to secondary school, the professions, and bureaucracy; rather, they would become the kind of farmer Africa so desperately needs—the modern cultivator who looks to the future, is not ashamed to work, and is prepared to take the advice of technicians and instructors. The school would be comparatively cheap to maintain. The school itself and the teacher's house would be built by the villagers and the students themselves, as an exercise in their education. "Such expensive obligations as the need to learn French, which is a foreign language in Africa," would be dispensed with, he says. The students would work on the land four hours a day and go to school four hours a day. The curriculum would be basic and practical. "A rural school of this kind," he says, "would very soon become the real center of agricultural progress in the village."[2]

After the effect of the new school system begins to be felt, he suggests, then the African countries can use an agricultural field service, agricultural radio, agricultural bulletins, and the other communication channels effectively. But they will not really be effective *until* a change in the schools brings about a fundamental change in attitudes toward manual labor.

It is not necessary for us to decide whether Professor Dumont has the correct solution, or whether he has underestimated what the mass media can do. The point is that he has gone about reaching his solution, not by putting the question, How should we use the mass media (or the field staff, or the schools, or rural discussion groups)? but rather by asking, *How can the needed change be brought about?*

This is where systems thinking necessarily begins. The planner has to know the culture well enough to know how the given change can be brought about: what can be done by information and persuasion, and by what kind of information and persuasion; and what must be done by allocating resources or providing opportunities other than symbolic ones. Then he has to plan some sequence of events. The physical resources and the informational resources have to be brought to bear when they will help each other, and when the audience needs them. So far as the informational part of the program is concerned, at given points in the campaign certain people will need to be reached, and the best channels will have to be found to reach them. Whenever possible, more than one channel will be used for a given purpose, to make sure that the word gets through, and, if possible, to permit one message to reinforce others. Beginning with the question of how a desired change can be brought about, the planner of a development campaign therefore finds himself working with an entire communication system, trying to use all its resources in the best combinations and sequences.

In a typical development campaign, audiences are usually first made aware of a problem or an event by the swifter media. Then come the more detailed treatments, the expressions of opinion, the arguing of different positions, the provision of more information, from whatever channel will appropriately provide those services at the times they are needed. Thus the sequence of need is met—first, for awareness; then for additional details, so that the conditions of decision will become clear; then for arguments pro and con, so that opinion can begin to form; then for additional information with which to undergird opinion; and finally, for the expressions of consensus and decision.

We know from studies of innovation in highly developed countries that the first step in this process is usually a contact with the mass media which provides information about a potentially rewarding new practice (and at the same time suggests the inadequacy of existing practices).[3] At this point, the prospective innovator is the more passive participant and the media are the active participants in the process. But if the message interests the innovator, then he becomes active. Typically he checks the information with persons he respects, or with other mass media. Usually he wants more details on what the practice involves. He wants to know what other people think about it and what they are planning to do. Above all, probably, he would like to see the practice in use; and therefore, about this time, a demonstration will be useful. If group decision is required, a meeting or a discussion forum will be helpful. If the innovator decides to try the new practice, he will then need really detailed information and guidance. For this he may go to an expert, a more experienced farmer, a "how to do it" poster or magazine, or a technical booklet. And so on. The point is that there is a sequence in which these different kinds of information are needed, the appropriate channels for different purposes and different targets at different times.

So if a developing country is to make best use of its facilities in the great campaigns of development, early in any given campaign someone will have to look at the problem broadly—more broadly, that is, than from the viewpoint of radio, or the extension service, or schools, or newspapers, or films. Someone must look at the needs for change, at the likely dynamics of change, and at the resources available, and then design the system of messages, channels, and events that promises to be most efficient at bringing about the change desired.

FOUR CAMPAIGN AREAS

Agriculture

One example of a broadly conceived development campaign is the Intensive Agricultural District Program, the so-called "Package Program" in India. This activity, which is designed to reach some millions of cultivators in selected districts in various parts of the country—one in each state, generally—is operated by the Government of India with some financial aid and technical assistance from the Ford Foundation. Other institutions are also assisting. The chief representative of the Ford Foundation in India has described the program in a thoughtful paper, from which we shall quote a few passages.

The Package Program includes, for one thing, a "package" of related practices:

Agricultural improvement work in India in recent years has stressed the adoption of single practices, such as use of improved seed, or of green manure, or sowing of paddy rice in rows instead of broadcasting the seed. The Package Program, however, emphasizes the simultaneous use of a "package" of several related practices, such as use of better seed, seed cleaning and treatment, better seedbed preparation, use of fertilizers at the right times and in the proper quantities, better water use, and suitable plant protection measures. The "package" of practices varies between areas, but always includes a group of interacting practices that are much more productive than any single practice can be when applied alone. The practices involved are those that are feasible for cultivators to perform under existing conditions, that can be supported with adequate technical guidance and supplies, and that the cultivators themselves agree to undertake.[4]

Another aspect of the "package" is logistic support sufficient to keep innovators from experiencing the frustration of adopting a plan and then not being able to carry it through. A soils laboratory, an implement workshop, a supply of fertilizer and seed, and opportunities to obtain credit for purchases are available close at hand.

All this is in addition to, but by no means separate from, the information "package." The intent is to make the information program as local as possible, and responsive in every way to the needs and culture of the villages. Therefore, each district in the program has its own information unit. Much reliance is placed on the Village Level Workers, who devote most of their time to agriculture, and on the block and district staff members who conduct meetings and have many individual contacts in the villages. The technique most used is that of demonstration:

The program relies heavily upon field demonstrations to educate cultivators in the use of new practices in tillage and planting, application of chemical and organic fertilizers, use of seed treatments and better selection of seed, water use and drainage, plant protection, and harvesting, drying, and storage of grains. From several hundred to several thousand field demonstrations of improved crop production practices were carried out in each of the seven districts during the crop year just past. . . . Inauguration of "demonstration villages," special demonstrations in water use, and development of "demonstration cooperatives" for service to cultivators are also planned.[5]

The program of demonstrations will be geared into a wider range of information activities:

A new avenue of mass education is now being opened up by the establishment of Package Program information offices at each of the district headquarters. According to official plan, the work of these information offices will be conducted as part of an integrated center-state-district information service. These units are the first district agricultural information offices to be established in India. It is their function to develop and use the available channels for mass dissemination of technical and program information to cultivators and the general public. They will produce and distribute simple visuals, leaflets, photographs, posters, and slides for use in their districts, and will aid in training of extension workers. To the extent feasible, they will make use of newspaper and magazine publicity, public speeches, radio programs, exhibits at fairs and melas, and motion pictures and film strips. They also will assist in activities with schools, youth groups, women's groups, local cooperatives, business groups, and the Panchayati Raj [village council] institutions so as to extend program information as widely as possible. . . . Together all these activities will result in the continuous communication of improvement information and ideas to cultivators, as well as the creation of necessary mechanisms for "feedback" of information to program officials. This work must close the existing gap between the culti-vators and the sources of knowledge and inspiration about new practices and their benefit.[6]

Thus a wide variety of media and interpersonal communication channels are combined to achieve a well-thought-out goal, based on knowledge of the local culture and supported by ample logistics. It is too soon to be able to assess fully the results of this activity, but the early increases in productivity are very encouraging.

Not every developing country, of course, can have an agricultural development program as well supported as the one we have described. In many countries, however, there are very interesting developments on a less elaborate scale, only a few of which we can mention. Many of these involve in an important way the use of radio. It is not difficult to see why radio should be particularly useful in rural development programs. It covers great distances and leaps all kinds of natural barriers. It is swift in reaching a listener. It is the cheapest of the major media in production, and reception can also be inexpensive. Now that transistor receivers are widely available, radio communication can be received even where there is no electricity. It is equally effective with literates and illiterates. And it lends itself to a great variety of content and forms.

For these reasons radio is very widely used, and in a number of different program styles. One of the simpler uses can be represented by the early morning farm broadcast from Radio Amman, in Jordan. This comes on the air daily at 6:15 A.M., and is largely made up of answers to questions. About 300 questions come in from farmers each week. "How do I treat the sickness that makes my cow have a calf before her time?" "What do I do about the insects that make the bark of my orchard trees fall off?" The broadcaster, a former agricultural extension agent, selects the most urgent of the questions and, when necessary, discusses them with specialists at the Ministry of Agriculture or elsewhere. When the best answer is determined, he reports it on the morning program, conversationally, in a friendly and interested manner. The number of questions that flood in to him testifies to the usefulness of the broadcast.[7]

It is worth pointing out that the Jordan program is *two-way* communication. Before the radio broadcast is prepared, the audience sends in its questions. The cultivators are therefore conducting a continuing dialogue with the agricultural experts, telling them at any given time what problems are causing trouble on the farm. When the cultivators don't understand advice, they ask another question. Doubtless it is this two-way circuit that keeps the program so practical and so popular.

Even in highly advanced countries, face-to-face communication takes precedence over the mass media at the point in the campaign where farmers are deciding whether to adopt a new practice. The farmers rely mostly on the media for information about new farming ideas, but when it comes to deciding whether to accept a new practice in their own farming, they consult other farmers or expert advisers.[8] The decision to change, whether the country is little developed or far along in development, is going to be made locally; it is going to involve discussion, advice, and personal influence; and it is much more likely to be a lasting decision if it is made on a group or community basis.

For this reason, the development and perfecting of the rural radio forum, combining expert advice with community discussion and decision, are most promising for the whole field of rural development. The forum need not be restricted to agricultural information; it can be, and has been, used for a variety of community development programs. It can be, and has been, used either with radio or with television. In any of these forms, it is potentially of great value in changing group-anchored attitudes and behavior, because the discussion permits an entire group to change without requiring an individual changer to deviate from the group. That is to say, it works this way in most countries. In cultures where discussion is regarded as a game, or a way to sharpen and demonstrate one's wit, a lecture will accomplish more than a planned discussion. But for most countries, the combination of mass media and group discussion is a most fruitful one, as was discovered in Canada, where the Farm Radio Forum was first started in 1941.

After ten years of the Forum in Canada, Unesco invited the sponsors to evaluate the practice as an instrument of adult education. It was concluded that the programs had been notably successful in developing leadership, in encouraging cooperation among farmers, and in creating a "sense of community."[9]

In France, rural discussion groups were organized around television. These were carefully evaluated and found to do precisely what it was hoped they would accomplish: carry information to their members and result in desirable attitude change. The evaluators discovered another thing of some importance about the clubs: they are more effective when the broadcast topics are selected and the programs planned in cooperation with prospective viewers.[10] This is another vote for "localness" in development information.

Japan also organized a number of forum groups around television. Interest was very high. The groups developed into community social centers. Said the evaluation report: "Though it was cold midwinter, the villagers, old and young, heads of households, wives and children, came to the community hall every Thursday evening. . . . [They] began to take an interest in the more serious subjects rather than in gossip and idle chatter. Television helped the farmers to open their mouths, to express their thoughts and to learn that it is not, after all, such a difficult thing to talk in the presence of other people. Moreover, after expressing their thoughts, they had a sense of satisfaction."[11] When Unesco's subsidy of the experiment came to an end, the Japanese government decided to continue the clubs under its own support.

The most extensive trial of the rural forums has taken place in India. Beginning with a pilot project of 20 programs broadcast to 150 village listening and discussion groups in five unilingual districts of one state, the activity soon spread to 3,500 village forums throughout the country. The third five-year plan provides for adding forums at the rate of 5,000 a year. In addition to the rural farmers' forums, there are about 1,400 women's listening clubs, and about 2,000 children's clubs in rural areas of the country.[12]

The research report on the rural forums was glowing: ". . . a success beyond expectations. Increase in knowledge in the forum villages . . . was spectacular, whereas in the nonforum villages it was negligible. . . . Forums developed rapidly into decision-making bodies, capable of speeding up common pursuits in the village faster than the elected *panchayat.* Frequently they took on functions halfway between those of a panchayat and a town meeting. . . . The forums thus became an important instrument of village democracy, and enabled many more people to partake in the decision-making process in the village. . . . The demand that [forums] be made a permanent feature was practically unanimous."[13]

The effectiveness of these forums, demonstrating the uniquely powerful combination of mass media and related group discussion, has encouraged the government of India, and other governments as well, to go ahead with plans to spot community radio receivers in as many rural villages as possible. In India, the central government subsidizes 50 per cent of the cost of village sets, up to a maximum of $25. Of the remaining 50 per cent, the village is usually asked to pay one-fourth; the other three-fourths, and the costs of installation, are ordinarily paid by the state. About 100,000 such community receivers have now been placed in villages in India, in addition to the somewhat larger number that are privately owned.

It must be emphasized again that rural forums are not used solely for information and decisions on agricultural production. Indeed, enlightened agricultural information programs of whatever kind are much broader than farm techniques. They are concerned with health, living conditions, education, literacy, participation in public affairs, and other topics which are only indirectly related to greater farm production. Ultimately, of course, anything done to meet these indirect goals will also be reflected in productivity. But the most successful agricultural information is addressed to the farmer as a man, rather than merely as a planter and cultivator.

Health

It is not necessary to speak at length of health improvement or other community development campaigns, inasmuch as these present almost exactly the same problems as the agricultural campaigns already discussed.

Linwood Hodgdon, a social anthropologist who has worked for

some years with problems of social and economic development in Asia, had this to say about health improvement programs:

The further we progress with programs of public health education, the more our educational efforts will have to be concerned with the individual, and with the sociological and psychological factors which influence his behavior.

In the initial stages of a malaria control program we are not directly concerned with either cultural values or individual attitudes and beliefs. Our efforts are concerned with doing things *to* people or *for* people, rather than *with* people. However, when we are interested in promoting a family planning program, or in changing the dietary habits of a group of people, we impinge directly upon the realm of individual attitudes, values, and beliefs. We must strive to help the people make a fundamental change in their personal behavior. In these instances we will find that progress can be made only as we understand and work through these values and attitudes. We will also discover that public health programs cannot be legislated into existence, but rather the focus must be upon the educational process.[14]

In health campaigns, then, as in agricultural improvement programs, so long as we are concerned with doing something *to* or *for* people, the task is not too difficult, and an information campaign, while useful, is not crucial. But as soon as we come to the point where it is necessary for the villager to make a decision and change his behavior, then effective information is crucial. And at this stage, as health development officers have discovered, if we expect our campaign to succeed and our information to be effective, then (1) we must base the whole campaign on an understanding of the life, beliefs, and attitudes of the villagers, and the social factors that help to determine how they live; (2) we must expect to provide face-to-face communication with field workers or other individuals who understand the village and villagers as well as the dynamics of social change, and use the mass media to support and extend the work of this field staff; and (3) we must use a combination of communication channels, employing each in such a way and at such a time as to contribute most to the total usefulness of the information.

A report of the Central Health Education Bureau of India indicates how that organization goes about applying information to the speeding up of community development in health practices. In the first place, there is an active field staff of public health workers, with traveling doctors and health clinics spaced over the country. To these people the Bureau and the state offices furnish a stream of materials, in the planning and selection of which the field workers presumably have a voice. The Bureau uses all the media of mass communication to reach the public health workers, the health educators, and the general public. It maintains a film library on health subjects, previews new films to advise other users, and helps the Information Ministry in the production of films on health problems. It also stocks filmstrips. It arranges radio talks and publishes the scripts in a monthly journal, *Swasth Hind*. It is beginning to experiment with India's one television station. It publishes pamphlets, carefully pretested with a target audience; issues press releases; takes advertisements; publishes posters. It has participated in a number of health exhibits. Now it plans a new nontechnical health journal in a vernacular language for people with minimum education. In a typical campaign, such as the one aimed at smallpox vaccinations, it produces brochures and pamphlets for popular use; posters on the need for vaccination for six different target groups; handbills, bus panels, and chalk boards, explaining about vaccination; feature articles and press conferences for newspapers; "talking points" and technical background material for the field staff; a special number of the journal; some radio features, advertisements, and a group of slogans for campaign use.

To the extent that facilities and personnel are available, a public health campaign in almost any developing country will resemble what we have just described. That is, it will be a broad spectrum effort with the mass media in support of an intensive interpersonal campaign. In dealing with rural, often illiterate, people, health information planners have found film and radio especially effective in support of public health workers. We can conclude with an example of each of these.

The government of the Philippines has been operating 22 mobile film vans, built on trucks, and carrying their own power generators, as well as projection screens, loudspeakers, microphones, and exhibits, pamphlets, and other supplies as needed. These vans go from community to community, showing films on health and sanitation, better agricultural practices, government organization and citizen responsibility, and so on. After the film showing, the microphones and loudspeakers of the vans are often used for a discussion of the problems introduced by the film. People throng to see the films. Audiences range from 500 to 3,000. In the course of a year, millions of people are reached.[15]

In South Korea, in an area where electricity and radio receivers were scarce, ingenious use was made of a limited number of inexpensive battery-powered radios. Twenty such receivers were obtained, and a 50-watt transmitter was built for a few hundred dollars. A program was designed to implant some needed information about tuberculosis, typhoid fever, and intestinal parasites, in an area where those were the principal health problems. This information was featured in a three-hour program, which also included a considerable amount of entertainment—a singing contest, local bands, a "man on the street" interview, and the like. The program was broadcast three times a day. After each broadcast, volunteers moved the receiving sets to another community. Thus, in three days, the broadcast on the 20 sets was heard in 180 different locations.

The broadcast was a huge popular success, and it taught the information it was intended to teach. A sample of viewers was pretested and post-tested. After the broadcast had been heard, less than half as many people as before believed any longer that tuberculosis was hereditary, almost everyone had learned how encephalitis is transmitted, and 50 per cent more than previously knew the source of typhoid fever.[16]

This, of course, does not guarantee that an audience in a developing country will necessarily learn from the mass media exactly what it is intended they should learn. One experience of the Peruvian Hacienda project mentioned in Chapter 1 is a case in point. As a part of the health program, a color film was shown on the transmission of typhus by lice. The hacienda dwellers were plagued with lice, and it was desired to point out some of the dangers of the situation. The film was previewed and judged to be effective. But when people were questioned about the film a week after the showing, it became apparent that the message had not been understood. People said they had seen many lice, but never one of the giant kind shown on the screen. Therefore, they judged that the dangerous animals must be a different kind of lice! Furthermore, they had seen many people sick with typhus, but never any like those in the film, who had a strange and unpleasant white and red color. They judged, therefore, that it must be a disease that afflicted other people but not them.[17] What was learned was obviously not what the film was intended to teach. The incident illustrates why it is necessary for a mass communicator to know his audience, and for mass communication in a developing country to be pretested whenever possible.

Literacy learning

In a thoughtful and enlightened paper considering the contributions various media could make to the teaching of literacy, the French National Commission for Unesco advanced the general hypothesis that literacy in the developing countries "must be regarded as a practical matter and, indeed, as a means to an end"; and from this hypothesis it derived the following points to consider in the fight against illiteracy:

First, the task of eliminating illiteracy must take different forms according to the social groups, the sectors in which development is aimed at, and the object in each case.

Second, in determining when literacy campaigns should be begun, development plans for these groups and sectors should be taken into account; in other words, the elimination of illiteracy is not necessarily the first step to be taken in a movement toward modernization and development.

Third, a literacy campaign must be regarded as part of a wider complex of measures which must be coordinated and consolidated.

Fourth, steps must therefore be taken to carry out the necessary preparatory work (a study of existing needs; measures to arouse a demand, based on existing interests, in places where the need for literacy is not yet felt; the production of more reading matter; the framing of a written form for languages which as yet have none; the production and distribution of supplies such as exercise books, pencils, etc.). To a greater or lesser degree, such problems as these will involve the structure of the economy as a whole, both in the sphere of production and in that of external trade; at a different level, they raise the question of priorities. For what use would it be to teach the people of a country to read if there were no printing-works capable of producing books or newspapers for those who have learnt to read, or if there were no organized distribution of imported newspapers and books, or if—as has happened on several occasions—the language taught in literacy class were not the one used in the current newspapers and books? Another essential aspect of the preparatory work, follow-up, and incidental features of a literacy campaign will be the training of general and technical staff and the administrative services required before, during, and after the campaign.[18]

This serves to emphasize again that any information campaign aimed at broad social change must be grounded in the local culture and the local situation, related to other developments, and adequately supported by planning and logistics. Success in one of these campaigns is by no means assured when one has a high-power transmitter, or the equivalent. As essential as the mass media are in any of these campaigns, they must march in an army and be assigned the tasks they can do best in relation to the other tasks and other channels.

Few campaigns are more closely related to the social setting and the other development plans than a literacy campaign. Literacy, as the French commission said, is a means to an end. It is a means to create more useful, more productive citizens, and to speed up national development. Therefore, its content must relate to the needs of the community and the development plan. Its incentives must grow out of assurance that to learn to read is a good thing from the point of view of the community and the individual, and will pay a reward in jobs and position within the community. The follow-up reading material must be related in a practical way to the life, problems, and opportunities of the community, or else the new literate is likely to decide the effort wasn't worth it, and give it up. In other words, as literacy experts from the Marxist-Leninist countries have often said, "literacy is a social problem," and when one begins to think about literacy information one begins first with the social situation.

When is a society ready for a broad literacy campaign? That is to say, when is it in position to make use of new reading and writing skills and to reward their possessors? Who should learn to read? Is there some group that needs it more than others? Is it sufficient to teach the children to read, and disregard the adults? *What* should new literates learn to read? They will be reading about *something* as they learn; cannot literacy learning be treated as a part of general community development, and used to impart knowledge of health, farming, citizenship, arithmetic, or whatever knowledge is most needed by the society at the time? Questions like these come up *before* one decides about information channels.

When one begins to think about channels, however, one finds three general patterns in use, of which two emphasize face-to-face communication and only one emphasizes mass communication. One of these is the great volunteer campaign. The countries with mass parties and with literacy already fairly well along generally have found it easier to concentrate a large number of people on the job of teaching others to read than to devise other campaigns. In Poland, for example, the electronic media played a supporting role —helping to build incentive, praise accomplishment, and so forth. The printed media made a very great contribution by furnishing primers and by printing materials with easy words and adult ideas to bridge the gap for new literates between literacy-class reading competence and newspaper reading competence. But the chief information channel was the volunteer teacher, who taught the illiterate the letters and the phonics, and monitored his early efforts to read and write.

A second pattern is to leave the whole job to the school. This means that many of the children will learn to read, but few adults will. The printed media will furnish the indispensable primers and readers, and there may be some help from films, radio, or television. But here the chief information channel is the schoolteacher.

The French Commission Report, quoted earlier, contains a paragraph on the school as center of literacy teaching:

The question may arise, therefore, whether the attainment of literacy in the countries requiring rapid development should be regarded as essentially or mainly a task for the schools. Schools are valuable—indeed indispensable—but their rate of achievement is too slow and the numbers they reach are too small to meet the urgent needs of those [developing] countries. While ceaselessly working for the extension of their school systems, they cannot rely on school education alone to lay the foundations of their future development. They need the new techniques and media, and, more particularly, television. Nor is there any conflict between such aids and the work of the schools. A literacy campaign conducted through the medium of television may well be based on school syllabuses, at least in some cases; or it may to some extent use the material facilities available in schools; or it may lay the foundation for school attendance. It is undeniable, however, that a teaching medium such as television is more flexible and more adaptable to individual, rapidly changing situations than is the school system. To give but one example, it would more easily reach the fluctuating population of rural adolescents without vocational qualifications or possessed only of a kind of training that is of little use in their actual circumstances—a group which is growing larger every day in the main cities of Africa and will long continue impervious to those forms of education and training which enjoy more traditional methods.[19]

To greater or less degree, most developing countries have felt the force of this argument and have tried to supplement their school teaching of literacy with out-of-school classes based on television, radio, or film. This is the third pattern of literacy teaching. At the time of the Unesco Expert Meeting on Literacy, in June of 1962, 13 of the 67 countries replying to a questionnaire reported that they were broadcasting literacy courses by radio, and the same number said that they were providing literacy courses by film. The precise number of countries now teaching literacy by television is not known, but it includes Italy, Brazil, Mexico, the United Arab Republic, Guatemala, the Ivory Coast, the United States, and Kenya.

In literacy classes taught by media, the general practice has been to try to station a teacher, or at least a volunteer chairman and supervisor, at as many centers as possible where students come to hear or see the literacy program. This is especially important in the case of radio, which is unable to present simultaneous sight and sound. Such a teacher needs little training, because the expert teacher on the broadcast or the film can carry most of the work. The local supervisor has proved to be helpful, however, both in explaining to the student and in feeding back student learning problems to the broadcaster.

Television is an appealing vehicle for literacy teaching, because it can present sight and sound together and because it is new enough to be especially appealing. The most extensive test of television as a vehicle of literacy teaching has been made in Italy. As late as 1960, there were still almost two million illiterates in Italy, mostly in the rural southern part of the country. Furthermore, there was a great deal of resistance among these people to literacy teaching. The Italian broadcasting system and the Ministry of Education combined their efforts and facilities to try to solve the problem. They created a continuing television program called "It's Never Too Late." This program was carefully designed so as not to embarrass or antagonize adult viewers. The teacher's desk and classroom never appeared in the picture; the teacher was chosen for his friendliness and for his resemblance to an ordinary person rather than an intellectual. Care was taken not to offend adult pride by talking down to the audience, by "playing games" with them, or by treating them like pupils. The program was leavened with humor, and with useful information in addition to the skill of reading. It was accompanied by specially prepared reading materials, and followed by additional courses which the student could take if he so wished. The Italians found it useful to station a teacher at each class meeting place to guide the students' drill, supplement the television teaching, and answer questions.

The Italian experiment, then, was an effort to teach a literacy class mostly by television to adults who were predisposed to be resistant. What were the results? Nearly every one of the adults who regularly followed the course at the viewing posts learned to read and write—some, of course, better than others. No precise data could be gathered on the progress of students who had viewed the course in their homes, but there were reports that some of them had greatly missed the help of the local teacher in correcting the students' own drill. The experiment, said the Ministry of Public Instruction, was very economical. The number of regular viewing points reached 4,000, and the number of viewers was approximately 563,000—more than one-fourth of all the illiterates in Italy, assembled at one time to be taught by one expert teacher.[20]

All adult literacy programs, and most particularly those that have leaned on media like television, radio, and film, have depended heavily on special, easy-reading materials for use following the class itself. Without them, the student quickly forgets his newly won skill. Furthermore, if these materials are well planned, they can disseminate a great deal of useful information about agriculture, health, sanitation, citizenship, national history and government, and other subjects of high priority in national development.

Different nations have handled these materials in different ways. Puerto Rico, for example, produces annually four books, several booklets, four issues of a poster, and eight to ten posters, all easily read and geared to the development program. Liberia sells (for three cents) a multilith monthly, *New Day*, written with the 1,200-word vocabulary of the literacy course. In Northern Nigeria, a group of tabloid news sheets, each eight pages in length, are available for new literates. In Lucknow, India, Literacy House assembles village libraries of books with simple vocabularies, publishes books suitable for new literates, and issues a fortnightly easy-reading family magazine. In other countries, special newspapers have been published once a week or once every two weeks to furnish news in easy-to-read form, and thus build the habit of news reading and civic interest. In still other countries, existing newspapers have carried a column or more of material especially written for new literates. These and other methods are satisfactory for delivering the material; the problem is to *prepare* material that new adult literates will consider useful and interesting and that will be easy to read, without being "written down."[21]

The functions of the mass media in literacy learning, then, become important at three stages of the process. They can help build interest and incentive to learn to read. When the students have been brought into the class, the media can play either a supporting role (as in Poland) or the main role (as television does in Italy).

When the students have mastered the skill enough to read a little on their own, the mass media must supply easy material to bridge the gap from class to normal adult reading.

Formal education

Schools and teachers form one of the largest items, except for industrialization itself, on the cost sheet of a developing country. The planner's question is, therefore, how can the mass media multiply scarce resources in this field? Any contribution that modern communication can make to reducing the cost per student taught, raising the efficiency of instruction, or extending it beyond present facilities will be an economic contribution of considerable importance.

Every school system in the world depends on printed materials, and audiovisual aids are used to the extent that schools can afford them.[22] Textbooks and teaching films do not appear automatically in a developing country, of course. There must be a book-publishing industry and skilled textbook writers if the country is to have its own textbooks, and a film-making industry, or at least arrangements for importing suitable instructional films and projectors, if a country is to have films for its schools. Failure in these respects is the reason why suitable textbooks are scarce and teaching films are much less used than they could be in many developing countries. But the efficiency and usefulness of these media in formal education are broadly recognized.

The newer media of radio and television are less well proved in schools in the developing regions, but they offer certain extremely attractive possibilities. To a country where highly trained teachers are scarce they offer the opportunity to share its best teachers widely. Where few teachers are trained to teach certain subjects, these media offer the hope that those subjects can be taught even before qualified teachers become available. Where projectors and films are scarce, television can serve as a "big projector" for hundreds of schools at the same time. And where schools are not yet available, or for people who, for one reason or other, cannot go to school, radio and television can offer some educational opportunity without schools.[23]

Henri Dieuzeide, research chief of the Institut National Pedagogique of Paris, has summed up what he calls substantial agreement already reached on the educational advantages and disadvantages of radio and television. On the one hand, he says, certain positive characteristics derive from their power of diffusion and penetration:

a) distribution of a single . . . message over the whole of a receiving network;
b) immediate, instantaneous, automatic dissemination of the message;
c) regularity of delivery, making possible the dissemination of a coherent series of messages permitting a coordinated action of an institutional character.

There are also some psychological advantages:

a) the character of particular immediacy and authenticity of "direct" messages which coexist with the psychological attention span of the spectator;
b) the personalized, intimate character of the message;
c) the feeling of belonging to a community of "receivers" and of participating in an activity of national importance.

On the other hand, there are some negative characteristics, stemming from the difficulty of adapting the broadcast message to the individual needs of the user:

a) fixed timetables which tie the audience to a specific hour;
b) uncertainty (more or less great) [on the part of the teacher] before the broadcast as to what the message will contain;
c) predetermined and immutable presentation of the message (structure, rhythm), all revision being impossible.[24]

Dieuzeide then lists four educational uses of radio and television which have been successfully undertaken in many places throughout the world. These are:

the *enrichment* broadcast, which is integrated into classroom teaching and makes a *qualitative* improvement in the teaching;

the broadcast designed to *palliate the deficiencies* of an existing educational system—for example, substituting for unqualified teaching staff or upgrading present teachers—and thus making a largely *quantitative* improvement in the system;

the *extension* broadcast, which extends or prolongs educational opportunities for individuals in their homes or groups of individuals formed for educational purposes, the individuals in this case having already had some schooling;

the *development* broadcast, designed to carry education to communities where there has never been a school. In this case radio and television conduct a mass educational activity which really *precedes the school*.[25]

The electronic media have been used successfully for years, in most or all of these forms, by the relatively highly developed countries.[26] During the last few years, a sufficient number of experiments and case studies have come in from Asia, Africa, and Latin America so as to leave little doubt that the developing countries, also, can with great effect use these media for education.

Concerning the usefulness of the electronic and film media for enrichment and palliative purposes in the developing countries, there can hardly be any remaining skepticism. Talks and music by radio, demonstrations and films by television have been used effectively in so many countries that it is useless to name the places. Research studies back up what has been reported from the trials. For example, Japan tested a course in English by radio in the seventh grade and found that the classes taught in part by radio were significantly superior to the conventionally taught classes.[27] They found also that third and fifth grades, whose classes in Japanese language were enriched by radio, did as well as or better than conventionally taught students in all test periods.[28] In Thailand, large groups of second- and third-grade pupils, and sixth- and seventh-grade pupils, were tested with and without enrichment broadcasts in music and in English language, respectively. The music students who had the broadcasts scored significantly better than the classes without broadcasts. The students of English who were assisted by the broadcasts did as well in aural tests as, and better in tests of reading and writing than, those who did not have the broadcasts.[29] In Delhi, India, two eighth-grade geography classes were compared on a 24-day unit of study. One of the classes was shown a number of films during the experimental time; the other class was not. Tested at the end of the unit and again some weeks later, the class that had seen the films did significantly better.[30]

In Turkey, rather than trying to develop a new course in physics, Istanbul educators adapted for use by Turkish school children the 162 half-hour lessons of the Harvey White physics course which had been broadcast successfully on television in both the United States and England. In Turkey, the programs were shown on film, and were intended to find out how programs of this kind might help to fill in the scarcity of well-qualified teachers. The experiment was therefore designed to compare what *lycée* students would learn (1) if taught by experienced teachers with the aid of the films, (2) if taught by inexperienced teachers with the aid of the films, (3) if taught by correspondence but given a chance to view the films, (4) if taught by the best teachers without the films, (5) if taught by average teachers without the films, (6) if taught by the films alone. It was found that students taught by the best teachers, using such teaching aids as they wished but not using the films, did indeed score somewhat higher than students who had the films but no classroom teacher. However, there was no significant difference between the test scores of students taught by *experienced* and by *inexperienced* teachers *if the films were a part of the course!* There was no significant difference between scores made by students taught by *correspondence* and film, and those taught by experienced *teachers* with the films. Students taught either by inexperienced teachers or by correspondence, using the films, did significantly better than students in another city taught by average teachers *not* using the films. These results are a remarkable testimony to the effectiveness of televised or filmed teaching.[31]

In 1942 an experimental radio school went on the air in Chile, supported at first by advertising on commercial stations. Its function was primarily enrichment of curriculum, but it soon branched out into extension broadcasts on such topics as "Knowing Our Children" and "Education for the Home," along with programs for teachers and other professionals. With each year, the school gained more acceptance and support. The Ministry furnished official backing and a considerable increase in staff. Teachers on their own raised money for receivers and amplifier systems. The Asociación de Radiodifusoras de Chile (Chilean Broadcasting Association)

placed at its disposal a chain of 14 stations, covering the whole
country, for 26 programs a week. The general verdict on this experiment is that it played a highly useful and significant part in the
establishment of the new curricula and new methods in Chile.[32]

In New Delhi, over 30,000 students are receiving enrichment lessons in language and science by the use of about 500 television sets
placed in the schools. Reports are encouraging. Both teachers and
administrators are quoted as saying that the television lessons, and
in particular the lessons in Hindi, provide as much learning for the
teachers as for the students.[33]

Western Nigeria has been broadcasting school television for
nearly three years. It has faced many of the problems that are likely
to recur in any school television program recently established in a
developing country, and a study of the Nigerian experiences would
be most useful to developing countries. The evaluation of results,
however, has been generally favorable, and the teachers and station personnel have been able to produce more programs than expected.[34]

One of the general results of instructional television and radio is
to upgrade teachers and improve classroom teaching. Henry Cassirer discussed this in a lecture to the 1961 Purdue Seminar:

Somebody mentioned to me that in Oregon a science teacher wrote to
the television teacher and said: "This year I'm not going to take you
in my class any more, because I've watched you for two years and I
think I can do the same thing you do and I don't think I need you any
more." To my mind this is exactly as it should be, particularly if the
television teacher didn't introduce physical elements that could not be
reproduced in some form in the classroom. If the classroom teacher has
the assurance that she can do it, then that is very good. And if she
learned it from television, so much the better. Another occasion when
I was in Pakistan, this question came up: "Should television be used
for primary education?" Obviously, it poses enormous problems to have
a television set in every primary school. There's no electricity in the
villages, there are thousands of primary schools, the cost will be very
great, the economics and many other aspects make it rather difficult.
But if you can use television to train the teachers, you have the double
effect of, first of all, using your television medium, but then also of avoid-
ing some of the handicaps of the television medium, namely the lack

education in the developing regions in the near future, still it looks as though the new educational media are going to contribute a considerable amount of excitement to the development of education in the next decade. For, as observers have pointed out, introducing the new media into a relatively new and rapidly growing system is not accompanied by the same restrictions as introducing them into a well-developed system where patterns of education have hardened. If the new countries take the challenge presented them, they will look imaginatively at the "new" media, and at their educational problems in relation to the media.

Let us dream with them a moment.

Suppose that a new country were to feel free to design precisely the curriculum it needs (not necessarily the one it inherited), secure in the belief that the new media could help it teach whatever curriculum it chooses.

Suppose that the country were to share its very best teachers as widely as possible, so that every student, by television, would have access to a considerable proportion of really masterly teaching.

Suppose, in addition to this, that the country would divide teaching duties according to abilities, with a few master teachers on television, others conducting classroom drill and discussion, still others (with very little training, perhaps) monitoring, correcting papers, keeping records.

Suppose that the country were to unfreeze the repetitious pattern of building schools with every room the same size. That is, suppose that the country were to observe that there are many learning activities a student needs to do by himself, and others for which he can efficiently use a very large room (for example, for televised classes), and still others for which he needs a discussion-sized room—and build accordingly.

Suppose that a country, with programmed instruction available, would make it possible for as many as possible of its young people to go forward in certain subjects at their own pace, so that the bright ones might go much further in the same time, and the slow ones would learn better what they have to learn.

Suppose that a country, short of secondary schools, long in dropouts, were to provide programmed correspondence courses, so that many of the young people who are in a region with no secondary school or who are forced to drop out of school for other than academic reasons, might still go further with their education.

Dreams? Perhaps. But not beyond possibility. The early years of a country are years to dream ahead. The early, pliable years of an educational system are good times to dream of how to use the new educational multipliers in support of the national goals. This is the time for educators in the developing countries, despite their pressing problems of budget and teacher training, to be imaginative about the new educational media. For as Robert Lefranc says:

Some countries, very little developed economically, have made colossal strides, passing without any intermediate stage from the age of the wheelbarrow and the bullock cart to the age of the aeroplane. We need have no fear that these countries, at least, will make the same slow pilgrimage to the temple of culture which has taken European countries some hundreds of years. On the contrary, they should undertake forced marches, and fight ignorance and illiteracy with modern methods and techniques, not with those available to Socrates, Montaigne, Rousseau, and Jules Ferry.[43]

6. Communication Research as an Arm of Economic and Social Development

An earthy proverb, which I heard for the first time from a cabinet minister in North Africa, sums up the point to be made in the following pages. Said the minister: "Don't juggle knives in the dark!"

The saying is quite apt. Given light, the juggler can follow the knives with his eyes, and move his hands in and out of the oval of whirling blades without injury. In other words, he gets a constant "feedback" from each knife he tosses into the air. He gets cues that tell him when the knife comes down, where to reach for it, how high to throw it the next time, and so forth. In the dark, those cues are missing.

When we talk about communication research in developing countries, we are talking about *feedback*. The developing country also is juggling dangerous tools. It cannot afford to set in motion the forces of social change and take its eyes off them. It cannot afford to use the powerful weapons of mass communication without an eye on their audiences. A basic task of communication research is precisely to meet this need: to provide continuing and systematic feedback from the audiences. Therefore, even nations overburdened with the practical problems of development, to whom communication research sometimes seems a "luxury," might well reconsider that opinion.

THE IMPORTANCE OF FEEDBACK

The mass media are concerned with feedback of two kinds. One of these is the kind of feedback they themselves can bring about through their programs. In many countries, this has been accomplished, with great effect, by building "localness" into the media. Radio becomes "local" radio; newspapers move into the towns and send their reporters into the villages. They abandon the idea that programs must be produced entirely in the radio or TV studio, films made wholly in the film studio, news found only in the cities or on the news agency wire. They go out to the villages and towns seeking interviews on farm plans and problems, films of what is happening in the villages, opinions from the "man in the street." They invite questions for the media to answer, letters to the editor, local speakers and panels on the air. In other words, they rely heavily on local production. And by so doing they bring about a feedback of local news and opinion into the media, and encourage the audience to think that it is indeed *their* channel—not merely a channel that comes *to* them.

This is important because any man would rather be talked *with* than *to*. A local leader in a recently independent state once expressed in these words the difference he felt: "When we are a colony," he said, "they come down and talk *to* me. When we are free, they come talk *with* me." Naturally, he preferred *two-way* communication. Every citizen of traditional society, faced with basic decisions on values and customs, would rather talk them over than be harangued about them. This is why two-way communication through mass media programs helps encourage development decisions.

Program feedback—two-way communication of the kind we have just been talking about—is intended to establish a flow of information and opinion from some users of the media to other users. *Research* feedback, on the other hand, is intended to provide a flow of information about audiences and the effects of the mass media, to the program and policy officers of the media and to the leaders of national development.

Research feedback of this kind is especially important to a developing country for the following four reasons:

1. A nation engaged in something as delicate as social change wants to work in the clear light of facts. It is desirable to make the process of change as efficient and as little disruptive as pos-

sible. Some groups will change faster than others; some will resist change more than others. Therefore, there will be different needs for information among different groups at different times. An explanation here, a demonstration there, a few questions answered in one place, a few assurances given in another, a problem to be studied and clearly understood in a third place—actions like these may make all the difference between a slow, resisted, unpleasant change and a cooperative change in which the people of a nation feel they are moving forward together.

In other words, the appropriateness of information directed *to* the audiences of the mass media depends on appropriate information *from* and *about* the audiences of the mass media. The *quality* of information from and about the audiences is of the essence. If it is to be useful, it must be based on facts rather than hunches; it must be adequate to allow for differences among parts of the audience, and for changes with time. This is why it is important that, so far as possible, the clear light of research be turned on the informational needs of the audiences.

2. A developing country cannot afford to waste resources on unsuccessful or inefficient campaigns. Even highly industrialized countries, where communication research is available, experience a certain amount of failure with information campaigns, especially those aimed at changing attitudes or behavior.[1] All the more reason to be on the alert for possible campaign failure in developing countries where research has not been readily available, where audience characteristics and differences are not fully known, and where most information campaigns in the course of economic and social development are directed toward changes of great magnitude. Furthermore, in developing countries the funds available for information campaigns are relatively less than in richer, more fully developed countries. A failure of any part of the expenditure to deliver the information where it is needed when it is needed is therefore doubly serious, and anything that can be done by research to make failure less likely, and the delivery of information more efficient, is likely to show financial as well as psychological gain.

3. In developing countries there is usually a diversity of audi-

ences and conditions, and a scarcity of detailed knowledge about them. In developing countries much of the audience will be new to the media and therefore unpredictable. Because traditional society maintains little contact between communities, the groups within the potential audience have grown up in relative isolation and may be expected to show a variety of cultural differences. Therefore, audiences in the less-developed countries are relatively less homogeneous than in many other countries. Furthermore, the cultural gap between producer and consumer is typically wider in these countries than in developed societies. Often the highly educated African or Asian producer or editor or information chief, trained, perhaps, in European or American universities, seems much closer to his European or American counterpart than to the village people in his own country. Unless he makes constant effort, through visiting his audiences and through research, to root himself again in the culture of his own country, his programs or films or printed materials are likely to be ill-adapted for the audiences that need them most.

4. New media have especial need to keep close contact with their audiences. The audiences in a developing country are changing rapidly; they need a great deal of information during the period of change, and different information at different times. But the media themselves are new, and changing very rapidly. There is thus no tradition to guide the services that the media provide for their audiences, and the media have good reason to think of their own development as occurring in partnership with their audiences, and their communication research programs as a means for determining the most appropriate audience service at a given point of change.

Caught up in simultaneous media change and social change, developing countries are discovering more and more the practical usefulness of research. Reporting on the first year of Nigeria's experience with educational television, George L. Arms wrote:

Underlying the whole matter of utilization . . . was the basic problem of research. Planning committees would be unable to work with any degree of confidence until they had a considerable amount of information about details of reception, impact, communicability, etc. For instance . . . there were some indications, from other areas of scholarship, that Africans may not be as visually sophisticated as could be expected, but there did not seem to be any real proof of this, and there was no information as to what, if any, impact it would have upon the learning process. On a considerably more elementary level, information was needed as to what happened when the set was turned on, what the attention span seemed to be, etc.

At this point, "some aspects of the experiment were successful" but others were not; "long-range planning [was] an increasingly necessary adjunct if the experiments were to be translated into an organ of permanent value," and the government had to "decide what it wanted to do." At this point, said Arms, systematic research ceased to be academic and became a matter of intensely practical importance.[2]

THE NATURE AND TASKS OF COMMUNICATION RESEARCH

Research is only one of several ways by which feedback on audience and effects is provided to the mass media and the leaders of national development. Its special usefulness, in comparison with the others, lies in its *reliability.*

When a letter comes in, praising or complaining, it is very hard to tell how much of the audience it represents. Even when a radio producer visits a village to find out reactions to his program, he can hardly be sure that the next village will have the same reactions. The more sophisticated the mass communicators of a country become, therefore, the more suspicious they are of unsystematic feedback. When a member of the audience reports that a program was "wonderful," they learn to regard it as one man's opinion, which may or may not be representative. When someone tells them that an information campaign was "a great success," they learn to ask for the evidence on which he bases the judgment. Many informal judgments of the success or failure of a campaign tend to be self-serving or based on inadequate observation. Many a campaign worker thinks the effort was a success, although a deeper study might show quite different results; many an informal observer has seen evidence of failure, when a more representative sampling of observations would indicate a large degree of success. Therefore, developing countries find, as more fully developed ones already have found, that they cannot place full reliance on any feedback or audience reports except systematic ones, which meet the standards and often use the methods of research.

There is nothing especially esoteric about research. It is simply the best way we have yet found to gather information systematically, accurately, and with safeguards that permit one to estimate how reliable the information is. This is accomplished through scientific sampling, adequate research design, uniform asking of questions or making of observations, skillful reduction of data, and the application of suitable statistics. It is not something that one undertakes without study or training; but neither is there anything magic or mysterious about it. Unesco plans a handbook on communication research especially for developing countries, and there are numerous places where one can obtain training or read about the methods that are used.[3]

Lasswell has described the sweep of communication research in terms of

> Who
> Says What
> In Which Channel
> To Whom
> With What Effect?[4]

"Who" is the study of communicators and of communicating organizations like the mass media. For example, what sources of development information are trusted and believed in the villages? How can the media be organized more efficiently? "What" is the study of content: what are the people being told about national policy or economic change? "Channel" refers to the study of different media; for example, how does a given kind of information come to the village, and what is the most effective channel or combination of channels for a given kind of information? "Whom" refers to studies of the audience—their characteristics, needs, information habits, reactions to the mass media and to development information, and the like. And "effect," of course, has to do with what communication accomplishes: what audiences remember from it, what effect it has on attitudes, values, and behavior. It is the last two of these, audience and effect studies, that are most immediately useful to developing countries.

The scope of methods and techniques available for communication research is very broad, ranging from content analysis to sample surveys, from participant observation to laboratory or field experiment. This is not a suitable place to discuss research method, but it should be pointed out that the technology of this kind of research is relatively mature, and has been perfected in many hundreds of surveys and experiments in a number of countries.

Two questions are frequently asked concerning communication research in developing countries, however, which represent opposite poles of opinion toward it. One of these goes something like this: Isn't this merely *common sense*? Doesn't research merely come up with answers which any intelligent person would arrive at, without research method and statistics and the other trappings of science? The other question is: Haven't these questions already been answered by communication research in developed countries? These questions deserve answers.

With regard to the first one, let us make clear that research is not in opposition to common sense, but is simply more reliable as a basis for policy. Here are some examples.

"Common sense" would certainly say that the best way to reach people and convince them of the need to change some of their customs would be in the language with which they are most familiar. And this is doubtless true in most cases. But an incident that happened in California illustrates the difference between the kind of guidance one gets from common sense and the guidance one gets from research. The Department of Health of the State of California wanted to print some pamphlets for the guidance of Spanish-speaking mothers who came to maternal and child health clinics. It was only common sense to give them publications in Spanish. But Spanish pamphlets had not worked very well. A little research showed that these mothers were very sensitive about language; they were acculturating toward American life and tended to be offended by the suggestion that they might not be able to use English. Therefore, they rejected pamphlets in Spanish. At this point, the "common sense" advice would have been, give them pamphlets in English. But research showed that they really couldn't read English satisfactorily. Therefore, the research recommendation (based on a small pilot test) was that the pamphlets be printed in a bilingual edition—English so as not to emphasize the ethnic difference, Spanish for easy reading. These worked very well. And the solution was doubtless "just common sense"—but it would have been a very long time before they would have come to it without the kind of systematic fact-gathering which we usually call research.[5]

Another example is one we have already mentioned briefly: the case of the "Mr. Biggott" cartoons. It is only "common sense" to believe that a good way to change a man's extreme attitudes is to get him to laugh at himself. This was the common sense reason why cartoons were the principal tool in a campaign to reduce prejudice. The campaign backfired. If anything, prejudiced people were more prejudiced than before. It took research to find out why, and to learn how to avoid similar fiascos in the future. Research showed that deeply prejudiced people hold to their prejudices with a desperate intensity—so desperate, indeed, that they will distort the most obvious meanings of what they read or see. For example, there was one cartoon that poked fun at "aristocratic" people who insisted they be given nothing but "blue blood" in blood transfusions within hospitals. People who are prejudiced in that respect typically did not laugh at the cartoon; they thought it was a good idea to be sure one got only the most aristocratic blood in hospitals! When this much became known, it was only "common sense" to try another approach to combating prejudice. But this was a conclusion to which "common sense" had previously given no guidance.[6]

Common sense, based on long experience with entertainment programs in well-developed cultures, advises that an audience should be sent away "happy." If something funny can be put at the end of a program, people will be more likely to come back for more. A comedy at the end of an instructional film showing is probably good public relations, and obviously relaxes the audience. But when this was tried in developing countries, development officers began to have doubts. They began to wonder how much of the health or agriculture or literacy taught in the earlier films was forgotten in the final comedy. "How many times," a film officer wrote ruefully, "have I seen the whole effects of teaching disappear in the gusts of laughter greeting Charlie Chaplin!"[7] The problem, therefore, is to balance the loss in learning against the increased motivation to come back for more—in other words, to find out the cumulative results of exposure. How much was learned over a period of time with, and how much was learned without, the final comedy; and how many people lasted through the course? Questions like these are research questions, for which common sense does not provide an adequate guide.

Therefore, research is used, not because people do not value common sense, but because they know where common sense is likely to give insufficient guidance.

The second question refers correctly to the fact that a great deal of communication research has indeed been done in economically advanced countries. The point in question is, how much of it is applicable to developing societies?

The more special and particular the findings of communication research are, the less applicable they are likely to be elsewhere. For example, take a finding that a certain television program attracted an audience of a given size and kind in England. The results of such a study are of very limited applicability to developing countries.[8] Clearly, if developing countries want such information about *their* programs or stations or newspapers, they will have to study *their* audiences. But how about more theoretical studies, for instance the series of findings by the Yale psychological group which was for a long time headed by Carl Hovland? They found, for example, that certain types of people are more susceptible to persuasion than others; that, under certain conditions, it pays to use a two-sided argument (that is, to cite the opponent's viewpoint also), and in some cases not; that very strong fear appeals usually result in rejection rather than acceptance of an argument; and so forth.[9] Are such findings more widely applicable? We are just beginning to find out. Or one might cite also the "two-step flow" theory of Lazarsfeld and Katz, which we have mentioned before—the idea that a certain amount of the influence of mass communication is exerted through opinion leaders at different places in the population who absorb more mass communication than the average.[10] All these findings have come out of advanced cultures. Some of them are doubtless applicable to other cultures, but we do not know, at this moment, how broadly they are applicable. It is necessary to replicate them in other cultures. So far as the most specific findings are concerned, then, the developing countries can expect to find very little use for them in their own planning. So far as the most general findings are concerned, until more of these experiments are replicated, the developing countries must proceed with caution in applying the results. The more *specifically* the results are to be applied to planning an informational program or campaign, the more cautiously the developing countries must proceed in making use of research results from highly developed countries.

It is the method, rather than the findings, which can be most directly applied. To build up a useful body of communication research results for their own use, the developing countries will have to use that method and *conduct* communication research.

Let us take some examples of how the method of communication research can be used directly as an arm of economic and social development.

Pretesting informational materials

In a certain Chilean clinic, women were being given directions for maintaining health during pregnancy. Among other things, they were instructed to "walk three kilometers a day." They dutifully learned this advice. But when someone asked them later how far three kilometers was, there occurred a lively argument in which the distance was interpreted variously from 9 to 81 blocks. Clearly, metrical distances meant nothing to these women, and the instructions should have been couched in more homely terms, such as "walk to the market and then to the church and back." A comparable event was noted at a Mexican clinic, when women were told to nurse their children "every three hours." Once again, the instructions were accurately learned, but they meant nothing because *hours* meant nothing to these women. They had no clocks. They measured time by the sun and the shadows, and had never had to learn the concept of hours.[11]

The lore of information services is full of incidents like these, in which otherwise simple facts were couched in a form that could not be comprehended by people in a particular culture. The record of mass communication in developing countries, when such a record is collected, will undoubtedly contribute to that list of communication failures. Where a doctor in a clinic is misunderstood by a patient, in many cases he can discover that fact and correct the misunderstanding. But if mass media are misunderstood, it may take a very long time to discover the misunderstanding and correct it. Therefore, the mass media must make special efforts to avoid possible failures in communication before these can happen.

This is where pretesting is of special use. It is relatively simple and easy to try out materials, before they are printed or broadcast, on a sample of the kinds of people for whom they are intended. In this way it can be seen where misunderstandings are likely to occur, where interest lags, and whether one form of material is likely to be more effective than another.

This is one level of pretesting. A second level is the "pilot project," in which a campaign is tried out in a limited area, and every aspect of the operation is closely observed and evaluated. The returns from a well-conducted "pilot project" are very rich.

Pretesting is something that can be used almost as a matter of routine with new audiences, new subject matters, and all significant materials until the communicators can be confident their materials and procedures fit the needs and capabilities of the intended audience.

Evaluating results of campaigns and programs,
to improve subsequent ones

Mass communication is always in a hurry. It goes from issue to issue, program to program, campaign to campaign, with little time to assess the results of what it has done and a great compulsion to devote its time to what must be done next. The reports from the audience that come to it are too late, too slight, or too unsystematic to be of much help in modifying future practice.

To make the results of past practice of real use in improving future practice, some of the most useful information can be obtained by studying a current campaign, or finding out what happened to a program, a film, or a piece of printed material among a given audience. What were the audience reactions? What did they like or dislike especially? What was misunderstood? How much of the factual content did the audience retain? What, if anything, did they *do* as a result? Were there any changes in opinion or behavior? To what extent was the object of the material or campaign achieved? And in each case, how were the reactions and effects different for different parts of the audience? Did some like it, others not? Did some misunderstand, but others not? Was it effective with some but not with others? If so, why? If evaluation questions like these can be answered, the results will be of immense help to any information system seeking to serve its national program of economic and social development. Indeed, if efficiency of information is an objective, then every major information campaign should have evaluation built into it; and evaluations should be made on a continuing sample of information materials.

Learning how innovation takes place
in a given culture

A few pages back, we spoke of an agricultural campaign that had failed because the wrong group of leaders had been persuaded:

the instigators of the campaign had dealt with the politically elected leaders, who had very little to do with decisions on agricultural innovation. This suggests the importance of knowing, for any given culture, how innovation takes place. It is very helpful to know who makes the key decisions, who are the leaders, how great is their influence, what is the importance of public opinion and how it is formed, what influence the group norms exert on individuals, and so forth. All these facts help a communicator to know whom to talk to, and what information is needed where. And all these are matters for research.

In a number of developing countries the process of agricultural innovation—how farmers decide to adopt a new kind of seed or fertilizer, or a way of taking care of livestock, or a different way of plowing the soil—has been studied repeatedly and in detail.[12] Much of what has been found out is doubtless generally applicable, but some of the evidence from developing countries suggests that by no means all of what has been found out can be taken over. Early results of innovation study in India, for example, suggest that under certain conditions, at least, adoption takes place very early in the process,[13] and most of the information seeking and evaluation trial—which in the classical pattern of agricultural innovation *precede* adoption—actually *follow* adoption and are concerned with reassurance and with learning how to put the practice into effect. There is good reason to suspect that in a culture that is less accustomed to innovations of any kind, where the pattern of trust in agricultural extension has not been built up as it has in certain other cultures, where the influence of group norms is felt more strongly in agriculture, and where religion and the supernatural enter into farming in a way they do not in most cultures that are economically advanced—in these cultures the patterns of successful innovation may be essentially different from those that have already been studied, and it is up to the developing countries to find out whether this is the case.

In many developing countries, for example, belief about the supernatural has a great deal to do with what and how innovation is accepted. A society on Luzon believes that each step of each act has to be given its effectiveness by a specific god; man has very little to do with events. In many Latin American countries, it is the custom to accept events as God's will or Fate. In such a case, as Margaret Mead says,[14] man is responsible for the performance, and God for the success, of the act. At worst, therefore, it is difficult to persuade people who hold these beliefs to use fertilizer or vaccinate animals, because the health of crops or animals seems to be in the divine department. At the least, this distribution of authority results in a relationship between the farmer and his occupation which obviously requires a different information treatment from the one typically expected of agricultural extension. Here is how Redfield and Warner describe this kind of farming as it exists in Yucatan:

It is not simply a way of securing food. It is also a way of worshipping the gods. Before a man plants, he builds an altar in the fields and prays there. He must not speak boisterously in the cornfield; it is a sort of temple. The cornfield is planted as an incident in a perpetual sacred contract between supernatural beings and man. By this agreement, the supernatural yield part of what is theirs—the riches of the natural environment—to man. In exchange, men are pious and perform the traditional ceremonies in which offerings are made to supernaturals. These ceremonies are dramatic expressions of this understanding.[15]

Agricultural information which enters into that culture had better be different from the kind that reaches the farmers of South Dakota or Saxony!

It may be asked whether this is not something that a local communicator—a community development worker, for instance—would know; and therefore, whether anything as sophisticated as research is really required. It is certainly true that a person from the local culture, sensitive to what is going on around him, would know of the existence of such beliefs in the supernatural as we have mentioned. He would very likely know who are the influential persons in making local decisions about agriculture. To the extent that qualified local representatives are available, and are continually reporting on such matters to the mass media, then they constitute a valuable resource whether we call it research or not. But the

media in a developing country are usually not very well represented locally; their feedback, as we have said, is thin; and they
cover large areas including many different communities. Therefore,
it is necessary to make special efforts and arrangements to collect
the information the media need.

Understanding the audience

Doob tells of one instance in which the same film produced radically different reactions in four different Nigerian societies—the
Yoruba, Hausa, Ibo, and Birom. In three of them the picture was
laughed at, but not in the fourth. Some of them understood the picture very well, but in one group even the commentator (who substituted in the native language for a sound track) seemed unable
to follow the message.[16] Obviously there were some differences
within the audience that had not been anticipated and, indeed,
that would not be thoroughly understood without some audience
research.

The media must be aware of how much the audience knows
about the topics on which information is to be sent; what attitudes
they hold that might affect their acceptance or rejection of the information; what kind of language and symbolism they can comprehend, and all the other sorts of information which one would
know or could speedily find out in talking face-to-face to an ac-
quaintance.

Take the apparently simple question of whether to use photographs or drawings in a development campaign. A missionary
wrote, "Take a picture in black and white and the native cannot
see it."[17] Told that they are looking at "a picture of an ox or a dog,"
they will "consider you a liar." But, he says, if you concentrate on
the boys in the group, and point out to them the horns of the ox
and the tail of the dog, they will learn to comprehend the picture,
and soon "the old people will look again and then they clap their
hands and say, 'Oh! Yes, it is a dog.'" There is some reason for
thinking that the ability to comprehend nondetailed pictures increases directly with the amount of education,[18] and it is doubtless
true that a measure of education will tell the mass media a great

deal about other characteristics of their audience, but there are many differences that are not predictable from education alone.

For example, some local customs have been known to get in the way of successful communication. Film in which the speaker gesticulated with his left hand would be regarded as insulting by the Ashanti of Ghana.[19] Competition is a perfectly good motivation among many peoples of the earth, but singling out a Samoan child and permitting him to skip a grade will cause him acute misery; similarly, singling out Navaho and Hopi children for special praise will be an egregious failure.[20] Most people of the earth expect to be questioned by a physician and to answer his questions freely and frankly, but many Zulus will not tell their symptoms because they feel this does not permit the physician to demonstrate his skill adequately.[21] These are examples only, but they indicate the range of differences in customs which may obstruct communication.

In countries where economic development is far advanced, it is common to say that people will accept almost anything if it is offered free. But this is by no means always the case in developing countries. In some countries doubt has been expressed that radio receivers given free to villages are valued and used as much as radios that have been paid for. Programs to give Colombian farmers seedling orchard trees, to provide powdered milk free of charge to poverty-stricken Chilean mothers, and to offer free medical care in a new clinic in Guatemala, all were viewed with the greatest suspicion by the people, and, in fact, were failures until tiny charges were made, in each case, for the article or the service. Even though the income made very little difference to the donors, paying it out made a great difference to the recipients of the assistance. They felt that something they had to pay for was probably worth having.[22] When a suspicion arose in Ceylon over a Rockefeller-supported program to give treatments for hookworm, a Moorish physician in the program took care of the suspicion by explaining that Mr. Rockefeller had once been very ill with hookworm, and, out of gratitude to Allah for being cured, had given all his money to cure others of hookworm. Reporting this, he concluded, "May Allah and Mr. Rockefeller forgive this deliberate falsehood, if it should come to their attention!"[23]

Where is the audience? is the question most commonly asked by mass media in developing countries. That is, how far along toward acceptance of change are they? How far along are they toward understanding the subject matter underlying the change? For example, if vaccine for animals is to be discussed, does the audience know anything about germs and how they cause diseases? In planning a campaign on housing, it is helpful to know what image the people in the particular culture have of what a house should be like; and what changes would have to be made in other parts of the culture if housing were to be changed. In planning information on agriculture, it is well to know how social status, family relationships, community values, and customs relate to farming. For example, it makes sense, generally, to fence pastureland and to plant trees to preserve land from erosion, but the chiefs of Basutoland have opposed it, as an attack on community solidarity and common ownership. One group of the Tanala people of Madagascar outlawed the change to more profitable wet-rice culture because it made for individual ownership and disrupted their custom of joint-family ownership and cooperative labor.[24] The need for information of these kinds may seem obvious, but it is not always met. Very often the study of the cultural matrix of communication and social change does not begin until professional researchers are added to a project or a staff.

Among the many other things that the mass media in a developing country need to know about their audiences is a set of questions directed at the relationship between media and audience: Who is in the audience? What do they read or listen to? What do they think of different media—different newspapers, radio, and so forth? What needs do they feel that ought to be satisfied by information? What *special* needs are felt by what *special* groups among them? Any publisher or station manager would think of many more such questions. To the extent that he can get helpful answers to such questions, to that extent he is in position to move confidently toward serving his audience better. And these are audience research questions.

Studying how information comes to people

Questions like the one just listed lead to the larger question of how information comes to people. In many countries where economic development is far along, these questions have been studied in detail. It is known, for example, what a given kind of individual is likely to read in a newspaper or a magazine, what kinds of films he is likely to see, what kinds of radio and television programs he is likely to select. About certain kinds of audiences—farmers, for example—it is known where they are likely to look for new agricultural ideas, where they are likely to look for additional information on them or to seek advice concerning them. This is very useful information which does not exist in any detail in less-developed countries. It is not a difficult research task to gather such data, and as the information systems develop more fully it will become increasingly necessary to gather it.

At present, when the mass media in most developing countries still do not reach the whole population, and many of their functions are delegated to the chains of interpersonal communication, corresponding information about the interpersonal channels is also possible to obtain, and often proves very useful. For example, it helps to know who are the influential persons in a community with respect to a given kind of social change or policy, and who are the people whose advice is likely to be sought in deciding whether to adopt a new health practice. Another example of helpful information of this kind is the pattern by which information flows through a society: Who talks to whom? Sometimes these channels are rigidly restricted. For instance, Doob cites the fact that among the Tallensi of Ghana face-to-face communication is heavily influenced by one's "genealogical relationships." These people are therefore relatively well acquainted with the other settlements of their clan and somewhat less well acquainted with the areas where their mothers were born, but almost completely ignorant of settlements and persons, even close at hand, where they have no kinship bonds.[25] Likewise, channels of communication to women in many Moslem communities are often hard to find. Among certain societies there are different channels for formal and informal communications. For example, in some societies of Africa, orders or directions must be transmitted very formally through the hierarchies of chiefdoms. The king cannot transmit such information directly to the people who are under a lesser chief; instead, a messenger must go to a subordinate chief, and *his* messenger to a still lower chief, until the tidings arrive at the level where they are intended for use. On the other hand, there are a number of informal channels by which news can travel through the same society without any such restrictions.[26]

Obviously, a knowledge of these interpersonal chains may save much trouble and inefficiency in an information campaign. On the one hand, it will be helpful to know who are the chief sources of interpersonal information, so that they may be informed. On the other hand, it will be helpful to know what resistances may be expected to interpersonal information. For example, when Dr. Margaret Clark found unexpected resistance to house visits during a health campaign in a Spanish-American community, she made a list of the strangers who would be most likely to visit a house in that community. Almost without exception they would represent *trouble*. That is, they would include police, the truant officer to report that a child was not attending school, a representative of juvenile court to report a child in trouble with the law, a government inspector to check on documents, another inspector looking at sanitary facilities, the tax assessor or collector, a building inspector, and so forth—all of them being potential threats to the poor people of the settlement. A major problem for community workers in that locality would therefore be to establish their role as friend and helper; and to know how to do that would take some study and a considerable knowledge of the culture.[27]

Another set of research questions in this area aims at better management of such information resources as exist. Inefficient distribution is a common difficulty in developing countries. It handicaps the local media, and it handicaps government information services.

Any developing country can therefore benefit from a close look at its circulation problems. Would more materials reach the village if they did not have to descend through the hierarchical levels of information offices? Would the flow be larger if printing could be decentralized more than it is? What changes in postal regulations or services would help to get more information to the places where information is scarce? Answers to questions like these, in most developing countries, would greatly assist the flow of useful information.

COMMUNICATION RESEARCH IN DEVELOPING COUNTRIES

That there are special problems involved in doing communication research in developing countries cannot be denied. These are due, for one thing, to the fact that little or no communication research has so far been done in most of the developing countries. Research of any kind becomes easier after a considerable amount of it has been done. More researchers are available. Facilities are available. The particular problems of doing research in the particular area have been discovered, and many of them have been solved. Enough has been found out so it is no longer necessary to study the whole problem; research can concentrate on learning in depth about *one part* of the problem. This is the enviable situation in countries where communication research is well developed. In most of the developing countries, however, it does not describe the situation, and for that reason certain administrative and working problems must be solved before any great amount of effective communication research can be accomplished.

Administrative problems

Researchers. Trained researchers are needed to design and supervise the systematic questioning and observation which constitute communication research. Where can developing countries get trained communication researchers?

Ultimately, the only solution is to train them. At first, some of them can be trained abroad, but as soon as possible training should be established in the home country.

But training of this kind requires three or four years of graduate study. What can be done in the meantime?

A number of interim measures are possible. A competent researcher may be borrowed from a country where communication research is well developed. He can supervise some research, and train a number of persons to perform competently as research technicians. Another way to meet the need on an interim basis is to find a scholar in the home country who is not trained specifically in communication research, but is interested in doing some of it, and has the skills of, say, a psychologist, sociologist, or anthropologist. He might derive some useful ideas and techniques from visiting a country where communication research is advanced; Unesco or some other international organization might be asked to send him a consultant briefly, or conduct an international seminar for such new communication researchers from neighboring countries.

One way to augment the supply is to assign more researchers and technicians to the early projects than are really needed. Thus, more people will acquire experience in communication research.

Still another way to combat some of the shortage of researchers in this field is to train media or information service personnel to conduct some of the simpler kinds of research. Radio audience studies, newspaper readership surveys, or elementary pretests, for example, could be made by resourceful communication personnel after only a minimum of training, providing they had careful instructions and, if necessary, some place to go for advice. The training required might be no more than a month-long course, taught by a skilled researcher, native or foreign.

A handbook for communication research in developing countries is being planned by Unesco with the aid of the International Association for Mass Communication Research.

Research and development. If communication research is to significantly affect information programs in the next few years, research must be considered closely allied to development. One of the chief functions of the communication researcher, in the early period, will be to use his skills to help the writer and producer turn out an effective product. The researcher will find himself assigned to an information campaign, with the task of helping to make the campaign as effective as possible. He will find himself trying to ascertain results that will be effective next week, not next year. He will really be playing an engineering role, rather than the traditional role of basic research.

This will sometimes be difficult and perhaps unpleasant for researchers trained in orthodox methods and procedures. Many of them will do it because of the urgency of the need, but the real solution is to train a number of students in this research engineering function. They would have to learn most of the skills of the orthodox communication researcher, but with a somewhat different emphasis; and they would have to learn and practice a different research role. The number of such persons who will be needed in the next 20 years is at least in the thousands.

Quick results vs. findings of permanent value. A fundamental problem is how to obtain quick, usable results and still have results "add up." Ultimately this comes down to a problem of research administration. A developing country must administer research as it administers other resources. It will undoubtedly feel, at first, that it must put most of its effort on the "engineering" problems we mentioned. But it must reject the impulse to put *all* its efforts on such problems. It should undertake some longer-term research, related to theory. Furthermore, the way questions are asked in the course of "engineering" research will have a great deal to do with whether the results add up to a principle or contribute to an insight that can be used again and again to guide information. Are questions asked the same way in different places, so that results will be comparable? Are clear questions asked and observations made in such a way that there can be no doubt about what happened? Are all the necessary facts collected that might help explain the results? For example, if the reaction to a piece of information is being observed, do the researchers know enough about the education, attitudes, and previous customs of the audience to put the results in perspective and to be able to compare them with the reactions of another audience? Careful attention to the way developmental research is done will result in capturing a great deal of it for long-term usefulness. Gradually a map of the audience characteristics of the country and a catalogue of effective and ineffective procedures under given conditions will emerge.

One of the most useful administrative acts of the developing country will therefore be to make sure there is some common planning as to what facts are to be gathered in different places, and that the facts gathered in different places are brought together, collated, and put into usable form for communicators and researchers.

An idea that has a great deal of promise for communication research in developing countries is one borrowed from scientific agriculture: the experiment farm. An experiment farm, in the agricultural sense, is a farm where new techniques and crops can be tried and demonstrated, and where some of the research can be quick and short-term, some of it long-term and continuing. The same idea would seem to be applicable to communication research. A communication experiment "farm" would be a laboratory of communication researchers and technicians where a varied research program would be under way all the time. Some of this research would be quick and short-term and might be conducted in conjunction with campaigns. On the other hand, some long-term research projects would also be on the program. The advantages of bringing a group of researchers and a group of projects together in this way are: (1) joint planning, and the opportunity to balance short- against long-term research, (2) the opportunity to assemble and collate research results from all the projects, (3) continuity of effort and experience, (4) opportunity to demonstrate desirable communication practices, (5) opportunity to train future researchers. Such a "communication experiment farm" would obviously be a major national resource for an information program.

Working problems

Sampling. Most social research depends, to some degree or other, on sampling—that is, selecting a sample of people from a population so that the results of the questioning or observation will be

representative of the total population. Statisticians and surveyors
have learned to draw samples skillfully in well-developed countries. In developing countries, however, the task is often very difficult. Elmo C. Wilson, head of an international research organization, has summed up some of the difficulties in the way of adequate
sampling in developing countries:

The lack of census data and the unreliability of existing statistics make
it difficult to apply any but the most primitive sample designs. . . .
The scarcity of adequate statistical sources also complicates the matter
of making projections or population estimates from samples. . . . There
are, moreover, no ready checks or controls on sample performance in
the absence of facts about critical population parameters. . . . Greater
costs are often involved in setting up even the simplest sample abroad.
. . . The orderly pre-listing of households [is difficult where there is
no] orderly arrangement of dwelling units, [where] there is a substantial proportion of the population living in makeshift shelters which rise
and disappear with equal celerity, [and where] there may be thousands
of floating, homeless individuals. . . . The random selection of respondents within the households often clashes with local custom or familial
protocol. In some countries, women lead wholly secluded lives. . . . In
some countries, the male head is the exclusive household spokesman.[28]

These points are all true of some or most developing countries,
and they make sampling a very difficult problem. As development
occurs, as population data become fuller and more reliable, sampling will become easier. But it is not necessary to wait for these
desirable improvements before putting communication research
at the service of development. It is necessary, however, to be
doubly careful in drawing a sample not to undertake more than
one can confidently do in the situation, and not to claim more than
one justifiably can as to applicability of results.

Furthermore, many useful kinds of research can be conducted
without sophisticated sampling. Case studies, carefully planned
and interpreted with insight, are an example of research which
would be highly useful at this stage of development in many countries, and which would require a minimum of sampling, if any.
Studies of a whole village, or a whole unit of any kind, are useful
if well done, and get around the sampling problem. Some partici-

pant observation studies can produce very useful results without sampling, as anthropologists have long ago proved. This is not to say that sampling is not an important and necessary tool for a large part of communication research, but merely that many things can be done without it.

Interviewers. The problem of finding and training expert interviewers is complicated in developing countries by the lack of a tradition of social interviewing, and, in many countries, by sanctions against the employment of women for such purposes. In industrialized countries, most interviewers are women, and there is a large group with experience and skills which make them easily trainable. Needless to say, this is not so in most developing countries. Furthermore, in many countries there are restrictions on who may interview people at a given social level, and there are also language problems that keep some interviewers from being effective except in limited areas. Problems like these complicate the situation, but do not make it impossible. Most developing countries will have to train the interviewers they need, to meet the particular kinds of interviewing problems they will have to face.[29] This is a job that could be done well by a "communication experiment farm." However, the situation will improve if each research project trains at least a few interviewers; gradually a pool of experienced and tested interviewers will become available.

Interviewing. Many communication research projects involve asking for opinions—of a program, a pamphlet, a film, a policy, a public figure, or something else on which most residents of industrialized countries would be expected to have an opinion, and to give it freely if asked. Unfortunately, this is not true in many developing countries. Some people are not expected to hold opinions on any except the most personal issues; these people neither think they should have an opinion, nor are able to articulate one. An attempt to interview a representative sample, therefore, often runs into obstacles. Lloyd and Suzanne Rudolph have described some of their experiences when trying to interview "opinionless" people in India.[30] When they would show their desired list of interviews to the village headman, he would exhibit consternation and would demand, "Why do you want to ask this poor *Harijan* woman any questions? I can tell you more than she can!" And the woman herself would protest, "Why ask me? I am only an ignorant woman. Ask my husband!"

In some cases, say the Rudolphs,

. . . the view that a "poor backward woman's" opinion counted for nothing was so strong, both on her part and on that of her neighbors, that they could only suspect the most mysterious and fearful reasons why an educated man from the city would wish to talk to her. "Police?" was a question the interviewers encountered more than once, and one woman was so persuaded that the questions were a preliminary to a criminal proceeding that she answered while weeping bitter tears. The interviewer decided that neither science nor happiness was being promoted by the questions, and gave up.[31]

All social research in such countries is plagued by problems like these, and must find a way around them. Often this is done by depending on observation for a large part of the data. Rao, for example, used a skillful combination of observation and questioning.[32] Sometimes it is necessary to interview officials, whether or not their answers are to be included in the sample, merely to establish the authenticity of the project. Sometimes it is possible to explain. The Rudolphs' interviewers found a useful explanation in an old Tamil proverb, "If you wish to know whether the rice is done, pick out a grain and taste it." Many subjects were entirely satisfied with the homely explanation that they were like the grain of rice, picked out to be tasted.[33]

In economically advanced countries, persons are usually willing to be asked questions, and to answer, in privacy. This is by no means always accepted in developing countries. It is often all but impossible to interview a person alone, and therefore other opinions and influences are easily mixed up with the interviewee's opinions. Sometimes a question generates an argument among the listeners, which completely blocks out the person being interviewed. Rao reports that his patience was most sorely strained when he was trying to interview wives in the presence of their husbands, who would constantly break in to tell their wives how to answer.[34]

As we have said, the giving of frank answers to strangers trying to conduct an interview is not in the customary behavior pattern of many people in traditional societies. In some ways, even more disturbing is the habit of giving *polite* answers. Many cultures teach that it is unkind to give a negative answer. Thus an interview may proceed for some time before the interviewer realizes that he is being told what the subject thinks he wants to hear. Only very skilled framing of questions will overcome this difficulty.

Understanding the dynamics of decision. Difficult interviewing has one advantage in that it forces a researcher in a developing country to consider whom he really needs to talk to. In industrialized countries, where people are used to giving opinions and where the population is fairly homogeneous, it is almost standard operating procedure to sample whole populations. In developing countries, there are many occasions when it is wasteful to sample a whole population. As Wilson points out, "Large masses in many countries are disenfranchised by poverty, ignorance, ingrained apathy, and the indifference or guile of those in power." Where that is the case, he says, if one wants to uncover significant attitudes, "it often makes more sense to start from the top and work down through opinion leader levels to that point where meaningful information can no longer be obtained."[35]

This, of course, would not apply if one wished to determine something about the health or living habits of a community. In that case, one would clearly need to sample an entire population. But if one is concerned with decisions that are to be made, or social changes to be accepted or rejected, then there is less reason to sample the whole population. Rather, one needs to consider how the particular decisions which concern him are going to be made. It may take research to answer that preliminary question, but if one knows something about the dynamics of decision making in that society, then he can probably save himself money and effort, and get better data, by talking to opinion leaders.

Data processing. As development progresses, and research progresses with it, the flow of research data will become such that any developing country must have facilities for swift processing of data. This means that punched-card machines must be installed, and ultimately computers. But this should not frighten a new country away from doing the research that needs doing. By the time it needs data-processing machinery for researchers, other units of the government, business, or natural science research will also need them, and time can be shared. By the time communication research needs computers, they will already have been installed and will be available elsewhere in the country.

Costs and Returns

It is easy to compute the additional costs of communication research, but less easy to compute the savings.

Good communication research in developing countries will require trained men. Inasmuch as most of the research will be done in the field rather than the library, there will be some research cost beyond the salary of researchers. The total will be a fraction of a per cent of the cost of information, and a still tinier fraction of the development budget. But it nevertheless represents an addition to costs.

How does one compare this cost with what it buys? Accounting figures are not available with which to ascertain whether communication research will actually save money on the cost of information packages and programs, although there is good reason to think that it might pay for itself simply by eliminating wasteful and ineffective information items. But how does one figure the savings resulting from more effective information as against less effective? A campaign that accomplishes its objective as against one that does not? A radio service or a newspaper that knows what its audience is, and what its reactions are, as compared with one that does not? A way to find out in advance whether a poster will be effective, as against the lack of such a way? A way to find out what kind and level of information will be understood by the people who need it, as against the absence of a way to find it out?

These are not intangibles, but they are not readily measurable in monetary terms. We think, though, that they are measurable in developmental terms, and that competent communication research can contribute to the efficiency of information and in turn to the pace and smoothness of national development.

7. Building the Mass Media

Describe almost any country in the early stages of economic and social development, and you will say these things about it:

Old and new communication systems are functioning side by side. Just as there are two social systems—the modernizing cities and the traditional villages—and two economic systems—industrialization and money exchange in the cities, subsistence agriculture and barter in the villages—so also there are two communication systems. In the cities, newspapers and transistor radios are in common use, there are many cinemas, and there may be television. In the villages, communication is chiefly oral and personal, as it has been for ages. The new system is reaching into the villages, but slowly, slowly.

There is a shortage of trained personnel for modern communication. The shortage includes writing and production personnel, engineers, management personnel, and maintenance men.

There is a shortage of newsprint with which to expand the coverage of newspapers; and a shortage of other paper, which might be used to make books and magazines more widely available to new literates.

There is a shortage of radio receivers, with which information might leap the literacy barrier and bring modern life to the villages.

There is a shortage of printing, broadcasting, and film-making and film-showing equipment of many kinds.

Small newspapers are in difficult financial straits. Indeed, financial problems stand in the way of every extension of modern communication beyond the cities.

There are conflicting demands for the use of radio. Some want it used for entertainment, some for information, some for culture, some for education.

There is pressure to bring in television (if it has not already been brought in), despite its frightening cost.

The facilities for distributing modern communication—telecommunications, electrification, transportation, postal services—are inadequate.

The country has reason to be concerned over its legislative and institutional arrangements for an expanding mass communication system.

There is neither plan nor mechanism for integrating and balancing its communication development: balancing the development of one medium against that of the others; integrating mass media channels into the interpersonal channels of decision making, teaching, and local government; integrating the "new educational media" into education.

This is where mass communication development starts—with a set of problems like these, and a commitment to solve them and the secondary problems that lie behind them. Development starts where the media and their related services are. Fortunately or unfortunately, this is where they usually are in early development.

We have been talking in earlier chapters about what is and what can be—the present situation of the mass media in developing countries, and the contribution a wise and skillful use of these media might make to world-wide economic and social development. Now we come to the practical question: how? How does a new nation proceed to modernize its communication system in the service of national development? Of many steps, what steps does it take first? And we shall have to answer as best we can by talking about some of the problems involved.

FINANCE

Let us get an idea of the orders of magnitude involved in financing mass media growth in the developing countries.

Unesco has estimated the cost of expanding mass communication facilities in the developing countries during the next 20 years at $3.4 billions. Of this total, $.6 billion is the estimated cost of services in support of education. The rate of expansion assumed for the media is the same as that estimated for general economic growth. Any such projection into the future must be highly approximate. Nevertheless, this estimate, by an organization which is in position to take a broad view of needs and means, gives an idea of the general order of the costs we are talking about.

We can put this sum into perspective by comparing it with certain other large sums estimated for related activities. A series of international conferences of educators and statesmen during the last few years have been engaged in fitting numbers to educational needs. The African governments meeting at Addis Ababa in May 1961 estimated that the cost of the present five-year plan for raising the school enrollments *in Africa alone*[1] would be about $4.15 billions. The Asian governments meeting at Karachi, the Arab governments at Beirut, and the Latin American governments at Lima and Washington came to comparable conclusions regarding the magnitude of educational costs which they faced. No one has ever dared to estimate the total cost of educational development in the next 20 years, but it would certainly be many times the cost of mass media development. In fact, if mass media, by aiding education, could save only a tiny fraction of the anticipated cost of education during the next two decades, they might save more than the total cost of all media development.

Mr. René Maheu, Director General of Unesco, recently estimated that $1,911 million might eradicate two-thirds of the adult illiteracy in Unesco Member States in ten years. This represents an average investment of only $5.79 for each of the 330 million illiterates to be rescued. The total investment comes to a mere 0.14 per cent of the gross national product, in 1961, of the nations included in the campaign.[2]

These figures are tantalizing. It would take only a small fraction of the annual budget of any one of the richest countries to eliminate illiteracy in the world. The total bill for mass communication development for 20 years is less than one per cent of the United

States gross annual product for one year. These are not astronomical sums, and it is not unrealistic to think that such amounts of money can be raised—particularly when one realizes that investments of this type should reduce the gigantic bill for education and contribute to general economic improvement.

The size of the bill itself is not the stumbling block in developing the communication systems of the new nations. Rather, it is the difficult management questions accompanying the investment: the need to allocate wisely in the face of great competition for resources, the need to husband resources so as to get the most out of mutual support (as, for example, education and mass media), the need to schedule and time the rates of growth so that a given investment will be most productive and least counterproductive (for example, producing literates at a rate at which a society can efficiently absorb them). These are key questions.

How does a country decide when it is investing *enough* in mass communication? And a developing nation, of course, would like to decide its media investments on the basis of such a yardstick as this:

> *X dollars invested in mass media, under given*
> *circumstances, will pay back Y dollars in*
> *economic development.*

For a number of reasons, however, it is unlikely that such a cost-benefit ratio can be obtained.

For example, consider one product which is clearly a goal of national development and to which national information is intended to contribute: an informed citizenry. How does one value, in money, a better-informed citizenry? It is conceivable that one might identify and put a monetary value on increased agricultural production resulting from agricultural information, or on the contribution of an information campaign to an increase in national savings. But is it possible to put a price tag on increasing interest in national policy, a greater sense of nation-ness, or a greater willingness to cooperate toward community betterment? Yet these are clearly national development objectives to which improved information can make a contribution.

Consider another relatively intangible value to be derived from making the communication system more efficient: leadership. Communication is of assistance to leadership at every level of society, and contributes to the *formation* of leadership as well as the exercising of it. Yet what is the monetary value of the mass media contribution to leadership?

Consider also the relation of investments and growth rates in different segments of society. There is a very widespread interaction. Speeding up the growth of mass communication contributes to the increase of some of these other rates, which in turn contribute to the faster growth of mass communication. For example, the growth of education and literacy would contribute to the growth of mass communication, but the growth of mass communication would also contribute to the growth of literacy and education, and none of these strands of development could go markedly faster than the others. General economic development in a society would contribute to the progress of electrification and the availability of newsprint, and thus make it easier to extend the mass media, which, in turn, would make economic development easier. And the *rates*, beyond the mere *fact*, of growth interact. A sudden surge of literates or of school graduates may not be absorbable by the economy, and will create a dissatisfied and unproductive segment of the population. Too few literates, too few school-trained citizens, will keep the economy waiting, and slow up the growth of industry. So the problem is not only to get all the related segments of society growing, in order that each one may help the others grow; it is also to manage and relate their rates and schedules of growth.

This means, then, that if a nation wants to speed up the growth of its mass communication, it must concern itself simultaneously with the growth rates of such related elements as literacy, education, electrification, and the like, as well as industry and agriculture; and the resources that can profitably be invested in mass media growth will be limited to some extent by the growth of these related elements. It means also that to sort out the precise contribution of the mass media to these interactions would be very difficult.

It is a ratio, rather than an absolute figure, that developing countries need. And in this respect, unfortunately, few developing countries have to worry that their investment in mass communication will run ahead of their investments in other segments of society. Usually, the situation is just the reverse. Communication has a very low priority when development investments are decided on. Pool comments in this way on the financial support of one outstanding national radio:

The practice in India is typical of the priorities. There are two radios per 1,000 persons in India. The First Five Year Plan allocated two-tenths of one per cent of outlays to developing of broadcasting. It allocated 14 times as much as that to posts and telegraph. It allocated about 60 times as much to education. But that was only the Plan. Across the board, actual outlays for the five years slipped 15 per cent below the Plan, but outlays for broadcasting were allowed to fall short by 45 per cent, leaving actual outlays at somewhat over one-tenth of one per cent of the total. In the Second Five Year Plan, development of broadcasting was given no greater role, being again allowed two-tenths of one per cent of outlays. In the Third Plan it is cut down to one-tenth of one per cent.

The willingness of countries faced by foreign exchange shortages to ration newsprint or impose severe excise taxes, tariffs, and quotas on radio and TV sets, and even to exclude TV entirely for fiscal reasons, attests to the fact that few non-Communist countries have assigned to the development of the mass media the same significance they have to steel mills, roads, railroads, and dams.[3]

The first requirement for accelerating the development of mass communication is, therefore, that a nation be willing to make a serious investment in media growth, an investment that is in some rational and equitable proportion to other related investments. Substantial progress could be made if nations could surmount the idea of *competition* for funds (which understandably arises from the funds going to different ministries, and the greater political visibility of some investments than others), and substitute for it the idea of *cooperation* for results. That is, a certain investment in education will benefit from a certain related investment in educational media. A certain investment in agriculture needs a certain related investment in informational media. And so on through the list of development activities to which mass communication contributes.

Let us say again that the basic requirement for developing the mass media at the rate at which they can make their greatest contribution to national development requires a serious and substantial financial commitment. Throughout the developing world, it is our observation that the mass media are underfinanced and underdeveloped and therefore are not contributing what they might contribute if fully and adequately used.*

If a new nation will demonstrate its own serious commitment to the development of the communication it needs for national development, it will find immensely easier the task of getting capital help. If it demonstrates its friendliness to private investment, it is more likely to attract such investment. If it demonstrates its willingness to implement a thoughtful set of priorities for communication, and to support these under pressure, then it is much more likely to be able to get technical assistance, loans, grants, or other bilateral arrangements to help build communication. But it must be ready to commit *itself* in appropriate measure.

PLANNING

It is not easy, in the cross-pressures of budget making, to allocate a sum of money to mass communication that might otherwise go into a road or a dam. It is not easy to decide to invite private capital or bilateral aid into mass communication rather than into industry or power, or to ask for grants for radio equipment rather

* We do not mean to leave the impression that all the cost of developing the media is necessarily *government* cost. Even under systems where the media are government-owned, newspapers, receivers, and movie admissions, among other things, are usually sold. The amount of government ownership of the media varies greatly among the developing countries. Most of the newspapers, however, are privately owned; most of the radio systems are government-owned; and most of the uses of media for education are government responsibilities. Even in some government-owned broadcasting systems, part of the support comes from commercial advertising. This is the case, for example, in Jordan, where income from radio advertising has been used, in part, to make possible the country's entry into television. Thus private financing can help to develop a nation's media, and government legislation and administration can help to make development easier for privately owned media.

than factory equipment. Even within mass communication itself, it is not easy to opt for the more necessary rather than the more prestigious and spectacular investments (radio rather than television, schoolbooks rather than international short wave, and so forth).

Yet this is precisely the order of commitment a developing country must make if it plans to develop its information channels congruently with its industry and its agriculture. The chief reason why communication growth has lagged in many countries is not so much lack of interest or lack of belief in its ability to contribute to national development, as simply unwillingness, under cross-pressures, to make the commitment to it.

The best basis for such a commitment, the best buttress against cross-pressures, is a well-thought-out plan that integrates the development of mass communication into the general pattern of social and economic development.

Making such a plan is essentially a national task. From time to time there has been discussion of a world-wide "plan" for building up the mass media. On several occasions suggestions have been made that Unesco should prepare an international plan for speeding media growth in the developing countries. Undoubtedly international cooperation could help enormously, and Unesco would be in position to advise and to guide some of this cooperative effort where it would do most good. But any such international "plan" would necessarily have as its chief goal to help the developing nations make their *own* plans and carry out their *own* mass media development. The communication system is such an intimate and essential part of national structure and function that responsibility for developing it cannot be transferred outside the country. Therefore, although we shall refer from time to time to points at which international financing might be called on, problems concerning which nations might share their experience, or needs that might better be met jointly, we shall be talking mostly about what a developing country *itself* can do to develop its mass communications —for this is how the task is going to get done.

How can a country go about planning its mass communication development? Here are a few suggestions. To some nations they may seem old-hat, because those nations have already done these things, or found a way to do them better. To some they may seem unnecessary, because they feel they know exactly what to do without any additional study or planning. To some, we hope, they will be helpful.

Who should make the plan? This will depend on the country where it is to be made. In some countries, responsibilities will naturally fall to the planning commission; in others, to a ministry or ministries; in still others, perhaps to a national commission representing both public and private sectors. Whatever the auspices, countries have found that it helps to have a broad base for the planning, and therefore to have the private sector represented wherever appropriate, and to bring in such related ministries as education, agriculture, health, and community development. The purpose is to make an *integrated* plan; this calls for broad participation.

The planning falls naturally into three phases. The first—taking stock of the present situation—requires the gathering of data, and is a point at which communication research can be of great help. The second—setting priorities and goals—is the step at which most of the important decisions must be made. The third—provision for review—is the continuing activity by which the plan is revised and priorities are rearranged.

Step one—taking stock. The first requirement is a basic inventory on which the remainder of the planning can rest. In Appendix B we have set down a number of questions to be asked and, by implication, some of the procedures that might well be followed, in making such an inventory.

At the outset, countries that have gone through such a planning procedure have found it useful to take each of the media in turn—radio, newspapers, films, books, magazines, and television—and inventory the present facilities, the area of coverage, the size and kinds of audiences being reached, and the kinds of services being performed (what kind of information is being carried, how much educational material, how much entertainment, what direct contributions to development programs, and the like).

Next it is well to inventory some of the related and supporting services, such as literacy training, schooling, electrification, transportation, post services, telecommunications, news agencies, and training for mass media. What is the present situation of each of these? At what rate are they to be developed? Ultimately, it must be asked whether this rate is adequate to meet the needs of developing mass communication.

It is also well to examine the kinds of import restrictions that affect the availability of newsprint, equipment for printing, broadcasting, and film making, and raw film stock; the tariffs that are collected on imports of such equipment, as well as on books and other educational and informational materials; and the taxes that are collected on communication materials and enterprises. How much are these restricting the growth of media?

Finally, it is necessary to look at what the media are now doing to further national development in fields such as literacy, education, agriculture, industrial training, health, and citizenship, and others where they are capable of making a contribution. What are they doing, and what more could they do if they were given the facilities and opportunity?

At this point it is possible to measure the present development of mass communication against some standard or standards. Media development can be compared, for example, with the Unesco minima (ten copies of daily newspapers, five radio receivers, two cinema seats, and two television receivers per 100 persons), or with the accomplishment of well-developed countries, or with the needs of the people or the schools. We should hope that one of the chief standards might be the projected needs of the national development program: what help will the development agencies and the educational system need?

On the basis of this work, it is possible to make a general estimate of requirements: for new and upgraded facilities, equipment, supporting services and materials, organizations, trained personnel, research guidance, government administrative and legislative action, and capital. Against this estimate of need can be put an estimate of help available to meet the requirements. How much of capital needs is it reasonable to expect private sources to meet? How much financial help can be expected from international funds or bilateral arrangements or loans? How much technical equipment can be supplied by private industry or international cooperation? To what extent can training needs be met by regional or bilateral cooperation? To what extent can experts be borrowed to speed the development? Is there experience in other countries which would reduce the cost and time of meeting the requirements? Answers to a series of questions like these should make possible a realistic appraisal of precisely how much will be required of the particular country itself, if it is to close the gap between present conditions and requirements.

All the activity up to this point might be described as *gathering the basic data* for a communication development plan. Essentially, it means that a developing country must survey and project its resources and needs in this field. In so doing, if necessary it can get a certain amount of help. Communication experts can be borrowed, through an international agency like Unesco or through bilateral relationships, to help study the resources and needs. It may even be possible to secure a grant of funds to help support the survey; indeed, a series of grants of this kind might contribute considerably to realistic planning for communication development, and the efficient use of capital, equipment, and skills. But basically the responsibility lies with the nation itself. It must satisfy itself that it knows accurately where it is in communication development, where it would seem desirable to go further, and what the requirements of doing so would be.

Then it is ready to take the second step, into the heart of planning.

The second step—priority and goal setting. We have been talking of what is and what could and should be. But in the sweep of national development there are always more things to be done than can be done. There are always more requirements than can be met, more competitors for an investment dollar than can be satisfied, more products needed than can be manufactured, more technical experts in demand than can be found. Therefore, the needs of communication must be considered in connection with the needs of other parts of the development program.

We have been careful not to say: the needs of communication must be considered *in competition with* the needs of other parts of the development program. Communication development is not *really* in competition with industrialization, agricultural modernization, educational development, health improvement, community development, the growth of nation-ness, broad participation in public affairs, or any of the other great goals of national development, although in budget hearings it is sometimes made to seem so. It is the *servant and ally* of each of these. It must go forward with them. It is society that moves forward—not agriculture or health or information. Skillful planning, therefore, will be concerned not with how much money should be given information in comparison with how much is given something else, but rather with the size of the information component needed for the curve of social development as projected.

Therefore, the first essential information in priority setting is the planned curve of development. What are the objectives in the next few years for agriculture and health? How fast are public education and literacy to be expanded? What are the general goals of the country as to how fast the informational level and resources of its people should be raised? And then, of course, what expansion and improvement of information services and facilities do these imply?

Even after the broad priority of communication is established, there must be priorities within communication itself. What most needs doing? Is the present the time to emphasize radio, or should television be brought in? Are the present needs of education more for additional books, or for projectors and films, or perhaps for radio broadcasts? In what respects are the information services lagging? For example, would a training program to upgrade information personnel now be more helpful than some additional facilities?

Decisions of this order on what most needs doing must be placed realistically against a recognition of what must be done before something else can be done. For example, there is no use to encourage the establishment of more newspapers if the present inadequate supply of newsprint is not to be increased. There is no justification for building more radio transmitters if more receiving sets are not going to be available. There is no use to bring in television before training television personnel. In any kind of development, efficiency lies to a great extent in establishing an efficient sequence of events.

Out of deciding how much can be done, what needs most to be done, and what has to be done before something else will come a set of priorities for what *should* be done.

Here, even more than in making the basic inventory, it may help to have an advisory committee representing all aspects of communication. Such a committee was recommended by the 1960 Bangkok Meeting on Development of Information Media in South East Asia. The Conference had in mind that the committee would provide informed advice to the planners and feedback information to the media, and thus make possible a high degree of understanding and cooperation.

The third step—providing for review. Planning and review should not stop when the basic data are gathered and the goals and priorities set. Quite the contrary. Although it will perhaps never be necessary to make a basic inventory again, still the problems and performance of information media in national development should be under more or less constant review. Communication development in many countries will be a part of national planning, and will be under constant study and revision along with the rest of national development. With or without this, a committee broadly representing government and private communication might well interest itself in the progress of communication development. Another possibility is to turn the continuing task of review over to an organization that specializes in communication study— for example, a center for communication research and training. But the important thing is to have competent people thinking about the rate and nature of communication development, and the part it is playing in national development.

What kind of information is going out to the people of the country? How adequate is the flow of news and public affairs information? Where, if at all, are the blind spots that information is not reaching? Are the great objectives of economic and social development—agriculture, health, community improvement, literacy, education, and so forth—being adequately supported by the media? Is the balance of culture and entertainment satisfactory as against public affairs and instruction? What changes or expansions in the communication system would help to equalize the balance of coverage?

What could be done to get more effect out of the facilities the country has? For example, could newspapers serve a substantial number of literates who do not now have a newspaper if better transportation were provided, or if public copies were made available,.or if additional press capacity were available? Could the addition of a few hundred receiving sets in the coverage area of a given radio station make a substantial difference in the effectiveness of the development program? Is there any way in which present media can serve more purposes? Are there unused radio hours that might be put to good use? Could film vans deliver films to schools in the course of their travels? Would it be useful to experiment with current operations? One example: at the present time in a certain developing country, the country's first television station is being used to broadcast a few school classes and a few forum talks per week. The country is therefore finding out some useful things about school television and television listening groups. But the station's signal reaches a number of villages; one or two of the unused broadcast hours might well be employed in trying out television as an aid to agriculture, health, and literacy programs in these villages. It would also be possible to experiment with certain elements of a general television service, well in advance of the time when such a service will come into use. Thus, more might be achieved from an existing installation.

The continuing review might well include an exchange of experiences and materials with neighboring countries, perhaps with the aid of regional seminars or personnel exchanges. It is reasonable to expect that many of the same problems have appeared in most or all of the countries of a region, and that some countries have found better solutions than others. It is also likely that different countries within a region have made broadcast programs, films, or printed materials on many of the same topics. These will furnish an outside standard by which to judge one's own work, and are likely to include some materials that could be shared by more than one country, perhaps with necessary adaptations. The more that superior materials can be shared, the more time and money each country will have to produce other superior materials.

But the essential point is that the responsibility for communication development should not be dropped when an inventory and a plan have been made. The responsibility should be an active and continuing one.

TRAINING

Trained persons are needed in a great variety of communication fields—information and development field officers, news personnel, program and production personnel, editors for book and periodical publications, teachers of mass media and information service personnel, broadcast and film engineers, printers, maintenance personnel, technicians, and others. This need is almost as universal in the developing countries as the need for capital, and the supply of trained persons usually runs far behind the provision of channels.

Ultimately any nation wants to train its own communication personnel, although it may still want to send some of its promising people abroad for experience. But it may be a long time before many developing countries have a sufficient supply of training institutions: schools of journalism, professional courses or institutes for film and broadcast training, professional training for publishing, technical schools for broadcast and film engineers and technicians, a school for printing, and perhaps a center for advanced training and research in mass communication such as India is about to set up.[4]

A new nation that already has one or more radio stations and one or more newspapers, and wishes to start additional radio stations or newspapers, can do some training in its present studios and newspaper offices, and can borrow experienced supervisors from those established operations. But suppose it wishes to introduce television. When television was to be introduced into Thailand, the future chief engineer was sent abroad for several years of experience in technical schools and television stations. When it was to be introduced in Nigeria, several production persons were sent abroad for training, and a foreign expert was brought in to supervise program production for the first few years, and to help train the program and production workers who were not sent abroad. In some cases, new nations have contracted with suppliers to furnish them television stations as "going concerns"—that is, with facilities built and operating, and personnel trained. Whatever the method followed, a developing country will be able to benefit from outside help in some aspects of its training program, even while it prepares to assume ultimate responsibility itself for that training.

On-the-job training. Throughout the world, the majority of all communication personnel are trained on the job. Future reporters go to work in a news room, are given minor tasks, gradually gain experience, profit from criticism, and finally either prove to the satisfaction of their superiors that they can report news or are dismissed. Future broadcast technicians with some knowledge of electricity go to work for a radio station or repair center, work up from simple jobs to more difficult ones, observe how more experienced workers solve problems, gain experience, and ultimately either prove their ability to do the work or try something else. The difficulty with this traditional way of training is that the more experienced workers usually have little time for teaching the younger ones. Furthermore, in this kind of training the standard is set by the present operation—there is no very good way to raise the standards of newspapering or broadcasting above the level of the present supervisors, who themselves probably came up through the same kind of school of experience and therefore were restricted by the level of *their* supervisors. And on-the-job training tends to encourage a fairly low educational average in the communication professions. During the years when a young man might be in secondary school or college, he is typically in an apprenticeship.

In an attempt to do something about these objections, several variations of on-the-job training have evolved. One of them is the "cadet" training system, which is used widely in the British Commonwealth in an effort to combine practical training with formal education. A young man is selected by a newspaper, put to work on a minor job, then sent to school or college part time. Over a period of three or four years he can thus both learn his craft and get a substantial education.

Another variation is the professional seminar for communication personnel. This takes many forms. The American Press Institute, at Columbia University in New York, brings in about 30 science writers, or city editors, or telegraph editors, or other groups, to talk over their problems for three weeks, with each other and with leaders in the profession. The International Center for Higher Studies in Journalism for Latin America, at Quito, Ecuador, has short courses for practicing journalists as well as for teachers of journalism. The International Center for Higher Education in Journalism, at the University of Strasbourg—which, like the Quito Center, is Unesco-supported—has likewise opened up its courses to journalists as well as to teachers of journalists, and it has conducted sessions in Dakar and Strasbourg for African journalists.

In still another variation of training on the job, the International Press Institute has sent experts through several developing countries to advise newspapers on their problems. It has prepared and published a textbook of newsroom practice for newspapers where training opportunities are slight. It has also conducted a number of seminars for practicing journalists, and has recently helped establish the Press Institute of India, to conduct training and research for newspapers in that country.

Also, there is correspondence study. At the Soviet universities, for instance, the correspondence course takes six years, the residence course, five.

Training in schools. Increasingly in the economically well-developed countries, training has come to be conducted in the *school* of journalism. This is based on the belief that the essence of an enlightened profession is to have educated, ethically responsible men in it. Therefore, if the most essential craft training (in reporting, editing, and the like) can be combined with a broad course of college or university study, and this experience set in the perspective of the history of human communication, freedom of speech and of the press, and the ethics and responsibilities of the communication profession, this would seem to be the basis for truly professional education. In most schools of journalism, the technical and professional work takes up 25 per cent or less of the total curriculum. Sometimes the technical training is scattered through the college years; sometimes it comes as a graduate year *following* four years of broad college study. In any case, the major part of a student's time is devoted to history, science, literature, and other subjects that will help him write with understanding of the world he lives in.[5]

We have been talking mostly about *journalism* training, because this aspect of communication training is more highly developed than others. However, it is only one of several important fields in which developing countries need trained communication personnel. Radio program and production personnel, film production personnel, book-publishing editors, and magazine editors need the same combination of broad education and skills training as do journalists, although, of course, the skills they need are not quite the same. The engineers and technicians who are going to operate the broadcasting stations and film studios and maintain the equipment need specialized training, as do the printers who are going to operate the composing and press rooms of the nation. In addition to these, almost any developing country will have a large number of general information personnel whose responsibilities are for the information which keeps the development program going, and who may have field assignments or assignments preparing materials or planning campaigns. Ideally, therefore, one might say that a developing country needs a group of schools for mass media training.

An inventory of training needs and facilities is needed before a country can project training needs some years ahead, and decide (a) what training can be done with the country's present facilities, (b) where it must ask for assistance from outside in "priming the pump," (c) what additional national training resources it needs, and where it might get help in establishing them, and (d) where it can benefit from regional cooperation.

By "priming the pump" we mean help which is necessary before the country can start some of its own training programs. If a country does not have television, it will probably have to send some of its own people abroad for training, or borrow experts from other countries for training. If it does not have a publishing industry, it may have to borrow experts to help it start one. If it does not have a school of journalism and wants to start one, it may have to send some of its people to school abroad, or borrow journalism teachers or administrators temporarily from abroad. If it wants to improve its on-the-job training, it can send some of its people to an international seminar on such a topic. For these and other purposes, it can send some of its practicing professionals to see how training is conducted, and how the media are run, in other countries. Assistance in such "pump-priming" activities as these is relatively easy to get. Training fellowships, travel grants, and the loan of experts are available in considerable numbers from international organizations like Unesco, or bilaterally.

A country can hope for assistance also in establishing *its own* training institutions. Experts are frequently made available to help plan for a school or institute. In many cases, teachers have been lent for the early years. Technical assistance of one kind or another for buildings, laboratory and library equipment, and some aspects of operations is often available.

Regional cooperation is a promising avenue for meeting some of the needs for communication training. Training seminars can more easily be financed on a regional basis. In some cases, training institutes can be established in one country, with international assistance, with the understanding that they will open their doors to students from neighboring countries also. Admittedly, there are difficulties in this sort of arrangement. Language may get in the way. Cultural differences may make it hard for a single curriculum to serve all students. And ultimately, each country will want to conduct its own training. But until this time comes, a regional training facility is better than none. Other useful regional cooperation is the exchange of professional personnel and teachers. When one country is more advanced than others in certain communication fields or in certain training activities, it can become a place for observation, provide some training opportunities, and send its own more experienced professionals or teachers to help others.

Professional associations. Raising the level of information handling from apprentice training to college-level training is bound to have an enormous influence on the kind of information that flows through a system. Professional organizations can also have a significant influence on information handling. Traditionally, these organizations are the custodians of professional standards of conduct, and often they are the continuing force behind professional improvement. In many cases, they have contributed substantially to in-service training. Therefore, a new nation, building its mass media, should consider very carefully whether it should not also encourage the formation of vigorous and active associations of newspapermen, broadcasters, film makers, printers, communication engineers, and the like.

EQUIPMENT AND MATERIALS

All developing countries have a shortage of mass communication equipment and materials. To most of them, this list will be familiar:

Newsprint—a world-wide imbalance as a result of which one continent produces more than 70 per cent, and a single country consumes 60 per cent, of the total supply. Few developing countries have any newsprint manufacturing facilities of their own, and these countries are therefore at the mercy of a market that requires foreign currency.

Radio receivers—too scarce and too expensive in the developing countries. Time is of the essence in solving this problem. Radio receivers are uniquely useful in the early stages of development, when illiteracy and isolation are high. Later they will still be useful, but not uniquely so.

Printing and broadcasting equipment (presses, typesetting machinery, transmitters, and so forth)—typically in short supply. Few of the developing countries manufacture such equipment.

Raw film stock and film equipment (cameras, projectors, and so forth)—also in short supply, and manufactured in relatively few developing countries.

There are only two real solutions to these shortages. One is to manufacture the goods within the country. The other is to ease the import restrictions—tariffs and quotas—so as to increase the flow from other countries.

The long-term solution for most developing countries will undoubtedly be to set up industries to make the equipment. In many cases this is a very attractive possibility. For example, South Asia, where there may be two billion people before many years have passed, is potentially the great newsprint market of the world. Yet it has very little local output, although many countries grow, or could grow, the tree stock to feed paper mills. In the case of radio, most industrial development plans include an electronic industry, toward which the manufacture of radio equipment would be a good start. The stage is set for the manufacture of the very low-cost but rugged receiver (ten dollars or less). A design has been made and Unesco is trying to get it manufactured. The transistor has greatly reduced the necessary size of sets, the amount of current required, and the frequency of maintenance. Therefore, if the skills and capital exist or can be imported into a country, radio manufacture is an attractive industry.

Advice and help are available from international organizations for any country that wants to begin to make its own communication equipment. The Food and Agriculture Organization of the United Nations has been giving special attention to the problems of making and supplying newsprint. The International Telecommunication Union and the International Labor Organization are able to consult on electronic communication equipment. Advice can also be had, in many cases, by bilateral arrangement or from the industries themselves in countries where they are well developed.

Manufacturing is undoubtedly the long-term solution. For the short term, a country can make it as easy as possible to import the mass media equipment it needs. National cooperatives in some countries can purchase larger amounts of newsprint and stabilize the supply to the small user. Regional cooperatives could conceivably furnish the same service to a group of countries. Efforts like those of the FAO to make available the excess capacity of existing mills are also hopeful. Regional cooperatives or even regional centers of manufacturing might also increase the supply of printing and broadcasting equipment, receivers, and film stock. But even arrangements like these will benefit from a review of import restrictions.

As we have said before, there is no reason why a developing country need retrace all the steps whereby a particular technology has been developed. There is no need, for example, to manufacture, first, crystal receiving sets; it is possible to start with transistors or whatever stage of technology best meets the country's needs. In the fields we are talking about there have been a number of recent developments that are of great potential significance to developing countries. Among these are:

—phototypesetting, which eliminates the need for casting type from hot metal, and greatly reduces the need of special skills in the composing room;

—offset printing, which works from a photographic plate, and therefore can use almost any kind of copy, thus giving great flexibility to a printshop without requiring a great variety of equipment;

—the transistor, which is replacing the vacuum tube in many places in broadcasting equipment, thus making it possible to reduce the size of components, the amount of electricity required, and the amount of maintenance needed;

—videotape recording, which makes it possible to record and ex-

change television programs as easily as ordinary sound recording;

—frequency modulation broadcasting, which, within a radius of 60
miles or so, is relatively free of electrical interference, and excellent in quality of transmission, thus recommending itself for use
in the tropics, for schools, and for services in which music is very
important.

Considering these and other new developments, when a country
decides what kind of equipment to import—and, more important,
what kind to manufacture—expert advice and a thorough investigation of available equipment will pay off.

But it makes no sense to import or manufacture the newest in
communication equipment without preparing adequately to service it. A technical institute is an excellent solution which a number
of developing countries have adopted. Sending technical personnel to study advanced machinery in an industrialized country is
a good way to "prime the pump." An advanced institute for the
study of printing and printing machinery, and for the training of
master printers, is being established in South Asia. Others may be
established elsewhere. Regional cooperation in such technical
training centers, as well as in the manufacturing or buying of
equipment, holds promise.

THE PROBLEMS OF MEDIA DEVELOPMENT

The central problem of media development is to extend modern
communication from the cities, where it already has a foothold, to
the rural regions. Planning, finance, training, providing equipment
are essential parts of this effort. Beyond these, however, is the
problem of an integrated, timed, and balanced development of
facilities and media. Radio must be available when illiteracy and
distance still bar the printed media. Newspapers must move toward the towns and villages in the path of literacy. In order for
news coverage and news distribution to be available in the towns
and villages, a national news agency is needed. Small newspapers
outside the cities will need special help and support for the first
years after they are established. Improved distribution systems

(for example, postal deliveries of printed material, telegraph and telephone) should accompany the extension of media information. The growth of these new channels should be integrated with the development of field staffs, volunteers, and adult educators. Above all, the media should be developed at a rate to make them as useful as possible to schools and to young people who have no schools at their level. This kind of balanced, integrated development is the ideal to which a developing country makes the best approximation it can.

In such a development each of the media presents certain individual problems, some of which we can suggest here.

The use of radio

The problem is not whether, but how, to use radio. This is because radio can do so many things.

Radio can bring news to people who can't read newspapers. It can bring instructions and advice to people who need help with farming or health improvement or community development. It can bring supplementary teaching to schools. It can bring extension teaching to individuals and groups who are unable to get to school. It can carry the classical music and drama of a nation. And it can carry light entertainment—popular music, light comedy, serial dramas, variety shows, sports, and the like.

Radio can do almost too much. Therefore, it is asked to do too much. When it is broadcasting to the farmers, it is not serving the city people. When it is broadcasting to the schools, it is not usually serving the adult population. When it is broadcasting the classical culture of the country, it is likely to lose some or much of its audience to the commercial station broadcasting light entertainment from across the border. So what should it do?

In a country like the United Kingdom, the national radio operates on three channels, at different cultural levels. This solution may not be possible for many developing countries, but they must somehow allocate their radio time by function and content. Should there be special stations for the rural regions? Should there be special stations for light entertainment? Should there be special educational stations? Should all these functions be combined in a single station or network, and if so in what proportion and at what times of the day? These are not easy decisions, and it is sometimes hard to know whether one has made them wisely. For example, is it a net profit or loss if a nation uses its national radio for serious purposes—news, instruction, high culture—and then loses much of its audience to a light entertainment station? On the other hand, if it offers light entertainment and keeps the audience, is the cost of that programming properly considered investment or consumption? Most developing countries prefer to offer a variety of programming on one outlet or network. What is the most efficient way to mix different kinds of service? This is the kind of question that faces a developing country deciding its radio policy.

One principle, it seems to us, should prevail here. Radio is so important in the early years of national development, and during those years it has such a unique ability to inform people outside the cities, that no radio policy should be adopted that would not use it as effectively as possible for informational purposes. This does not mean that radio should not carry entertainment and culture, as well as information; nor that its information should all be of one kind. It can carry news, development information, information to help people participate in public affairs. But whatever mix of entertainment, culture, and different kinds of information is carried by the national radio, it seems to us that the policy should be first of all to make sure that there is the kind and amount of information needed by people in the developing villages who still do not have printed media available. And if the radio is privately owned, it seems to us that national interest still requires that information be adequately represented.

The small newspaper

A high proportion of the vernacular newspapers outside the great cities of developing countries are in desperate financial plight. Yet the small, native-language, rural newspaper is one of the great movers of national development. It serves the literate elite. It serves the new literate, and gives him reason to learn to read better. It furnishes much of the public affairs information without which public participation in government would be at a very low level. What can be done to make it easier to found and maintain these small newspapers?

A nation that wants the newspaper to move out of the cities toward the newly literate and rapidly changing population can well consider giving tax relief to such newspapers during their early years. If possible, a preferential rate on newsprint might be offered, and newsprint quotas should be set so as not to penalize the newcomers to publishing. Many small newspapers cannot afford the full services of a news agency, and the lack of such a service penalizes the very readers who most need it: therefore, why not provide a skeleton news service at lower cost? In the United States, free postal carriage within a certain geographical area had a great deal to do with enabling weekly newspapers to operate profitably and still serve a wide audience; some similar help in distribution would aid new and struggling newspapers in developing countries. A pool of used printing machinery to be made available at cost to small newspapers; management help; fiscal guidance—these and other forms of assistance might well make it possible for newspapers to survive in their early and most vulnerable period.

Nor should the mimeographed newspaper be overlooked. Such a project has recently been launched in Liberia, and has led to the establishment of 30 low-cost self-supporting roneoed papers serving local communities. From such beginnings a truly rural press should develop.

National news agencies

For most countries the problem is not whether to have a national news agency, but how to establish, staff, and develop it. Most developing countries would say flatly that, if they do not already have a national agency, they must have one as soon as possible. Without it, their news is less likely to be covered well, either inside or outside the country. Without it, there is likely to be less cooperative news gathering and handling among the newspapers of the country.

Building a news agency involves, among other things, equipment, training, cooperation. There must be ways to circulate the news—if possible, teletype circuits. There must be correspondents, inside and outside the country. This implies the cooperation of the country's own newspapers, and the possibility of regional cooperation in pooling correspondents. Above all, a news agency needs expertness. The job is complex and highly competitive. Newspaper experience alone does not necessarily qualify a person to operate a news agency. Therefore, it is to the advantage of a developing country to seek training grants, expert missions, and other competent advice and assistance when entering this field.

Films

The problem is not whether there shall be films, but where film-making belongs in the country's plans for development.

In most developing countries, the great impact of the entertainment film has already been felt, and the schools have discovered the potency of the instructional film. The various field services, the adult education centers, and the industrial training programs will feel the need of training and informational films. The national program of information will doubtless require documentary films. And above all these will be the clamor of the general audiences for entertainment pictures.

This will require a supply of projectors, repositories of films, distribution systems for films, and, most important, sources of films. A developing country must therefore decide the extent to which it wishes to produce its own films. Doubtless it will want to make at least some documentaries. Will it make its own instructional and training films? Will it adapt films from other countries? Does it want an entertainment film industry? If it does, what more will be required in the way of studios and theaters? If not, what arrangements does it wish to make about importing entertainment films? What restrictions does it plan to put on the showing of entertainment pictures? Most countries have some sort of board to review films, and some are restrictive as to what films may be seen by children.

These questions should be decided as early as possible. A study

of the experience of other countries will be useful in answering
them, and so also will be an examination of different types of films
available from abroad.

Television

Every new country is under some pressure to install television. It
is a badge of prestige. It is an invitation to entertainment. Therefore, a developing country's first problem with television is to decide when to start to use it. In the course of making that decision,
the country must also decide *what kind* of television.

Some hard policy decisions are called for. The considerations
are much the same as those for radio, except that all costs are much
greater. Transmitters, studios and studio equipment, programs,
and receivers, all cost several times as much as corresponding items
for radio. Maintenance is more costly, and operation in general
requires more skills. Therefore, if television is to be installed in a
country, these costs and training needs must be faced frankly in
advance, and plans made.

One question that is sure to occur is whether the nation wants
to support its television, in whole or in part, by advertising. With
regard to both advertising and private ownership, it would be
helpful to examine the experiences of some other countries with
television—notably the developing countries, but also such forms
of control and organization in the more fully developed countries
as the public corporation (BBC) in the United Kingdom, the private and publicly owned systems side by side in Japan, the "educational" television stations operating under nonprofit regulations in
the United States, as well as the patterns of total government ownership or total private ownership. There is no apparent reason
why a new state, if it wishes to, should not support its television
so far as possible through the proceeds of advertising and still control the content of the broadcasts to its tastes and needs.

But the essential question, as for radio and film, is where television belongs in national development. What the people are usually asking for, when they clamor for television, is the succession
of entertainment programs which have made the medium so pop-

ular in many countries that are further advanced economically. These are the "Westerns," the crime mysteries, the advanced programs, the comedies, variety shows, and sporting events. It is hard to argue that these have much to do with economic development. On the other hand, in a given country it may be highly desirable, at a given point in development, to offer some of this relaxing program fare, and it may be that the bonus of news, public affairs, and instruction mixed with the entertainment programs might be enough to justify the expenditure for television in development terms as well as entertainment terms.

Receiving sets in a tropical country are likely to cost somewhere in the neighborhood of $300 each. The number of families able to make this purchase may be small. Most of the viewing is likely to be in public places. This, as we have said, implies school use, adult center use, viewing groups, public sets, and so forth. Use of this kind seems to call for a practical and serious kind of programming, rather than the entertainment service which is more typical of television in advanced countries.

There is little doubt of television's effectiveness in a public affairs and instructional context. But when is a nation ready to make maximum use of it? One or two hours a day is a wasteful use of such an expensive tool as television. School broadcasting by day, adult education and rural broadcasts in late afternoon and early evening, a mixture of entertainment and public affairs in the evening—something like this would seem like a reasonable use to expect of a station.

And this must be said—that television has never been used to its full capability in support of economic development. It may be financially impossible to use it this way. But still the possibility is tantalizing: What if the full power and vividness of television teaching were to be used to help the schools develop a country's new educational pattern? What if the full persuasive and instructional power of television were to be used in support of community development and the modernization of farming? Where would the break-even point come? Where would the saving in rate of change catch up with the increased cost?

Television, whatever the kind, has an almost insatiable appetite for programs. It may be some time before a new nation, if it makes maximum use of its television, can produce all its own programs. It will be necessary to exchange films and tapes with other countries, or purchase or rent them. Regional cooperation commends itself, not only because it is a way to obtain more programs, but also because the countries of a region may have to get together to decide on channel allocations and standards in order to minimize interference and maximize the ease of exchange. In this respect, developing countries might wish to look at the example of Eurovision, which circulates programs through Europe, or National Educational Television, which serves 75 U.S. educational stations that are not connected by telecommunication networks.

Integration of media with personal communication

Developing countries find that this doesn't happen just by doing what comes naturally. They have to work at bringing it about.

Any teacher is willing to show a film occasionally as a "breather" from classroom activities. Any agricultural field agent is glad to have a radio broadcast on the subject of his current campaign. But to work a series of films into a course so that they are an integral part of the learning experience—this requires effort and planning on the part of the teacher, and understanding of the teacher's needs on the part of the film maker. Similarly, to make active use of a broadcast in a village is not always an easy thing for a field worker to do, and he certainly cannot do it unless there has been mutual planning in advance. The rural radio or television forum has often been cited as an ideal example of this kind of coordination, but even the forum requires careful advance planning, in which field knowledge must be represented.

Therefore, one of the great problems of a country developing its communication system is to devise arrangements and organizations to make this cooperation efficient. The media ordinarily go their own way. The field staffs and volunteer organizations ordinarily go their own way. If these are government organizations, they probably report to different ministries. Government servants or not, the field people are ordinarily not well trained in the mass media, and the media people are not well informed about field operations. Where a unified command is needed, therefore, it seldom exists.

Three suggestions, derived from the experience of developing countries, may be of help. For one thing, one of the most common points where coordination is needed but does not exist in many countries is between the Ministries of Education and of Information, or whatever the top governmental units are called which are concerned, respectively, with the schools and with the mass media. Unless these see their common problem, coordination is doubly hard along the chains of command. At this writing, for example, a television station in one developing country is dark throughout the school hours of the day despite the fact that the schools are sadly in need of audiovisual aids and master teachers. In that country, unfortunately, there is very little cooperation between the education and the information ministries. This is wasteful. The schools in a developing country have a stake in the mass media, just as do the information services. The mass media, on the other hand, have a stake in the schools, because through them the media can make one of their largest contributions to development, and furthermore because the children now in the schools will be the greatly expanded media audiences of tomorrow. It makes sense that whatever mutual suspicion is held by educators and mass media people should be put aside so they can plan together.

Many developing countries have found it helpful to let the media personnel have some experience in the field, and the field workers some experience in the media. Other countries have formed information planning teams, made up of both field and media personnel. Still others have set up a centralized top policy group, representing all the ministries concerned with this cooperation and familiar with both field and media operations.

A third suggestion comes from experience with development: it is possible to use the mass media to upgrade and inform a country's communication personnel. Films can be used to help train printers. Radio broadcasts can provide in-service training to newspaper employees outside the major cities who have a hard time getting training of any kind beyond the trial and error of their daily work in a shop where everyone is too busy to teach them. Perhaps the most useful training of all can be provided to field information workers, primary teachers, volunteer "animators" or group leaders, health workers, forum discussion leaders, and the like. These people are somewhat isolated, and often in need of new information. Why not use radio to talk to them, so to speak, over the shoulders of their audiences?

LEGAL AND INSTITUTIONAL CONSIDERATIONS

By Fernand Terrou

[*Mass media development, like other aspects of national development, takes place in the most rational and orderly fashion only when it is within an appropriate framework of law and institutions. Communication law is a specialized and increasingly important branch of legal studies. Therefore, we have asked one of the great scholars in this field, Dr. Fernand Terrou, Professor in the Institute of Political Studies of the University of Paris, and Director of the French Institute of the Press, to write the following pages (through p. 245) on the part that communication law can and should play in information development.*]

What have strictly legal considerations to do with a study of the general conditions under which, and methods by which, the mass communication media can contribute to economic and social development?

The basic truth is that there exists a fundamental diversity of legal systems, and this diversity is both the reflection and the inevitable consequence of the variety of mentalities, cultures, economic levels, and social needs. How can the common elements of regulation be discerned in these local systems, especially in a field like information, where their diversity and their subordinate character are accentuated by the preponderance of political factors; and especially when to the variety of traditions and cultures are added such vast differences in economic development as separate most of the developing countries from the highly industrialized countries? Can it be seriously argued, for example, that the legal provisions governing the establishment and use of the great information media in the United States or in Western Europe or in the USSR could be applied, immediately and successfully, to ensure the right to information to the Ife family of West Central Africa or the Bvani family of Southern Asia?

There can be no question, in the present stage of social development, of imagining standard regulations which would be equally valid for all countries. It is nonetheless certain that the efforts now being made to improve the mass communication media and ensure the contribution that they can and should make to economic and social development might be seriously compromised if consideration were *not* given to the characteristics of the legal factors in this field.

The expansion of legal regulations is a phenomenon characteristic of the contemporary development of societies. This expansion may be observed, in various degrees and forms, under all regions and in all countries. It is the inevitable consequence of the strengthening of social organization, of economic growth, of the increasing number and complexity of the mechanisms to which this growth gives rise, and of the need to adjust and regulate these mechanisms. This need brings about the generalization of planning methods. Now there can be no planning, however flexible, without the reinforcement of legal regulation. The expansion of this regulation is further accented by its diversification. The latter is not only or even chiefly the reflection and the consequence of the differences between the ideas and the regimes which characterize the various national communities. It is, on the contrary, an element that tends to bring together these ideas and these regimes, for it is caused by the identity of the specific nature of the techniques and of their social functions, whatever may be their differences of form and degree in the various countries.

These techniques and these functions dictate similar imperatives, which, in spite of the persistence and sometimes the resurgent virulence of ideological divisions and conflicts of interest, create a rapprochement, a sort of osmosis of the norms of collective organization and individual behavior and their translation into institutional terms. The old adage "There is no society without law" takes on new power and new meaning in the formulas of contemporary sociologists. "It is institutions," says M. Monnet, "which prescribe the relations among men and are the real support of civilization." And information, because it is one field particularly noteworthy for the progress of its techniques, and for their similarity in nature, in functions, and in the social needs which they create, is also one of the fields in which the increasing importance and convergence of institutions are most strikingly manifest.

The experts who during these past years have studied the problem of information in the regions where it is insufficiently developed—and particularly the experts from these regions themselves—have come to realize the importance and the increasing specificity of information law.

Sometimes this realization may still be somewhat delayed or hindered by the idea that this law consists essentially of the provisions enacted by the public powers to restrict the extent of freedom of expression. But, under the pressure of facts, the narrow limits that this notion implies are becoming more and more outdated. For example, if the report of the seminar on freedom of information organized in 1962 by the United Nations in New Delhi, in its chapter on Press Laws, takes into consideration mainly state control or regulation of the content of publication, it is nevertheless true that even in this chapter it was unavoidable that other categories of regulations — anti-trust legislation, for instance — should be evoked. And what is more significant still, in all the other chapters, which have nothing to do with the legal aspects of the problems involved (organization and functioning of information enterprises, circulation and exchange of information, practice of the journalistic profession, etc.), stress is laid on the importance of the choice of suitable institutions or regulations—whether these be enacted by the public powers or drawn up and applied by professionals.

Thus information law already appears in its full extent, as far as its object is concerned. According to a convenient and generally admitted division, this law now includes four branches.

The branches of information law

The first and most traditional may be described as the statute of *content.* This statute sets, either by enacting precise restrictions or by indicating criteria of guidance, (*a*) the limits or conditions imposed on the diffusion of facts or the public expression of ideas by the need to safeguard the basic interests of the national community or the rights and dignity of individuals; (*b*) the processes of sanction or of prevention or of guidance intended to ensure the respect of these limits or these conditions.

This statute also determines the rights attached to the content of publication (copyright, neighboring rights, protection of news, etc.).

The second branch of information law, the statute of *enterprise,* includes all the provisions applicable to the material means of publication (establishment and functioning of enterprises, their economic and fiscal regime, the special rules and formalities imposed on these enterprises in connection with publication operations). The third branch, called the statute of the *profession,* which has arisen from the professionalization of informational activities, includes the particular institution and regulations which concern the status of professionals and the exercise of their activities. Finally, the development on the international plane of institutions, conventions, and legal acts of cooperation has given rise to an *international* statute, which constitutes the fourth branch of information law.

The expansion of the object and the content of this law has been facilitated by the diversification of its methods of formulation or application and by its gradual specialization and transformation. The rules enacted by the public powers—legislation, governmental or administrative regulations—or interpreted by the courts are more and more supplemented by norms established by convention or by delegation of power by the professional organizations. This new institutional category is continually expanding in many countries, thanks to the establishment of professional councils and to the increasing number of professional codes of ethics and collective agreements. Certainly it cannot be substituted for state regulation in the most serious cases, especially where the repressive provisions of the latter are concerned; it has not the coercive force. In many cases, it makes possible the prevention or restraint of the excesses of this regulation, while at the same time it takes into consideration the increased need for legal rulings created by the development of the mass communication media and their social functions. Furthermore—and under the best possible conditions, since these rules are drawn up by professionals—it accentuates the specialization of information law as well as the change in its role, which is less and less to restrict and more and more to promote action; these two are the latest but not the least characteristics of the development of this law.

Information law in the developing countries

This expansion and specialization, this transformation of information law, may be observed chiefly in the highly industrialized countries. They are nevertheless imposing themselves gradually in those countries that have not yet reached a normal degree of development, for they are precisely the condition, the support, and also the sign of development. What is more, is it not in these states that they can be achieved under the best conditions? It is frequently noted that in the states where industrialization is most highly developed, especially where information is concerned, there exists a certain divorce between the new structures and functions of information on the one hand and the applicable legislation on the other. This divorce also appears in cases where information activities continue to be legally guaranteed and regulated as if they were individual activities, whereas they have become collective activities, both because of the importance of the means they require and by the nature of the social functions they fulfill. Is it possible that the legal institutions or rules conceived at the end of the eighteenth century or even in the nineteenth century to protect the individual's right to free expression against state power can suffice to ensure adequate information in the time of Telstar and the laser and of the industrial concentration of the mass communication media?

This divorce also exists in cases where information activities were originally considered and regulated simply as ways of exercising state power, to which all individual activities, whether intellectual or material, were subordinated; whereas, later on, social development and the rise in cultural and economic levels revealed the need for a continual broadening of the role left to the individual's freedom of initiative and choice.

The situation is different for the new countries and, in a general way, for those that must, in the interest of national consolidation and economic and social growth, construct or thoroughly revise their structures or mechanism. Unhampered by the weight of old regulations and interests, or the modes of behavior which these have brought about, they can benefit from the sum of the experiences accumulated in the world to help them choose institutions and rules adapted, on the one hand, to the most recent progress of information techniques and functions, and, on the other, to the particular characteristics of their own social needs. Certain conditions must, however, be observed. The first is to proceed by stages, with a clear understanding both of the need for these stages and of their transitory character. In regions where illiteracy is high, incomes low, and communications difficult, it would be useless to install presses big enough to print numerous copies of voluminous dailies. It would be just as useless to work out, at the start, minute and complex legislation in regions where the population has not yet sufficient political experience, a feeling of national solidarity, or a sense of economic perspective. In these regions political consolidation, national cohesion, and, naturally, economic and social development require a mobilization by the public powers of all intellectual, moral, and material forces.

In the field of information, this mobilization sometimes means, inescapably, the taking over and management by the state of the great mass communication media. It is at this price that these techniques, especially radio, can be fully utilized, not only under the conditions analyzed in this book, for economic and social development, but also (for all these tasks go together) for political unification and the creation of a real "public opinion." This imposes on the methods of organization and management obligations or restrictions of such a nature as to promote the action of the central power. What is important is that these special regimes be closely linked to the first phases of development, and that they be conceived and set up in such a way that they not only do not prevent, but on the contrary prepare the way for the *new* institutional choices—whatever may be the political doctrine that inspires the choices—which are called for by the rise to a normal stage of development.

This is not the place to draw up a catalogue of the many questions that may be the subject of legal provisions in each phase of development or of the various means of regulation that may be adopted. It may be useful, however—even at the risk of seeming overbold—to pick out a certain number of elements or criteria for guidance. Information involves one of the fundamental rights of man, that of expressing himself and knowing what others are expressing. This right was set forth in Article 19 of the Universal Declaration of December 10, 1948. In general, written constitutions, either in the text itself or in the preamble or declaration which precedes it, recognize this right. But it is generally expressed in a concise way as a right of the individual. However, information has also become a real social power. This does not imply that this power should be considered as a power of the state; it is a power within the state. It fulfills functions of general interest, among the foremost of which is its contribution to economic and social development. For the exercise of these functions, various methods may be chosen. But it must never be forgotten that economic and social development is not an aim in itself. It tends to promote the flowering of human values. One of the principal functions of law is to protect these values. Sociologists note a close correlation between economic growth and the development of education and information media. This correlation takes its full force and value only insofar as it is based on law and as the law serves to introduce into the mechanisms of these parallel developments the norms necessary to guarantee the full use of the material resources and intellectual progress that they should ensure to each individual in the interest of all. And this is particularly true in regions where, to raise them to a normal level of development, the central power is led to take charge of, or control strictly, the means of information.

It is indispensable that the action of this power be guided and limited by precise legal provisions which will guarantee that its control of information is really in the service of the *general interest of the country,* as this interest is perceived at each stage of development, and not in the service of an oligarchy or a faction.

This implies, first, that the *power of information be defined in fundamental legal acts* which determine the organization of the national society, and that the principles establishing power be defined in such a way as to exclude arbitrariness or the abuse of power at all the stages where governmental or administrative authority may be exercised. The existence of means of recourse to a legal authority endowed with executive powers is obviously one of these principles.

This implies, second—in order that the principles may be put into practice—*a special legal status for information.*

Whatever may be the imperatives linked to the construction phase, this status may be conceived at the start and gradually worked out with consideration for the division mentioned above. In certain cases the division and specialization of rules may be made difficult in the beginning, and apparently superfluous, by the concentration of powers and the integration of information enterprises and activities in a general system of administrative organization, which is sometimes rendered all the more inflexible by the rigidity of economic planning and the requirements of priorities in the educational field. This division and specialization should nonetheless be gradually achieved, just as far as possible, because they bring about an improvement in legal regulations which is one of the conditions for development.

Developing the statute of content

Thus that part of the statute of content which concerns itself with the protection of the interests of the community should include precise definitions of the obligations or restrictions that this protection requires, even in cases where information is entirely or partly, at least during an initial period, directed or controlled by the political power or diffused by public enterprises. These definitions serve both to guide and to limit the action of the power and to guarantee the right to information of all the members of the national community. The guidance given to the holder of the power of information to ensure as complete information as possible in all fields (civic, economic, technical, cultural) should be coupled with the prohibitions that this obligation entails (violation of military secrecy, false news, criminal provocations, etc.). These prohibitions may be extended exceptionally and temporarily, as they are under all regimes. Even so, this extension should be foreseen and limited by a precise legal text.

That part of the statute of content that tends to ensure the protection of the material and moral interests of individuals, including respect for their private life and for the dignity of persons and their legitimate beliefs, is also a factor of development to the extent that this development has for its condition and aim the promotion of human values. The progress of distribution techniques, their increased penetration, and their social influence give rise everywhere to a need for the reinforcement of this sort of protection. It should be particularly ensured in developing states. The jurists of these countries may refer, certainly, to the numerous processes already tried· out or proposed in the world to contend against calumny, libel, or outrage, but in choosing rules to protect the dignity and thus the activity of individuals, which is a condition of all social progress, they should give strong consideration to the peculiar characteristics of their own traditions and customs.

Another and still more delicate problem of adaptation—for it involves legal systems which are solidly implanted on the international level—is raised by the working out of the rules included in the third part of the statute of content: those intended to protect the productions of the various information media. The African meeting on copyright problems held August 5-10, 1963, showed the difficulties which this necessary protection may cause in countries of insufficient material resources.

The statute of enterprise

The statute of enterprise is the one which, *a priori,* is most important from the point of view of economic development. While it is not possible to indicate here the various rules of establishment and management which may be adopted—and which vary according to legal systems—two points may be raised:

(*a*) Experience shows in general the advantage to be gained from the gradual adoption of a cooperative status for organizations entrusted with services of common interest (news agencies, for example, and, in the field of the press, services for supplying newsprint, or distribution services). It also shows the need, for the most important enterprises, of a flexible status which, going beyond the traditional opposition between commercial and public enterprises, permits both professionals and the representatives of the various social forces to be associated in the management of the information services.

(*b*) On the economic level, it is the duty of the state to give special encouragement to information enterprises in proportion to the importance and the special characteristics of their social functions. A number of methods may be used, from the total or partial payment of equipment expenses or the provision of special facilities for the supply of raw materials (newsprint, for example) to reductions in telecommunication or transportation rates or to tax exemptions; these various methods are and have long been practiced in many countries.

But it is also a fact shown by experience that the granting of such advantages, whatever their nature or extent, cannot serve economic and social development unless it is done as a matter of public interest and not used as a means of economic pressure for partisan ends. Here again, precise legal rules are called for to set forth the conditions and procedures for granting these advantages and (this is the essential criterion for judging regimes) to permit recourse in case these conditions and procedures are not observed.

The professional statute

The professional statute depends, naturally, on the development and the specialization of activities in the information field. It is advisable to encourage the establishment of professional organizations as this development progresses, and to broaden their role gradually by extending their competence or associating them as closely as possible with the formulation and application of the provisions which govern their status or the practice of the profession. This implies, at the start, a clear legal definition of professionals and the choice, for the issuance of their credentials (professional cards), of a procedure in which they can participate. On this point too it is easy to find valuable elements of guidance in past experience throughout the world.

The international statute

Finally, there is hardly need to stress the importance of the international statute of informaton where underdeveloped countries are concerned. The special attention which they should pay to it does not derive only, or perhaps even chiefly, from the fact that the provisions or institutions which this statute includes are the supports or the instruments of the international assistance given to their development. It should be essentially inspired by the concern which they should feel—and which is decisive for their future —for taking their rightful place in the building of that international information structure which, in spite of accumulated obstacles, will eventually be created by the astonishing progress of telecommunication techniques.

Conclusions

From this rapid summary of the reasons for and conditions of the role of law in the development of the mass communication media four conclusions can be drawn, which are, moreover, closely linked:

1. The first is the need for a special statute of information drawn up simultaneously with any plan for economic and special development and adapted, through successive revisions, to the phases of this plan or of its fulfillment. It is superfluous to stress this first point: it serves as a kind of *leitmotiv* in all the explanations made above.

2. The second is the importance of collecting complete documentation on the various institutional regimes governing the mass

communication media and on the way these regimes are applied. Those entrusted with drawing up the statute of information and adapting it to the progress of development need to know about all the experience of other countries. We have noted this on several occasions in connection with the characteristics of each branch of information law. And the same thing was emphasized by the experts who, at regional conferences organized by Unesco, studied the conditions for the development of the information media in Africa, Latin America, and Asia.

3. In the third place, it is indispensable that considerable emphasis be laid on institutional problems in all programs adopted by developing countries for study and research concerning information. The first condition for such studies is the legal documentation of which we have just mentioned the need. Often, however, this documentation is insufficient (all too many examples could be cited of regimes in which the number of rules is in inverse proportion to their enforcement). It is necessary to be able to determine the practical effectiveness of these rules, the social needs to which they correspond, the behavior that they provoke. The institutional study should be made as thoroughly as possible, with the aid not only of legal sociology but of all the other disciplines which may lead to a better understanding of the information process.

4. Finally, the fourth conclusion has to do with the role that specialists in information law should play, not only—it goes without saying—in the formulation or study of regimes, but also in the carrying out of plans for economic and social development. The final report on the new uses of mass communication media for economic and social development, presented at the United Nations Conference on the Application of Science and Technology for the Benefit of the Less Developed Areas (Geneva, February 4–20, 1963) stressed the usefulness of the assistance which can be furnished in this field by specialists in mass communication, "even though they may appear likely to contribute only indirectly to the increase of industry or the formation of capital." Is it utopian to hope that among these specialists a modest place will be reserved for specialists in information law?

8. Review and Recommendations

Let us review the path we have traveled to this point.

The proposition we have been exploring is that an adequate flow of information, and in particular an appropriate use of the mass media, could make a substantial contribution to national economic and social development.

We began with two families, the Ifes and Bvanis, because they are really what this book is about: the human meaning of under-development and development. Attractive, talented, interesting, in many ways admirable and even enviable, these two families also personify many of the things that the developing nations are try-ing to develop out of—poverty, illness, short life span, illiteracy, lack of education, lack of the knowledge and skills to participate actively in building a new nation. From the viewpoint of their nations they are unused, undeveloped resources. The human prob-lem of a developing nation is to mobilize resources like these fami-lies, to modernize many of their life patterns, and, in so doing, to bring about the necessary social change as speedily and painlessly as possible.

This is where information enters the calculus of development. Social change of great magnitude is required. To achieve it, people must be informed, persuaded, educated. Information must flow not only to them, but also *from* them, so that their needs can be known and so that they may participate in the acts and decisions of nation building; and information must also flow vertically so that decisions may be made, work organized, and skills learned at all levels of society. Here is where *mass* communication enters the calculus: the required amount of information and learning is so vast that only by making effective use of the great information multipliers, the mass media, can the developing countries hope to provide information at the rates their timetables for development demand.

In Chapter 1 we looked more closely at the relation of mass communication to economic and social development. Wherever new skills and new attitudes are to be learned, wherever people need to decide to do new things, wherever traditional society trembles on the verge of modernizing, there a more efficient form of communication can be helpful. Efficient communication is needed to help modernize the primary sector, where ancient agriculture and subsistence economies must give way to new; to help teach the new skills required for the industrial sector; to help in the gigantic task of education where schools and teachers and materials are in short supply; above all, to help provide the "climate" of modernizing. National development moves very slowly in a climate where innovation is feared and distrusted, where fatalism leads men to believe they can do very little about their situation, where men do not believe in the dignity of labor and have little wish to better their lot, where attitudes toward taking animal life stand in the way of better health practices and better nutrition, where counterproductive social patterns like class or caste systems greatly restrict men's ability to cooperate with other men, where counterproductive customs obstruct a modern way of life, and where villagers are little interested in anything outside their villages. This is the climate to be modified.

We looked at four cases, from four regions of the world, where scholars had made some observation of mass communication in economic and social development. Lerner found in the Middle East that mass communication helps to develop the "mobile," empathic personality, by which he means a person who can accept change and take new demands in stride. This, he says, is the predominant personality pattern in modern life, and it is spread by the mass media. He concludes that mass communication is "the great multiplier" in development, the device that can spread the new ideas, attitudes, and knowledge more rapidly than ever before. Studying two villages in Asia, Rao found that mass communication was even more important in smoothing development than in speeding it. He tried to decide whether economic development or communication development is the prime mover—which chiefly stimulates the other—but finally rejected the question as futile. There is an *inter*action between the two, he concluded, and it is constant and cumulative. Studying village culture in the Andes, Holmberg decided that the real problem is to bring these villages into the life and attitudes and stored knowledge of the nation, and in this task radio, newspapers, and films will play a leading role as soon as the stage of the first patient face-to-face explanations and demonstrations is past. In the fourth case, Doob decided that communication is "at the very center of existence" for developing Africa. We pointed out that communication, by its very nature, is *always* at the very center of existence for any society, developing or not. It is the basic social process. Wherever dangers or opportunities need to be reported, decisions need to be made, new knowledge needs to be taught, or change is imminent—there information flows. It is not surprising, therefore, that the efficiency of communication is a consideration in determining the speed and smoothness of national development, where all these needs for information are vastly intensified.

In Chapter 2 we examined the flow of information, both the flow within developing countries and the flow between these and other countries in the modern world. The flow is sadly inadequate. The impacted channels between countries penalize the highly developed as well as the less-developed countries, but the situation is particularly cruel for the countries that are in an early stage of development. They find the world's store of technical information and informational materials and equipment most unevenly distributed, and centered in countries that have already gone through the development process. Although modern technology makes such information and materials more swiftly and easily transportable than ever before, still the shortage of credits and the strength of tariff and trade restrictions make it difficult to move informational materials across borders.

The effect of this situation is to deprive the developing nations, in part at least, of a right and a tool. Information, as we have said, is one of the basic rights of mankind, and an indispensable requirement for the freedom and dignity of the world's people. Beyond that, it is a tool for accomplishing certain things the overwhelming majority of nations want. It is the basis of international understanding and mutual respect. It is an aid "in the cause of enlightenment, at a time when more than half the world's population is still illiterate, and vast areas, underdeveloped or devastated by war, lack the means to dispel ignorance."[1] It is one of the chief hopes of all nations for speeding the process of economic and social development. Therefore, an inadequate flow of information is of world-wide concern.

Within the developing countries, the flow of information, already too slight, greatly thins out as it moves from the cities toward the villages, and still more as it feeds back from the villages to the centers. Where it is most needed, there it is least available. The result is to perpetuate the difference between the modernizing and the traditional cultures, and to make change more difficult.

We looked, in Chapter 3, at the distribution of mass media in the world, hoping to find, perhaps, that the media are there but not being used adequately. We found, however, that underdeveloped countries have underdeveloped communication systems, too. The band of economic scarcity around the world is also the band where literacy is lowest, where newspapers, radios, television receivers, and cinemas are least widely available, where newsprint is scarcest, where electrification and telecommunications lag, where children are least likely to be in school. Latin America is ahead of Asia and Africa in communication development, and, throughout the developing countries, radio is somewhat nearer the "Unesco minima" than are newspapers and film. But there is a long way to go before the mass media in the developing countries are adequate for the work that will be expected of them. They are underfinanced, underequipped, understaffed (at least with highly trained personnel). There is an encouraging rate of media growth, but the question, as we said, is whether it is fast enough for countries in a hurry.

Next we considered, in Chapter 4, how mass communication may be used most effectively in the service of national development. Beginning with a few pages on how social change occurs, we tried to identify some of the requirements for effective use of the media in accomplishing change. For one thing, it is necessary to know the local culture into which the media go. It is therefore helpful to increase the amount of feedback from the target culture, a topic on which we had more to say in Chapter 7. But one of the chief requisites of effective use of the media is to realize the limits of what they can do well. In general, the mass media are quite capable of handling the basic informational tasks of development by themselves. The decision-making functions of development, however, in many cases require the changing of strongly held attitudes, beliefs, and social norms; and therefore the mechanisms of interpersonal communication and group decision, rather than mass communication, are the key ones. This does not mean that mass communication cannot contribute powerfully to the decision process. It can feed information into the discussion, carry the word of the leaders, make the issues clear. It can confer status, broaden the policy dialogue, enforce social norms, help form tastes, affect attitudes lightly held, and make slight changes in more strongly held attitudes. But the strength of the mass media does not lie in frontal attack on strongly held beliefs or long-valued customs. Changing these is in the domain of personal influence; mass communication can only help indirectly. A third group of tasks—the teaching function—can be handled in part directly by mass communication, in part by combination with interpersonal communication. For example, the media are perhaps best used in a classroom where they can be part of a total educational experience under the guidance of a teacher; but where teachers or schools are not available, or where teachers are not sufficiently trained, the media can fill in. Likewise, radio cannot demonstrate an agricultural skill as well as a field agent can, but once the skill is learned, radio can supply additional information, answer questions, and report results.

Then, in Chapter 5, we noted how the mass media are being used effectively in some of the great development campaigns—agriculture, health, literacy, and formal education. Particularly in the last of these the challenge is to be imaginative in the use of the "new media"—instructional television and radio, programmed instruction, and the like. As Robert Lefranc says, there is no need for the new countries to "make the same slow pilgrimage to the temple of culture" as older countries have had to make; on the contrary, "they should undertake forced marches, and fight ignorance and illiteracy with modern methods and techniques."[2] In all the campaign areas, however, examples were found of successful use of a number of different media; perhaps the most useful principle that came out of this chapter was the concept of information systems. The great battles of development are continuing ones, and the results come less often from the impact of single messages or a single medium than from a succession of impacts of related messages and cooperating channels—in other words, from the use of a whole information system. In a campaign the nature of the message, and the choice of channel or combination of channels, will change as the campaign progresses. Effective planning for a development campaign therefore begins not with the question *How should we use a particular medium* (or the field staff, or the schools, or whatever), but rather by asking *How can the needed change be brought about?*

This led to a discussion (in Chapter 6) of the usefulness of communication research in providing feedback to guide the use of mass media and the planning of development messages and campaigns. It was argued that research of this kind is not a luxury in a developing country, but rather a very practical way to get reliable information, to avoid "juggling knives in the dark." A number of examples were given of useful tasks research could do—pretesting materials; evaluating results of campaigns and programs in order to improve subsequent ones; learning how innovation takes place in a particular culture; understanding the audience; studying how information on a particular topic comes to people. And whereas there are certain special problems in doing research of this kind in developing countries (not the least of which is a scarcity of trained researchers), still the rewards, in greater efficiency of mass communication, can be considerable.

Finally, in Chapter 7, we discussed some of the problems and ways of building up the mass media in a developing country—costs, planning of balanced and measured growth, training the necessary skilled workers, providing equipment and materials, developing individual media (including such special problems as what to use the radio for, how to aid the small local newspaper, whether to put in television, and how to integrate the media with personal communication), and providing a wise legal and institutional framework for the mass media. The desirability of planning ahead in all these areas was one conclusion that came out of Chapter 7. Another was the relatively modest cost of mass media development in comparison with some of the other costs of economic and social development. For example, if mass communication could save only a small fraction of the cost of educational development in many new countries, it might save more than the total cost of its own development. And yet, in the skirmishing for the development dollar, mass media development all too often comes off very poorly.

In brief, then, our conclusion is that mass communication, if used adequately and well, can indeed make a substantial contribution to national economic and social development. There is nothing on the horizon, except possibly formal education, which has any such potential ability to carry new ideas and skills from the modernizing cities to the traditional villages and to build the spirit of nation-ness in a new country; and the mass media, as we have seen, are swifter than formal education, serve the adult population whereas the impact of education is chiefly on youth, and are in no sense competitors, but rather extenders and enrichers of formal education. Furthermore, we have now had enough experience with the mass media, in developing countries as well as in economically advanced countries, to understand what patterns of use are more effective than others, what supporting services are required, how mass communication must be related to personal communication and to other segments of national development, and, among other things, the danger of raising aspirations through mass communication which cannot be satisfied by the political or economic segments of developing society. The conditions for effective use of mass communication in national development exist. But, as we have noted, in most developing countries the mass media are underused and underdeveloped, and consequently the flow of information is thin and slow.

Therefore, at the end of the long path we have traveled in this book (from the Ifes to the cost of television!) let us set down a few recommendations to developing countries and their friends and aiders, concerning what they might do about the mass media.

1. *A developing country should examine the flow of development information within its borders.*

Change will not take place unless those who are expected to change know and accept the reasons, the methods, and the rewards for changing. New skills will not be learned unless they are taught, and unless individuals are motivated to seek teaching. Decisions that involve changes in group norms and customs will not be made unless people have a chance to talk them over. And true national participation in economic and social development will never come unless communication flows up as well as down the channel between the national leaders and the rural people.

These are truisms, well recognized, unnecessary to say again. And yet, what do we find in many developing countries? The flow of information drying up as it moves from the national and state capitals toward the villages. Dependence on *telling* the people, rather than encouraging them to seek information, or talk over decisions, or express their needs and wishes. Lack of coordination between the great channels of development information—the mass media, schools, extension and field staffs, and local government. A persistence of old counterproductive attitudes, and a disturbing lack of the information that is essential for the making of a modern nation.*

* Of which an example comes as this is written. A study just completed by a nearby university of a "typical" village in one of the largest countries of the world shows that the villagers have "only the haziest ideas about their own nation, its leaders and its problems." The political information of some of these people is 15 years old. The national leader, a world figure, is variously identified as "some Brahmin," "chief of the local district council," "ruler of the world." (*New York Times,* October 27, 1963, p. 28: "Nehru Unknown in Indian Village.")

These observations do not necessarily reflect national negligence. They do not reflect on the people who do not have the information that we, looking from the outside, think they should have. Rather, such failings result from centuries of informational blackout, and they will undoubtedly persist to some extent as long as two social systems, two economic systems, and two information systems exist side by side, as they do in most developing countries.

But we have seen in the preceding pages that it is not necessary to take lack of information for granted. Modern communication provides a way to do something about it. And change begins where one is. Therefore, the first step in putting modern communication at the service of national development is a thorough and candid appraisal of the flow of information through the country. What information on economic and social development is being sent out, and how much of it is being received? Whom is it reaching, whom failing to reach? Where is it going in insufficient quantity? Where, and on what subjects, is the need to know not being satisfied? Where is information on a one-way track, when it needs a two-way track?

Many countries have found such a self-study to be an eye-opening experience. They have found, to their surprise, that much of the information they were sending was never delivered; that some they were able to deliver was being misunderstood or rejected; and that groups they assumed to be informed on a given topic were ignorant of it. Knowing these things, they found, is the basis for improving them.

2. *A developing country should examine the use it is making of the mass media in multiplying the flow of information on development.*

The mass media, the great multipliers, are a nation's best hope of filling in some of its informational lags, and keeping (so far as information can help to keep) its timetables for national development. Therefore, a developing country needs to look hard and carefully at the use it is making of these tools of modern communication.

Where are the media reaching? Where are radio receivers available, where do the copies of newspapers go, where can films be seen, how many schools are making use of the media? Where, and with what people, are the media "blacked out"? And what are they being used *for*? To what extent are they helping agriculture, health, community improvement? Contributing to the needs of formal and adult education? Feeding the forums of interpersonal discussion? Carrying the public affairs information that people need if they are to participate in government? Helping to build the climate of national development and the empathy needed for national cooperation?

Where are the bottlenecks that impede faster growth and greater use of the mass media? Lack of stations, newspapers, or cinema facilities? Lack of receivers and other equipment? Lack of electricity or newsprint? Lack of training? Lack of sufficient economic support? Lagging literacy? Lack of understanding by development leaders of how mass communication can help them? Policies that neglect the development uses of the media in favor of entertainment or other nondevelopment uses?

In other words, a country needs to take stock. If it is not using the mass media adequately in its development program, then it needs to ask why, and what more it can do. The answers may prove surprising. Countries that have looked hard at their performance in this respect have usually found that, whereas they need more of everything in mass communication, still they can make more efficient use of what they have. They have been able, at least to some extent, to increase the impact of their mass media on national development even while they assemble the resources to enlarge the system.

3. *To the extent that planning is possible, a developing country should plan a balanced and measured growth for its mass media, with a view to relationships among the media and to those between the media and other aspects of development.*

In Chapter 7 we have made a number of suggestions on how a nation might plan the development of its mass media. There is no need to repeat those suggestions here. It is recognized, however, that the prominence of private ownership in a nation's mass media, and the general attitude of the country toward centralized planning, may make some difference in the amount of planning and the kind of planning that will be useful.

The most typical pattern of media ownership in developing countries is a mixed one. Most often the radio is owned by the government and the press by private industry, whereas some of the films are made by government and others made or imported privately. Most of the related services and powers—education, adult education and other development information programs, telecommunications, import restrictions and tariffs on newsprint and other mass media equipment and supplies—are in government hands. Even in cases where all the media are nationalized or where all or most of them are in the private domain, however, there is still good reason for the persons chiefly responsible to take stock, lay down a set of priority needs, and plan together toward meeting them. Where all the media are nationalized, the planners will probably come from the government. Where all or some of the media are privately owned, it is sometimes found useful to assemble a national council on mass communication, representing private industry, government, and the public. In this latter case it is not suggested that the representatives from outside the media should take over any of the prerogatives of private ownership; but rather that when resources are as scarce as they are in developing countries and when the growth of media is intimately involved with other aspects of national development and dependent in part on government actions and plans, all parties concerned can benefit from broadening the base of media planning.

For example, take the situation in which a country is trying to develop its local media—small-town newspapers, local radio stations, and the like. These usually have a very hard time financially. The government, however, is in position to help them survive, if it will adopt certain friendly policies. (We shall say more about these in the following pages.) Even if the local media are privately owned, therefore, this is a point at which national interest and private interest intersect, and there is everything to be gained by the people who are responsible for the local media sitting down with the people responsible for relevant policy, to look ahead together, mesh their plans, and help each other.

By "balanced and measured growth" we mean a rate of development at which a maximum amount of mutual assistance between the media and other aspects of development can be generated. We have demonstrated that the growth of mass communication interacts with other aspects of economic growth and social change— with the modernizing of agriculture, for example, the spread of a money economy, the acceptance of favorable attitudes toward modernizing, the growth of literacy and education, the learning of technical skills. The media help bring these about; they help the media grow. But in each of these interactions there is some optimum balance. It is counterproductive to teach people to read before printed media are available for them to read, or to introduce printed media into an area before there are literates there to read them. The rate of modernizing agriculture will depend to some extent on how much the mass media press for such development; and when the decision is taken to modernize, new and different needs are created for information. The media needed for support of agricultural modernization will depend on the stage of literacy and education in the population. The people must not be pressed to modernize faster than technical skills, supplies, and equipment can be made available; on the other hand, the decision to learn such skills, to use such equipment and supplies, should not lag too far behind their availability. In other words, as we have said, a developing nation marches forward together. Investment will be more productive, social strain will be less, if the strands of development that interlock can be moved forward at approximately the same rates. A nation that has no resources to waste and no time to lose has a special interest in achieving that kind of balanced and coordinated development.

4. A developing country (and its friends and aiders) should not hesitate to invest in a well-considered program of mass media development and use.

A nation's achievement in the development of mass media is measured not only in the *quantity* of media growth, but also in the *quality* of their service to the nation. Unfortunately, either increased quantity or improved quality is likely to cost more. The countries that want to realize the full potential of the mass media will therefore almost certainly be required to invest in them.

We say "invest." In the materialistic universes of some economists, all expenditures on mass communication have been lumped together as "consumption," whereas expenditures in such productive sectors of society as industry and agriculture are "investments." Whether or not most of the expenditures on the great entertainment media of developed countries should be considered consumption costs, the situation is vastly different in the developing countries. In those countries an effective communication system is an essential element in modernizing agriculture, in producing healthy, literate, and trained workers for industry, and in bringing about effective participation in the making of a nation. The consumption aspect of informational expenditures in developing countries is therefore a small part of the total. Investment in information, in a developing country, is investment in the most essential social and economic changes which make up national development.

A high proportion of developing countries have now found out, from their own experience, how crucial information is to their development programs. Yet, even in many of these countries information is still a poor cousin. It is starved for operating funds, equipment, training. It has had only a tiny fraction of the support available from international organizations and bilateral loans and grants. We should like to urge that these priorities be reconsidered, both by the developing countries and by their friends and aiders. If a considered plan can be worked out to relate information development to other strands of development, then the evidence on the use of mass media in national development seems to us clearly to indicate that it will be for the good of the country to support the plan.

This is the *sine qua non* of mass media development. A nation must decide whether its mass media are or are not on its national development "team." If they are on the team, if they are to be used seriously as instruments by which to speed and smooth economic and social development, then their support must be commensurate with the tasks assigned to them. Half measures are no more effective with the mass media than with factories or dams.

5. *A developing country should try to establish a cooperative relationship between the organs of government responsible for its mass media development and those responsible for education and other related developments.*

Typically, the mass media activities of a new country are represented by one ministry, the educational program by another, and some of the supporting activities such as transportation, postal services, telecommunications, and electrification by still others. It is not altogether surprising that these separate ministries sometimes do not cooperate as fully as they should, and consequently that related developments do not march ahead together, and one activity does not take advantage of the opportunities offered by others. Many such reports come in. To take one example only, in a certain country the new television station stands dark for all the school hours, even though the schools are desperately in need of expert teaching and audiovisual enrichment for their courses. The chief trouble seems to be that there is little cooperation between the ministries of information and education. This is a wasteful condition which developing countries can ill afford, and should get rid of as soon as possible.

It is hardly necessary to say that the development of education and literacy in a country has such an intimate relationship to media development that it is almost impossible to separate the two. This is not only because one helps the other, but also because of the effect of education on the information-seeking and information-giving patterns of people. An investment in education contributes more than a harvest of skills which can be utilized in industry and technological development. It does more than raise the average level of abstract knowledge in the country. In school, one "learns to learn," and, in a nonprofessional sense, one "learns to teach." An educated man has acquired the habit of seeking information, and will seek it throughout all the rest of his life. He will read books, magazines, and newspapers, use libraries (or help establish them if they do not exist), seek out expert advice, use technical handbooks, be interested in news and the interpretation of it. And be-

cause he does have a store of knowledge and a certain articulate-
ness in expressing it, he becomes a *source* of information for his
friends, neighbors, and co-workers. Thus, the effect of education
is to stimulate enormously the flow of useful information to and
from an individual.

Literacy brings to an adult much the same experience as school
brings to a child. He gains a tool for learning. With a little experience, he gains the habit of learning, and acquires information
which he can both use and dispense. In his case, it is specially important, because for at least a generation he and his age-group will
be in charge of policy and administration in the villages of his
country. Literate leaders are likely to be more forward-looking.
They are likely to bring more knowledge to their task, for they are
able to use mass media and technical materials. In other words, the
percentage of literacy among the influential adults is likely to have
a fairly close relation to the interpersonal flow of development information, the use of the printed media, and the overall pace of
development.

Every planning commission on earth is aware of the importance
of investing in education and literacy. We are concerned here, not
primarily with the need to develop these services, but rather with
the need to develop and use them cooperatively with the mass
media. The same thing applies to the development of roads and
transportation, postal services, telephone, telegraph, telecommunication networks to carry electronic messages, and electric mains
to make it easy to use radio receivers, film projectors, and printing
machinery. These are not only part of the arterial system of communication; they are also part of the arterial system of commerce
and industry, and most planning commissions are aware of their
usefulness. Because they do have a close relation to development
of the mass media, cooperation in planning and extending them
would be mutually beneficial.

6. *A developing country should take steps to facilitate the circulation of news.*

News is a basic commodity of the information media. It is a na-
tion-maker, drawing together diverse people around common na-

tional problems and interests. It is the principal window on modern life for traditional and isolated societies. It is the password to participation in public affairs.

There are a number of things a developing country can do to help the news circulate, beyond the obvious action of expanding the news media and improving telecommunications. One action a country should certainly consider is the establishment of a strong and healthy national news agency, if it does not already have one. Such an agency would gather the country's own news, distribute it to the country's own newspapers and broadcasting stations, and make it available to the world agencies. Furthermore, such an agency could express the news needs of a country to the world agencies more effectively than it can be expressed by individual newspapers or broadcasting stations, so that, for example, if the flow of news from neighboring countries is inadequate, something is more likely to be done about it. National news agencies greatly increase the possibilities for cooperation, both among the newspapers and broadcasting stations of the country and with the news agencies of other countries. Therefore, such a development as the organization of 20 new national agencies in Africa since 1951 is a most promising one.

In the second place, a great deal could be done by nations working together to make it easier and cheaper to transmit news internationally. At the present time, rates for similar services may vary by as much as 500 per cent in Latin America, 600 per cent in Africa, and 700 per cent in Asia. And in some cases, rates for messages sent in one direction are over twice those for messages sent in the opposite direction.

Some of those inequalities grow out of old political and commercial ties. Others are due largely to a lack of sufficient telecommunication facilities or to differences in methods of fixing rates. The Organization of American States in cooperation with the International Telecommunication Union is assisting the development of a network for Latin America, and the International Telecommunication Union is helping with similar projects in Asia and Africa. When these needs are met, it will become much easier to send

news at reasonable cost, and without being restricted to a few pathways. Meanwhile, Francis Williams has made some sensible suggestions as to how to begin to even out rates and services.[3]

Finally, the flow of news could be greatly eased if news censorship could be eliminated, and if newsmen could be freed from fear
of reprisal for reporting or printing a story as they see it. These political restrictions are more widespread than is generally realized.

7. *A developing country should try to make it as easy as possible
to establish and maintain "local media."*

By local media we mean such units as small-town newspapers
and local radio stations. These come into existence slowly in developing countries, where the media tend to huddle in the cities. Yet
local media are of great importance in social and economic development, not only because they are in better position to know and
serve the particular needs of a region, but also because they make
it easier for more people to have access to the media and therefore
to take part in public affairs.

Local media typically have a hard time financially. As an illustration of that, on pp. 102–4 we quoted A. R. Bhat's graphic account of the problem of survival facing a local vernacular-language
paper in India. Such an account as Bhat's is disturbing not only
because it shows how precarious is the existence of local media, but
also because it demonstrates that when a small newspaper or radio
station is holding desperately on to life, as many of them are, it is
too hard pressed to do its best job.

Government can in many cases help these useful but impover-
ished media to survive and grow. Is it possible to decrease the tax
burden on the new medium for its first few years? Is it feasible to
establish a pool of used printing equipment from which new and
small newspapers may draw? Can newsprint be made more easily
available to small newspapers, which typically come late to the
market with small orders and therefore often have to pay a high
premium? The government can help newspaper circulation by
speeding the literacy programs in the area of the new paper. It can
help increase the radio audience by speeding electrification in the

area, by distributing school and community sets, and by encouraging cooperation with the school and adult programs. Not only the government, but also the foundations, friendly governments, and international professional organizations can, and do, contribute to the skill and competence of these small and new media, by establishing training opportunities and by offering professional advice.

If the local media, by policies like these, can be helped over their first precarious years, they can survive and serve effectively on the front lines of development.

8. *A developing country should give special attention to combining mass media with interpersonal communication.*

Mass media can be effective, and interpersonal communication can be effective, but, as we have seen (Chapter 5), the two together can sometimes be uniquely effective. We have shown a number of examples of such successful combinations: radio broadcast and group discussion combined in the rural radio forums; classroom teaching and film or television combined into a learning experience more effective than either alone; radio or print used to follow up or reinforce the information a field worker gives the people he serves. The effectiveness of combinations like these is one of the lessons that many developing countries have learned and are incorporating into their information strategies.

But it takes skill and effort to bring about a successful marriage of interpersonal and mass communication. The skill of planning a successful group discussion around a radio broadcast, or planning a broadcast to stimulate group discussion, is something that has to be learned. Working a television broadcast into a classroom lesson must be studied and practiced. The timing and content of a broadcast or a poster to reinforce a field worker are also matters of some delicacy. If in any of these cases the media and the personal communication *just happen* to fit effectively together, it is a rare and fortunate accident.

We are not implying that a developing country should be wary of combining mass media with interpersonal communication. Rather, it should seek out all appropriate opportunities to bring about the combination. But it should also be aware that such combinations, potent as they are, are not automatically successful. They take special attention, and richly repay care and skill.

9. *A developing country should review its restrictions on the importing of informational materials.*

It is shocking to reflect that, although the world has become more interdependent in almost every other way, the exchange of materials of information has, in the last half-century, actually become more difficult. Two wars, with their military and political censorship, a tense and suspicious international situation, and a new prominence for political propaganda, have contributed to this situation. There have also been economic problems, particularly in the new countries that are trying to make their financial resources and hard currency go as far as possible. The result has been, as we have pointed out, that informational materials have been caught in a general pattern of import restriction and tariff and tax collection, where they really do not belong. Textbooks, instructional films, newspapers, teaching materials, newsprint, raw film—these and other types of informational materials are restricted from crossing many frontiers today by quotas and the need to secure import licenses (which may be withheld for either economic or political reasons), by import charges, tariffs, and sales taxes.

The question is whether the developing countries, with their great need for information, can afford such restrictions on the import of informational materials. It seems to us that every developing country should review the difficulties it places in the way of such imports, and balance the currency it saves or the charges it collects against the potential gain from being able to add such imports to its own internal flow of information.

During the last decade, Unesco has taken the leadership in pointing out actions that may be taken internationally to relieve such restrictions. It has proposed a series of international agreements—for example, conventions on the importation of educational, scientific, and cultural materials; on the international circulation of audiovisual materials; on the importation of goods for display or use at exhibitions, fairs, meetings, etc.; and on the temporary importation of professional equipment. The purpose of such agreements has been to provide a common intergovernmental standard for granting customs and import dispensations to such materials. Unesco has also instituted certain arrangements such as the International Coupon Scheme, which makes it easier for a soft-currency country to buy publications, films, and scientific equipment from a hard-currency country. There has also been developed an internationally standardized label, which permits packages of instruments to be sent customs free across international borders between scientific laboratories. Unesco has also worked closely with the Universal Postal Union, the International Air Transport Association, and other such organizations to secure reduced rates for the transport of informational materials. Reaction to these efforts has been very gratifying.

Eventually, however, the problem always comes back to an individual country, not usually as an international agreement or arrangement, but rather as a policy question: How much does it stand to gain by restricting the imports of informational materials, and what would it stand to gain by facilitating the flow of such materials as much as it possibly can?

10. *A developing country should consider the possibility of establishing communication industries.*

The need of communication equipment and supplies and the need to invest in productive industry together point to the need to establish communication industries. Newsprint is typically in short supply in a developing country. Radio receivers are far too few and too expensive for truly mass distribution. Projectors, raw film stock, and many other items important for communication development are scarce and expensive. A developing country faces a choice of doing without these things, making it easy to import them, or making them.

The idea of establishing an industry to make newsprint, radio receivers, or other communication materials is an extraordinarily attractive one to many countries. Many such industries, once the capital is found and a sufficient number of skilled men found or trained, not only would serve a country's needs and save money, but also would generate additional capital. For example, if a South Asian country could establish an adequate newsprint industry, it would find itself, within a few years, in a newsprint market where the needs were almost limitless and the potential rewards very great.

Therefore, a developing country can well review its needs and its resources for establishing communication industries of its own.

11. *A developing country should provide adequate training for its information personnel.*

A developing country can hardly afford to turn its information program over to untrained and inefficient persons. There can be no greater mistake than to build communication facilities or import equipment without providing the skilled persons such facilities and equipment require. A developing country will therefore need training programs for all the mass media, for technical, writing, editing, production, and managerial personnel. And this is but a part of the total training of information workers. For instance, teachers and administrators must be trained for the schools and for adult education, and field representatives and supervisors for community development and other government information services. Some of these training programs will be very large—for example, teacher training. Others will be very specialized—for example, the first group of television engineers. But all these in their own way are important, and it is beneath the dignity and contrary to the interest of a developing country to trust its facts and ideas to untrained communication workers.

In Chapter 7 we have made some suggestions on how training for mass communication can be conducted. This is a matter of first-rate importance to any developing country that wants to get the most out of its information system. Even if used unskillfully, an adequate communication system will contribute something to the flow of information, although much less than it potentially could; as will an *in*adequate system, skillfully used. But an inadequate system, unskillfully used, will compound its failings and magnify its weaknesses. A developing country does not often have an adequate system, and it seldom has enough extra capacity in its system for inefficient use of it. Therefore, such a country must be concerned with training and upgrading its communication personnel.

12. *A developing country should seek as much feedback as possible from its mass media audiences.*

In the predominantly oral communication of traditional society, feedback is automatic. A communicator can tell instantly what effect his message is having. In the mass media communication of modern society, however, feedback is slight and slow in coming. A communicator can only guess what effect his message is having, or even whom it is reaching, until the trickle of letters, telephone calls, complaints, compliments, canceled subscriptions, and, in economically advanced countries, audience rating reports, begin to come in. It usually takes a while for developing countries to learn that they must work hard at obtaining reliable feedback from audiences to guide the media.

The most efficient way to obtain reliable feedback for the media is by audience research. As soon as possible, a developing country should train research men in this field and take advantage of their ability to pretest messages, measure and describe audiences, and report on the effect of the mass media. Even without formal research, however, it is possible to increase the feedback by means of reports from field staffs and workers and from volunteer observers and local officials, and by encouraging comments, suggestions, and reports from members of the audience.

The point is that adequate feedback will not come to the mass media unless they work actively at obtaining it. And without a considerable amount of feedback, the media will operate blindfolded. They will not know whether they are meeting the needs and wishes of the audiences they are reaching, or whether one kind of message or treatment is more effective than another in accomplishing what they are expected to accomplish. Therefore, the problem of feedback is one of the basic problems that a country must solve in order to use its media efficiently and give its people the information they need and want.

13. *A developing country should draw up a special statute of information at the same time that it draws up a plan for economic*

and social development, and the statute should be adapted, through successive revisions, to the successive phases of national development.

Professor Terrou, in his section, has written very convincingly of the importance to developing countries of an adequate statute of information. Smooth and rational development in this field, as in others, is most likely to occur within the framework of law. In this field, however, the rule of law is especially important because it helps to safeguard the rights and freedoms that are associated with information.

Professor Terrou has also sketched the principal subheads of such a statute, but points out that the statute must develop with the country. The latitude that a government feels it can allow the mass media may not be precisely the same at an early stage of national development as later. The responsibilities to be expected of the mass media may not be the same at each stage of development. Therefore, a developing country must be prepared to reconsider its statute of information in the light of its progress, its changing immediate goals, and its national aspirations.

In devising an adequate statute of information, a developing country has, in a certain sense, an advantage over older and further developed countries. The new countries, as Terrou says, are "unhampered by the weight of old regulations and interests." They can benefit from "the sum of the experiences accumulated in the world to help them choose institutions and rules" to fit their needs and their information system. But this accumulated experience is of no use to them unless it is collected and easily available. There is no such collection now. Professor Terrou's own book, *Legislation for Press, Film, and Radio,* is perhaps the best existing guide to statutes of information in different countries. But much more needs to be done toward assembling and describing the statutes and institutional arrangements that shape information in different countries. Just as new countries will benefit from the counsel of specialists in information law, so will these specialists need all the information they can get about the experience of other countries with different kinds of statutes and institutions. This is a need that inter-national organizations might well help to meet.

14. *A developing country should not hesitate to make use of new technical developments in communication, in cases where these new developments fit its needs and capabilities.*

In earlier sections of this book we have spoken of new technical developments, and therefore shall not discuss them at any length here. The important point is that developing countries can jump many steps in communication technology. It is not necessary for them to advance through the hand press to the steam press to the electrically driven rotary to the offset press; when appropriate they can go to offset printing at once. It is not necessary for them to go through hand setting to type casting to "cold type" methods; when appropriate, they can go to photosetting and cold type immediately. Where a new way of teaching mathematics, or a new method of learning such as programmed instruction, seems promising, a developing country can try it without first trying all its predecessors. In some cases, certainly, these newer devices and methods will save time and money, and get the information flowing more efficiently. A developing country will benefit from keeping itself informed about these newest developments, and need not be afraid to try them.

Countries where technology is further advanced have a special obligation and opportunity to make their experience with new communication devices available to the developing countries. And this leads into recommendation 15.

15. *Countries should share their experience in using the mass media and other information channels to speed economic development and social change.*

The flow of expert advisers and advice, through Unesco, great foundations, and bilateral arrangements, from economically advanced countries to developing countries, has been encouraging and fruitful. Certainly the expertise and the training opportunities of the countries more experienced in mass communication can usefully continue to be offered to the less-experienced countries. But we want to suggest that the developing countries, too, have experiences to share.

Country A has tried programmed instruction; 50 other developing countries would like to know how well it worked. Country B has found a way to give in-service training to teachers by radio; Country C has used a combination of radio and correspondence study to educate children who have no secondary school in their areas; Country D has a new program for training printers; Country E has a new and efficient way to maintain village radio receivers. All these and many other experiences are potentially capable of saving other countries from mistakes and loss of money—and not only developing countries. The rural forums are a case in point. Canada's pioneering work with such forums was of great help to India, and India's experience in turn was of aid to Japan and France. France made them into *television* forums, and this experience with television was helpful to Japan, and aided India to establish its first teleclubs. A number of other countries have now been able to review all this earlier experience and make their own plans for forums.

Obviously, experience of these kinds deserves to be shared. How can it best be done? Publication is one way. The rural radio forums in different countries were described in a series of books and articles. A world-wide series of case studies in the application of mass communication to national development would be of very great value. Another way to share experience is by exchanging communication personnel between countries. Visitors can be invited to see especially interesting applications or demonstrations, and regional workshops can be held to exchange experiences. The communication equivalent of the experimental and demonstration farm does not exist, and yet the idea is feasible; a series of such "farms" throughout the developing world might be of incalculable aid to the whole region.

There is so much to learn about the use of information to aid economic and social development, and so little margin for error or waste in the developing countries, that it is both moral and prudent to share what is found out.

A final word. After so many pages spent analyzing the problems —the difficulties, the complexities, the things to be done—let us not lose sight of the essential challenge of the idea. How fortuitous, how almost miraculous it seems that, at this moment of greatest need for swift and widespread information in the developing countries, modern mass communication should be available to multiply informational resources! It is hardly possible to imagine national economic and social development going on at its present pace *without* some modern information multiplier; and indeed, without mass communication, probably the great freedom movements and national stirrings of the last few decades never would have come about at all.

But we must remember that the full power of mass communication has never been used, in any developing country, to push economic and social development forward. This is the really exciting question: how much could we increase the present rate of development, how much could we smooth out the difficulties of the "terrible ascent," how much further could we make our resources go, how much more could we contribute to the growth of informed, participating citizens in the new nations, if we were to put the resources of modern communication skillfully and fully behind economic and social development? This is the challenge of the evidence presented here.

Appendixes

A. Mass Media in the Developing Continents

Unless otherwise stated, figures given in the following table are for 1961, except for the last column, Literacy, where they are for 1950. Figures for other years are identified by superscript numbers; e.g., [59] indicates a 1959 figure. An asterisk indicates that data are estimated; — indicates a figure less than 0.1 (usually nil); ... indicates that data are not available. Source: Unesco, 1964.

AFRICA

	Daily Newspapers Copies per 100	Radio Receivers per 100	Cinema Seats per 100	Television Receivers per 100	Number of Dailies	Number of Radio Transmitters	Literacy, % (age 15+ except as noted)
Algeria	2.4	6.0	1.8[59]	0.6	8	16[60]	15–20
Basutoland (U.K.)	—	0.6[60]	...	—	—	...	50–55
Bechuanaland (U.K.) . . .	—	0.6	0.5[56]	—	—	1[60]	20–25
Burundi	—	...	...	—	—	...	...
Cameroon Republic	0.2	0.3[59]	...	—	2	7	5–10
Cape Verde Islands (Portugal)	—	1.2	1.6[60]	—	—	3[59]	21 (all ages)
Chad	0.03	0.3	0.1[59]	—	1	2[59]	...
Comoro Islands (France)	—	0.3[59]	...	—	—	1[60]	20–25
Congo Republic (Brazzaville)	0.1[59]	1.3[60]	...	—	3[59]	12	...

AFRICA (continued)

	Daily Newspapers Copies per 100	Radio Receivers per 100	Cinema Seats per 100	Television Receivers per 100	Number of Dailies	Number of Radio Transmitters	Literacy, % (age 15+ except as noted)
Congo Republic (Leopoldville)	0.1	0.2[59]	0.08[59]	—	7	12 AM[60] 2 FM	35–40
Dahomey Republic	0.1	0.3	0.2	—	2	4	...
Ethiopia	0.2	0.5	...	—	10	6	1–5
Gambia	0.5[59]	0.9	0.8	—	1[59]	1[62]	5–10
Gabon Republic	0.1	5.6	...	—	1	3	...
Ghana	3.2	1.9	1.0	—	4	7	20–25
Guinea Republic	0.02[59]	1.3	...	—	1[59]	4[59]	...
Ivory Coast Republic	0.3	1.7[60]	...	—	1	5	...
Kenya (U.K.)	1.4	0.8	0.2	—	6	13 AM[59] 1 FM	20–25
Liberia	0.08	7.7[60]	...	—	1	9	5–10
Libya	0.7	6.2[59]	1.7[55]	—	2	5 AM 1 FM	13[54]
Malagasy Republic	0.9	2.2	0.2	—	12	9[60]	33[53] (14+)
Mali Republic	0.02[60]	0.2	...	—	1[60]	3[60]	...
Mauritania Republic	—	2.5	...	—	—	3	
Mauritius (U.K.)	*8.7	6.6	5.7	—	10	2	52[52]
Morocco	2.2	4.6	0.8	0.04	12	19	14[60]
Mozambique (Portugal)	0.3[60]	0.6[60]	0.25[59]	—	4[60]	19[59]	1–5
Niger Republic	0.03[60]	*0.3	...	—	1[60]	2[59]	...
Nigeria	0.8	0.4	0.2[60]	0.02	23	26 AM 1 FM	10–15
Portuguese Guinea	0.2[60]	0.3	0.1[60]	—	1[60]	1	1–5
Réunion (France)	6.5[60]	5.3	1.8[60]	—	3[60]	2[60]	39[54]

...odesia and Nyasaland	2.0[59]	1.8	0.2	0.3	5	21	20–25† 5–10
Rwanda	—	...	...	—	—	...	
St. Helena (U.K.)........	—	0.5	12.0[60]	—	—	...	95[56] (16+)
Sao Tomé and Principe (Portugal)	—	1.4[60]	1.6			1[59]	15–20
Senegal Republic	0.6[60]	4.7[50]	...		1	8[59]	...
Seychelles (U.K.)	1.9	1.4	2.0		1	1[59]	46[60]
Sierra Leone	0.7	0.4	0.06[60]		2	2[60]	5–10
Somalia	0.15[59]	1.2	0.7[58]		1[59]	4[59]	1–5
South Africa	5.7	6.6	...		21	45[59]	40–45
South West Africa (Rep. of South Africa) ..	1.4[60]	3.5[58]	0.7[50]		2[60]	...	20–25
Spanish Equatorial Region	0.5	...	1.1[56]		1	2	20–25
Sudan	0.4	0.09[60]	0.6[57]		7	4	12[56]
Swaziland (U.K.)	—	0.8	0.2[59]		—	...	23[56] (all ages)
Tanganyika	0.4	0.4	0.2[60]	—	3	6	5–10
Togo Republic	0.4	0.4	0.1[57]	—	1	3	1–5
Tunisia	1.9	6.3	0.9[60]	0.5	4	5[60]	10–15
United Arab Republic......	2.0[58]	6.6	1.0	0.3	35	28	29[60]
Uganda	0.8[60]	1.3	0.2[59]		5[60]	5[60]	(10+) 25[59] (16+)
Upper Volta Republic.....	0.01	0.8[59]	...	—	2	3	...
Zanzibar and Pemba.......	0.3	1.6	1.1	—	3	2	5–10

† The percentage 20–25 is for Southern and Northern Rhodesia; 5–10 is for Nyasaland.

ASIA

	Daily Newspapers Copies per 100	Radio Receivers per 100	Cinema Seats per 100	Television Receivers per 100	Number of Dailies	Number of Radio Transmitters	Literacy, % (age 15+ except as noted)
Afghanistan	0.5	0.2[60]	0.07[60]	—	12	4[59]	1–5
Bahrein	—	9.9	*8.2[60]	0.7	—	2	25[59] (16+)
Brunei (U.K.)	—	7.5	*9.5[60]	—	—	3[59]	43[60]
Burma	1.1[60]	0.5	1.3[60]	—	39[60]	5[60]	58[54] (16+)
Cambodia	0.6[60]	0.6[60]	...	0.006	9[60]	2[60]	31[58]
Ceylon	3.6[60]	3.8	1.9[58]	—	10	23	68[53]
China (Mainland)	1.9[55]	1.0[59]	...	0.003[60]	392[52]	233[59]	45–50
China (Taiwan)	6.6	5.5	4.0[59]	0.001	31	125	54[56]
Federation of Malaya	6.7[60]	4.1	2.2[60]	—	28[60]	21	47[57]
Hong Kong (U.K.)	22.0	5.4	2.5	0.3	44	5 AM 2 FM	71[61]
India	1.1[60]	0.5	0.6[58]	0.01[60]	465[60]	59[60]	24[61] (all ages)
Indonesia	1.1[59]	1.3	0.6[57]	—	94[59]	62[59]	15–20
Iran	1.5	6.5	0.7	0.2	27	22[59]	15[56]
Iraq	1.0[57]	2.1[60]	1.3[60]	0.7	16[57]	5[59]	10–15
Israel	21.0[57]	21.5	6.9[59]	—	28[57]	11[59]	90–95
Japan	41.6	18.7	3.4	9.8	157	394 AM 6 FM	98[60]
Jordan	1.8[60]	3.8[60]	...	—	6[60]	4[59]	15–20
Korea (North)	...	7.1	...	—	...	8	35–40
Korea, Republic of	6.9	4.6	0.7[59]	0.08	45[60]	39 AM 25 FM	77[55]
Kuwait	0.4[60]	34.8	0.9[59]	0.6	1	2[60]	34[57] (all ages)
Laos	0.06[57]	1.1	0.3[60]	—	1[57]	4	15–20

278

Lebanon	9.7[59]	6.1[60]	6.2[60]	1.6	46[59]	3[59]	45–50
Macao (Portugal)	11.2	2.1[60]	4.2[60]	—	5	2[59]	70[60]
Mongolian People's Republic	10.3[57]	2.3	...		3[57]	3[59]	55–60
Muscat and Oman	—	0.2	...				1–5
Nepal	0.08[60]	0.1[59]	...		13[60]	2[59]	5[52]
North Borneo (U.K.)	3.7	4.4			8	2	24[60]
Pakistan	0.7[60]	0.3	0.2		8[60]	19 AM 4 FM	19[61]
Philippines	1.8[60]	2.2[59]	2.6[58]	0.2	22[60]	120 AM 7 FM	73[60]
Portuguese Timor	—	0.1[60]	0.08[60]	—	—	1	1–5
Qatar	34.8[56]	...	...			...	5–10
Ryukyu Is. (U.S.A.)	2.5	...	4.0[59]	0.4	15[58]	6	75
Sarawak (U.K.)	0.4[60]	5.5	2.6[60]	—	8	4[60]	22[60]
Saudi Arabia	20.8	1.2[59]	...	0.1	4[60]	4[59]	1–5
Singapore	1.9[58]	8.8	2.7	—	8	8	50[57]
Syria	1.9[58]	5.7[59]	0.9[59]	0.02	40[58]	16[59]	25–30
Thailand	1.1[60]	0.6[60]	0.5[60]	0.3	27[60]	20[60]	68[60]
Trucial Oman	—	...	1.7[60]	—	—	...	1–5
Vietnam (North)	...		...	—			15–20
Vietnam, Republic of	2.8[58]	0.9	0.6[58]	—	26[58]	18[59]	15–20
West Irian	0.2	1.3	0.6[57]	—	1	7[60]	5–10
Yemen	—	...	...	—	—	1[59]	1–5

MIDDLE AMERICA

	Daily Newspapers Copies per 100	Radio Receivers per 100	Cinema Seats per 100	Television Receivers per 100	Number of Dailies	Number of Radio Transmitters	Literacy, % (age 15+ except as noted)
Bahama Islands (U.K.)	11.1	16.7	2.1	0.2	2	1	85[53] (5+)
Bermuda (U.K.)	41.9	48.4	5.8	21.8	2	2 AM 1 FM	97 (14+)
British Honduras	4.3	2.6	6.1[60]	—	2	3[59]	88[60] (10+)
Costa Rica	9.4	6.6	6.3[60]	0.6	6	48[60]	79
Cuba	8.8	18.8	4.8	7.2	10	119 AM 23 FM	78[52]
Dominican Republic	2.7[60]	4.8	1.2[60]	0.6	5[60]	76 AM 9 FM	60[56]
El Salvador	*4.9	14.1	*2.1	0.8	13	24[59]	48[61] (10+)
Guadeloupe (France)	1.1[59]	2.3	2.7[54]	—	1	2	65[54]
Guatemala	2.3	5.4	1.9	0.9	6	82	29
Haiti	1.1[60]	0.5	0.2[58]	0.05	6[60]	20[60]	11
Honduras	2.4[59]	2.6	2.2[60]	0.2	6	23[59]	45[61]
Martinique (France)	1.8	6.8[59]	2.2[60]	—	1	5[59]	74[54]
Mexico	8.3	*9.7	5.5	2.5	190	400	65[60]
Netherlands Antilles	12.9	20.1[60]	4.7[60]	4.1	5	9[60]	70–75
Nicaragua	6.6[59]	6.6	3.8[60]	0.3	8[59]	37[60]	38
Panama	10.4	17.2	4.9[60]	2.8	10	64[58]	78[60]
Puerto Rico	6.1	15.0	3.3[59]	...	5	...	81[60] (10+)
St. Pierre and Miquelon (France)	...	20.0	14.0[59]	—	...	1[60]	99[52]
Virgin Islands (U.K.)	...	...	2.1[60]	—	...	...	93[60]
Virgin Islands (U.S.A.)	11.2	...	4.7[59]	—	3	...	85–90

Barbados (Federation of West Indies)	8.5	15.9	2.5	—	2	...	91[46]
Jamaica (West Indies)	6.3	12.8	2.4[57]	—	2	8 AM[60] / 4 FM	82[60]
Trinidad and Tobago	7.0	8.6[60]	5.1[60]	0.002	2	4 AM[60] / 3 FM	74[46]
Leeward Islands:							
Antigua	0.1[60]	0.5	...	—	2[60]	1[60]	89[60]
Montserrat	..	0.4	...	—	..	1[60]	80[60]
St. Kitts, Nevis, Anguilla	0.3[60]	...	...	—	3[60]	...	88[60]
Windward Islands						8 AM / 1 FM	
Dominica	..	0.4[59]	..	—	—		59[48]
Grenada	*0.2	0.3[58]	0.2	—	1		76[46]
St. Lucia	..	0.2	0.3	—	1[54]		52[46]
St. Vincent	0.2[60]	..	..	—	1[60]		76[46]

SOUTH AMERICA

	Daily Copies Newspapers per 100	Radio Receivers per 100	Cinema Seats per 100	Television Receivers per 100	Number of Dailies	Number of Radio Transmitters	Literacy, % (age 15+ except as noted)
Argentina	15.5[59]	19.0	5.2[60]	3.3	233[59]	78[59]	85–90
Bolivia	2.6	7.3	1.3[58]	—	6	43[59]	32
Brazil	5.4[60]	6.4	2.9[60]	2.2	291[60]	876 AM[60] 54 FM	49
British Guiana	7.9	7.2	5.5	—	3	5	75–80
Chile	13.4	13.0	5.2[60]	0.04	47	119	84[60]
Colombia	5.5	14.9	3.9[59]	1.4	32	160[62]	62[51]
Ecuador	5.6	3.9	2.0	0.1	24	135[59]	56
Falkland Islands (U.K.)	—	45.0	15.0[60]	—	1	2	90–95
French Guiana	15.6	3.1	5.5[60]	—	1	1[60]	65–70
Paraguay	3.7	8.3	0.8[60]	—	7	12[59]	66
Peru	4.7[59]	10.1[60]	3.0	0.8	49	95[59]	45–50
Surinam (Netherlands)	3.3[59]	14.5[60]	1.8[55]	—	4	5[60]	70–75
Uruguay	21.5	35.1	5.2[59]	2.1	27	97[60]	80–85
Venezuela	8.2	17.1	6.8[59]	3.5	29	78[59]	66[61]

B. A Pattern for a Basic Mass Communication Inventory in a Developing Country

Development starts where a country is. The first step in planning communication development is to find out, as accurately as possible, where the country is, in relation to need, in its communication development. This calls, in the first place, for a basic inventory of facilities and services.*

The basic inventory. Imagine a chart like this:

Medium	Present Facilities	Coverage Area	Audiences Reached	Services Performed
Radio	_____	_____	_____	_____
Newspapers	_____	_____	_____	_____
Films	_____	_____	_____	_____
Books	_____	_____	_____	_____
Magazines	_____	_____	_____	_____
Television	_____	_____	_____	_____

The first objective of a basic inventory is to complete such a chart. Now of course the answers cannot very well be set down in the form of a chart, because the questions are too many and the answers would take too much space. But the chart can serve as a checklist of answers to be sought.

For example, here are some of the things to be known about radio:

How many transmitting stations are there, what is their power, and what areas do their signals reach? Are the transmitters and studio equipment modern? How many receivers are there, how many of them individually owned, how many in public places, how many in working order? How many and what kind of people listen

---

* We are not specifying who should do this planning. It will depend on the country where it is to be done. In some countries, it will naturally fall to the planning commission; in others to a ministry. In countries where part of mass communication is privately owned, it is assumed that the private sector will be brought into the study and the planning. Some countries have discovered, for example, the usefulness of a national committee on mass communication representing both public and private sectors.

to the radio, so far as that is known? What programs have larger audiences than others? What do people use the radio for, what services do they expect of it, what do they think of it? Is it being used in schools, or otherwise for training, and if so to what extent and with what result? What content is the radio carrying, what sorts of needs and interests are its programs designed to serve, and what language groups can use it?

About newspapers: How many are there and where are they? What kinds of printing equipment have they? How many of them are served by news agencies? What is the supply and cost of newsprint? To what areas do they circulate copies? How large are their circulations, and how reliable are circulation figures? How do circulation totals compare with numbers of literates? What is known about secondary uses of copies—that is, copies read by or to persons who are not subscribers? What kind of picture of environment would a person get by reading one of these newspapers? How well do they cover local news? National news? Foreign news? How well do they represent the news and themes of national development? What do the people think of the newspapers? Do they trust them? Do they feel the papers are serving major needs for information?

About films: Where are films made in the country, how many and what kind of films? What kinds of film-making equipment do the studios have? What facilities exist for exhibiting films: how many theaters, projectors in schools or other public places, film vans? How many and what kind of films are imported? What is known about the size and composition of film audiences? Are films being used in the schools or otherwise for training, and if so to what extent and with what results? What kinds of films are available for viewing in the country, and what kinds of needs and interests do they seem to serve?

About books: What are the country's facilities for publishing and printing books? What percentage and what types of books are printed locally, and what percentage and kind are imported? What facilities exist for selling or otherwise distributing books? How nearly adequate, in number and quality, is the supply of schoolbooks? Technical books? Reference books? What is the annual sale of books by type? Can they be bought in all parts of the country? Where are libraries available and what kind of contents do they maintain? In general, how does the supply of available books represent the topics most urgent to the country at a given time?

About magazines: What types of magazines are published, and what printing and publishing facilities exist for the purpose? Where do they circulate, and what are the facilities for circulation? How large are their circulations, and how reliable are these estimates? What type of content is going to readers through these magazines? What needs and interests do they seem designed to serve?

About television, the same questions may be asked as for radio, with slight adaptation.

Now imagine another chart of elements and services that relate to mass media development, like this:

Element	Present Development	Projected Development	Measure of Adequacy
Literacy			
Schooling			
Electrification			
Transportation			
Postal service			
Telephone and telegraph			
News agency			
Training			

About each of the blanks in the preceding chart a series of questions can be asked, of which these are examples:

Literacy. What is the best present estimate of illiteracy in the country? Where are the illiterates? How can they best be reached with information? At what rate is the proportion changing, and what future rate of change may be counted on? Could the society absorb more literates if they were produced?

Schooling. What proportion of children of different ages are in school? How long do they stay in school? How many of them stay long enough to acquire and retain functional literacy? What is the proportion of people with different amounts of education at present, and what is it expected to be ten years from now? Where are primary schools not available? Secondary schools? Technical schools? To what extent are the developmental needs for educated persons now being met?

Electrification. Where is electricity now available? What proportion of the villages are connected to the mains? What expansion is planned? To what extent now, and to what extent ten years from now, will the lack of electrification retard the use of radio and the growth of other mass media?

Transportation. To what extent does the availability of roads, public transportation, and vehicles now handicap the circulation of printed materials and films, and the maintenance of electronic communication machinery? What is the situation expected to be like in ten years?

Telephone and telegraph. How extensive and efficient are these services? How costly are they? Do they retard the coverage and circulation of news? What expansion is planned, and is it likely to be adequate?

News agency. Is there a national news service? If so, what news exchange does it have, outside the country? How adequate is the flow of news to it within the country? What correspondents does it maintain? What kind of service does it give subscribing newspapers? Is it able to offer its service at a cost small newspapers can pay? What plans has it for expanding its service?

Training. Is development or efficient use of the mass media now being held back in any way by scarcity of trained personnel of any kind? If so, what kind and how many trained persons are likely to be needed? What facilities are there in the country for training these kinds of employees? What facilities and programs are there for upgrading present staffs? What are the likely dimensions of future needs for trained personnel?

In addition to these, the basic inventory ought to include two other areas. One of these is a review of import, tariff, and tax policies and legislation as they relate to mass communication. For example:

Type of Policy or Law	Present Situation	What It Accomplishes	Effect on Mass Communication
Import restrictions (e.g., on newsprint; printing, broadcast, and film equipment; film stock, etc.)			
Tariffs (on communication materials of kind mentioned above)			
Taxes (on communication materials and enterprises)			

We shall not cite questions for the first column, inasmuch as we have talked about the problem several times before. Here a country should review its present quota, tariffs, and taxes as they apply to the needs of the communication industry. Under the second column, it should try to arrive at a clear picture of what the policy or legislation now accomplishes. Does it protect local industry? How much money, if any, does it bring in? How much foreign currency does it save? And finally, under the third column, an effort should be made to find out what the policy or legislation does to mass communication. Is it in any way harmful to growth? Does it reduce the supply of newsprint, projectors, cameras, presses, radio receivers, or any other supplies below the level of need? Does it make it hard for privately owned media to operate profitably? What other effects on the media or their services can be attributed to it?

Finally, a country should look at what the mass media are presently contributing and what they might contribute to some of the great programs of development:

Development Area	What Are Media Now Contributing	What Media Could Contribute if Able
Literacy		
Education		
Agriculture		
Industrial training		
Health		
Citizenship		
Others as desired		

Here the problem is to obtain a clear picture of what the mass communication system is now doing to further national development in each of these areas, and an estimate of the needs that could be met by the media if they were better equipped or staffed or financed or otherwise prepared to do their development job.

For example, let us take *education* as a sample area. An inquiry might begin by finding out about the adequacy, both in numbers and quality, of schoolbooks available. It would be desirable to know how many schools have projectors, and what variety and number of instructional films are available to be shown on the projectors. How many schools have radios—or television receivers, if television is available—and what school programs are available? How are these media used in the classroom—how often, for what purposes, and with what results? What might the media contribute to education that they are not now offering? Are more receivers, more projectors, more films, more programs needed? Are different programs and films needed? Could the media undertake responsibilities they may not now be facing up to, such as furnishing in-service training to teachers, or helping relatively untrained teachers with some of their classes, or offering classes to people who must study at home or in villages where there are no schools?

Is there a need in the country to try new media such as programmed instruction? Is there need for workshops or training to help schools make best use of the media? This is the kind of question that must be asked.

On the basis of many questions like the ones we have suggested, a country will be in position to sum up its present state of communication development. Where and on what subject is the flow of information now inadequate for the purposes of national development? Are there language groups or rural groups not now being adequately served? Are the media being used to their capacity to bring illiterates into the stream of modern facts and ideas? Are the schools, adult centers, and industrial training programs being helped as much as mass communication can help them? Are field workers being provided with the print, film, radio support they need? Are the ordinary people being provided the information they need to be at home in the modern world and take active part in public affairs? And is the system working so that all the information goes downward from the central government and the cities to the villages, or are there also channels by which information can flow laterally and upward? In other words, taking stock of things as they are, where is the country not getting the information it needs? When a country arrives at questions like these, then it needs—

Standards for communication development. Given that basic appraisal, a developing country usually seeks a standard against which to measure communication development. How big should its system be? Some help may be found in the measuring stick listed below:

a) The Unesco general standard—the so-called Unesco "minima" of ten daily newspaper copies, five radio receivers, two cinema seats, two television receivers for each 100 persons in the population. As we have pointed out, the radio standard is relatively easy to achieve, whereas the daily newspaper standard is much more difficult, mainly because it depends on a considerable growth in literacy and education. Considering the importance of radio in the early stages of national development, a nation might be well advised to aim for more radio receivers than the Unesco standards require. If seven or eight radios, rather than five, are available per 100 persons, it is much easier to fill the information gap until printed media are widely read.

b) The standards of industrialized countries. For example, it is noted that Europe has 23 daily newspaper copies, 21 radio receivers, five cinema seats, and seven television sets, per 100 people. Or a single country can provide a standard. Asian countries can compare their development with that of Japan (42 daily newspaper copies, 16 radio receivers, four cinema seats, ten television sets). Latin American countries can compare their development, for example with that of Uruguay (22 daily newspaper copies, 35 radio receivers, five cinema seats, two television sets). And such a comparison should not be limited to the four items we have been mentioning. It might well also include literacy, education, community development services, newsprint, electrification, flow of news, and others of the items mentioned in the previous section.

c) Standards based on the available audience. What mass media development could the present audience absorb? For example, the number of literates limits the number of newspaper copies that can be used. But suppose that the present literate population were served adequately with newspapers: how many additional copies would there have to be? Similarly, suppose that radio were made available wherever it is needed in the population: how many additional receivers and transmitters would that take? Suppose that schools and adult education were to be served adequately by radio and film: how many more radio receivers, film projectors, instructional radio programs, film libraries, and so forth, would be needed? How many more books do the schools need, and what additional capacity for printing does that imply? And in general, what kinds of need for information does the audience feel? Do some groups feel deprived of public affairs information? Do they feel that information does not circulate so well upward as downward in the hierarchy? Do some feel the need of how-to-do-it information, or cultural programs, or language training? In a developing country as well as in one that is economically advanced, the wishes and needs of the audience are a matter of importance, and a policy of enlightened audience relations is much to be desired.

d) Standards based on the needs of national development. In most countries the agencies responsible for modernizing agriculture will be making statements of this kind: if we had X amount of additional radio coverage, we could do better or faster with campaign Y. The agencies responsible for modernizing education will say: If we had A more film projectors and B more books, we could raise the level of education by an amount C. The agencies responsible for special training of industrial and service employees will be expressing their need for audiovisual training aids. The responsible officials of the literacy program will be able to estimate what they could do with more help from radio or films or printed materials. The community development officials will have an estimate of what additional help they need in order to get information into the villages. The political leaders will be able to estimate the amount of increase in the flow of public affairs information that is needed to increase public participation in government. In other words, it should be possible to estimate the order of magnitude of the informational needs now perceived in the national development program, against which to measure present capabilities.

e) Projecting needs into the future. It is necessary to consider not only what needs are now perceived, but what order of need can be foreseen. Any development program has to work several years ahead, and its plans must therefore be made to intersect society at a point where society has already changed and its needs are already different from the present. Therefore, an effort must be made to forecast communication needs 5, 10, 15 years from the present. What is the expected rate of increase in literacy? How many school children will there be? What needs can be anticipated for industrial training? With economic betterment, what increase can be anticipated in the market for radio sets, newspapers, books, films? What different needs for information will come with the different phases of the development plan?

Given answers to questions like these, then a developing nation is ready to make an—

Estimate of requirements. If the resources revealed by the basic inventory are to be increased to meet the needs and standards decided on, then there will be certain requirements that must be spelled out as realistically as possible. What will the nation require in the way of—

a) New and upgraded facilities? How many new radio transmitters and studios will be required, or how can the range of present transmitters be extended? Where are new newspapers needed? Theaters? Libraries? What expansion, if any, is indicated in the printing industry? If television is in the plan, what will it require in the way of transmitters and studios? What expansion, if any, is needed in film-making facilities?

b) Equipment? How much printing machinery must be added? How much radio and television transmitting equipment? Cameras, sound recorders, and other film equipment? Radio and television receivers? Film projectors? Film vans? And so forth.

c) Supporting services and materials? What order of need can be forecast for newsprint? For the extension of electric mains throughout the country? For the development of a radio manufacturing industry? For radio and television maintenance services? For the provision of raw film? For additional telecommunication services? For improved transport or postal service?

d) Organizations? If there is no national news service, should there not be one? Should there be organizations to distribute films to schools or adult education centers? To what extent should community development, health, and agriculture field organizations be expanded or altered? Are state and national information organizations adequate to provide the information materials needed, and if not, what are the requirements?

e) Trained personnel? What will be the needs of the mass media, over the next years, for trained personnel in both technical and editorial-production activities? What training institutions or programs will be needed to provide them? What information service personnel, field or central, must be trained in efficient use of the mass media, and what are the requirements for training them? Who will train the trainers, if they are not already available? What in-service training will be necessary to upgrade present personnel of the media or the information services?

f) Research guidance? How extensive are the needs for communication research likely to be over the next years? How much call will there be for pretesting, audience studies, studies of campaigns, evaluations of programs? What research personnel or research facilities, in addition to those already available, will be required? What, if any, arrangements must be made to train research personnel?

g) Government administrative and legislative action? What is indicated that the government should do about import restrictions, tariffs, and taxes on informational materials and services? What legislative actions will help to establish the positions of the media?

h) Capital? What price tag can be put on each of these requirements? How much for capital investment, how much for operating funds? How much for import, how much for use within the country? How much will go into productive industry (e.g., radio or newsprint manufacture), how much into service activities (e.g., radio broadcasting)? How much can be expected of private capital (e.g., investment in privately owned media), how much must be government capital? How much is recoverable (e.g., advertising, sales, receiver license fees, and the like)?

C. What Communication Satellites Mean to the Developing Countries

In 1962, space communication became a fact. Through small communication satellites, orbiting the earth, it became possible to relay telephone, telegraph, radio, facsimile pictures, and television between points many thousands of miles apart. This dramatic new chapter in the history of man's communication is potentially, although not immediately, of great importance for the developing countries. Therefore, we are appending this note to try to make clear just how communication satellites may enter into national development.

A useful popular introduction to this very complex matter is provided by a recent Unesco publication, *Space Communication and the Mass Media.* This report goes into the possible developments and uses of communication satellites in more detail than can be done here, and is especially recommended to readers who are interested in national communication development but are not able to handle the vocabulary of telecommunication engineering.

Perhaps the most important thing to bear in mind is that communication by space satellite is presently in a very early stage. As the science matures, different kinds of communication satellites will appear, and they will have very different uses.

Communication satellites are described, in general terms, as being either synchronous or nonsynchronous, and as having high or low power. A nonsynchronous satellite (like Telstar) orbits the earth at an altitude of a few hundred miles, and is visible from any given point on earth for a period of minutes. A synchronous satellite (like Synchron) orbits at a much higher level, usually about 22,300 miles, at a speed that keeps it always over about the same point on earth. Therefore, a nonsynchronous satellite is useful to any two communicating points for only a short time, and requires a very sensitive and responsive tracking apparatus, so as to keep a receiving horn always pointed directly at the moving satellite. A synchronous satellite, on the other hand, requires no such responsive tracking apparatus, because the satellite appears to move little or not at all; but it does require a very sensitive receiver, because the weak signal of a low-power synchronous satellite comes from 22,000 or more miles away.

At the present time, the signals of neither the synchronous nor the nonsynchronous satellites are receivable by home apparatus, and indeed they are not receivable in any dependable way except by highly expensive apparatus, skillfully manned. Therefore, designers and communication engineers look forward to the time when high-powered communication satellites will become available. The "power" of a satellite refers to the strength of the signal it can send out. Now this power is very small indeed, corresponding to that of a very tiny electric light bulb. Ultimately, it will be possible, unless a better power source is found, to orbit nuclear reactors in communication satellites, so the signal will become powerful enough to activate home receivers. This, however, is for the future. Now we have only low-power communication satellites.

The first use of these new instruments which is likely to be important to developing countries is an expansion of facilities for telecommunication. Telstar and its immediate successors offer a chance to use more circuits for telephone, telegraph, radio, facsimile pictures, and television. These circuits must necessarily at the present time run from country to country; for example, the television system of Country A can be connected up with the television system of Country B through elaborate transmitting, tracking, and receiving apparatus. If an individual in Country B sees a television program or receives a telephone call from Country A via satellite, he receives it over Country B's facilities. That is, the program is rebroadcast from Country B's television stations, or forwarded on Country B's telephone lines. There is, as yet, no direct satellite communication from Country A to *an individual* in Country B; when this becomes possible, many varieties of international problems are sure to arise.

Perhaps the first effect of communication satellites in most of the developing countries is likely to be felt by news agencies and news media. Such satellites will make it possible to circulate more news and to extend live coverage of widely important news. It may be that satellites will help fill in some of the areas where radio coverage is still scant. Certainly satellites will exchange live television programs from country to country, continent to continent. Already, remarkable results in exchanging television programs have been achieved. The quality of both sound and picture has been excellent in transmissions between Europe and North America, and between North America and Japan, and there will doubtless be many occasions in the near future when the viewers of European international networks like Eurovision or Intervision will be seeing the same program as the viewers of the American networks, or even Asian networks. ★

Of course, such exchanges of television programs or live coverage of news will be limited to events and occasions of timely nature and high importance. Public events of international importance, like the Kennedy assassination and events that followed; sporting events of great international interest, like the Olympic Games— this kind of coverage will get priority. Operas, lectures, entertainment, and other less timely events will continue to be circulated by tape or by cable. But even before the satellite channels reach directly to developing countries, they should make direct coverage more easily and quickly available everywhere.

Even with low-power satellites, therefore, the channels between continents and nations should grow wider, and events of worldwide importance should come nearer to being seen and understood by a world-wide audience. But when high-power satellites come into use, then opportunities of an even more exciting kind will offer themselves to individual countries.

When satellites can rebroadcast a signal to ordinary receivers, then a country (if it is not too large) can, if it wishes, provide instructional television for all its schools from one studio and one transmitter. It can activate every radio station and serve every newspaper and radio news room from one central headquarters, if it so wishes, without a microwave or telephone network. In other words, the high-power synchronous satellite offers an opportunity for truly national communication, where desired.

Let us repeat that high-power synchronous satellites are still far in the future. It should also be pointed out that when they *do* become available, they will bring with them certain problems: overlapping of signals between countries, copyrights, performers' rights, assignment of channels so as not to interfere in the enor-

mous coverage areas these satellites will have, agreement on standards, the need to fit languages to the needs of a variegated audience, the problem of scheduling classes over a wide area for instructional broadcasts. These and many other problems will prevent such opportunities as the later satellites will offer from being
won easily. Long before satellite communication is fully developed, however, nations can plan toward meeting the problems and
opportunities it will bring.

Notes

Notes

Complete authors' names, titles, and publication data are given in the Bibliography, pp. 311–27.

INTRODUCTION

1. Deshmukh, p. 126.
2. For example, Max Weber, in *The Protestant Ethic,* explained much of the development of Western Europe in terms of a social norm that valued hard work and accomplishment over pleasure.
3. Forrest D. Murden, in *Headline Series* (New York: Foreign Policy Association, 1956, p. 6), reprinted in Pentony, p. 7.
4. Nehru, p. 414.

CHAPTER 1

1. The several studies of Tepoztlan in Mexico are classic records of what a highway does to village culture; for example, see Oscar Lewis. Rao examined the effect of a new road in an Indian village in "The Role of Information in Economic and Social Change."
2. For example, in some Latin American countries the chief cash exports are fruit, coffee, and sugar.
3. The classic economic theory of how capital is built by releasing some of the agricultural population to industry (labor in this case serving as capital), is by Ragnar Nurkse.
4. On this point, see the very clear exposition of the development process in M. F. Millikan and D. L. M. Blackmer, *The Emerging Nations* (Boston: Little, Brown, 1961), pp. 47ff.
5. These figures are found in a most useful issue of *Scientific American* (209, No. 3, September 1963) devoted to articles on economic development: "The Development of Nigeria" is by Wolfgang F. Stolper, and there are parallel articles on the development of India, by Pitambar Pant, and the development of Brazil, by Celso Furtado. Brazil's agricultural production has been increasing at an average rate of nearly 5 per cent for the last 15 years, but the increase has largely been nullified by population growth. The country now saves about 17 per cent of its national income, and plans to invest about 18 per cent from public and private sources combined. India plans to increase its

rate of savings to 20 per cent by 1975, and its present five-year plan calls for an investment of 11 per cent. The goals of the plan are, by 1966, to expand agricultural production by 27 per cent, industrial production by 70 per cent, and national income by 30 per cent.

6. Millikan and Blackmer, p. 23.

7. Frederick Harbison, "Education for Development," *Scientific American,* 209, No. 3 (1963): 140.

8. *Ibid.*

9. *Ibid.,* pp. 144–47.

10. Coombs, pp. 14–19. For a statement of the economic importance of education, see Strumilin, "The Economics of Education in the USSR," *International Social Science Journal,* 14, No. 4 (1962): 633–46. That entire number of the journal is useful for students of human resources in economic development. It contains a consideration of "The Concept of Human Capital," by M. Debeauvais; W. Arthur Lewis on "Education and Economic Development"; and a report of the 1962 Warsaw conference on the Marxian theory of economic development. See also Adiseshiah, "Education and Development" and "Human Resources"; Schultz, "Education and Economic Growth"; and Max F. Millikan, "Education for Innovation" (Council on World Tensions, *Restless Nations*), pp. 131–47.

11. For treatment of some of these problems of innovation, see the papers on culture change and economic development in Hoselitz (*Progress of Underdeveloped Areas*), Spicer, and Foster. Lucian Pye has a good discussion of middleman roles in "Administrators, Agitators, and Brokers."

12. Zinkin, pp. 132–41.

13. Nair, *Blossoms in the Dust.*

14. John Condliff, in *SRI Journal–1963,* 1: 16.

15. McClelland, *The Achieving Society.* See also the use E. E. Hagen has made of the idea of achievement values in his volume *On the Theory of Social Change.*

16. Weber, *The Protestant Ethic*; Schumpeter, *Theory of Economic Development.*

17. Staley, pp. 390–91.

18. Rao, "The Role of Information."

19. Mead, "Applied Anthropology, 1955," pp. 94–108. Quoted and commented on in Foster, p. 264.

20. One of the reports to come out of Mainland China is that "everyone *hsueh hsi*"—studies.

21. Daniel Lerner, "Toward a Communication Theory of Modernization," in Pye, *Communications and Political Development,* p. 341.

22. *Ibid.*

23. *Ibid.,* p. 348.

24. For an example of this new interest among researchers, see Pye, *Communications and Political Development.*

25. Lerner, *The Passing of Traditional Society.* Lerner is professor of sociology at the Massachusetts Institute of Technology.

26. *Ibid.,* p. 43.   27. *Ibid.,* p. 45.

28. *Ibid.*, p. 60.   29. *Ibid.*, p. 50.
30. *Ibid.*, p. 52.   31. *Ibid.*, p. 54.
32. Whereas traditional man would tend to reject innovation by saying, "It has never been thus," the mobile modern man, says Lerner, is more likely to ask, "Does it work?" and try it. (*Ibid.*, p. 49.)
33. For supporting data, see the study by Hirabayashi and El Khatib on Egypt and one by Ozdil on Turkey.
34. Y. V. L. Rao is now Associate Director of the Press Institute of India. At the time he did his field study, he was a research fellow of the Institute for Communication Research at Stanford University. His study will be published by the University of Minnesota Press.
35. Compare the effect of the new road in a Mexican village, reported by Oscar Lewis.
36. Rao, summary, p. 2.
37. *Ibid.*, pp. 2–3.   38. *Ibid.*, p. 5.
39. *Ibid.*, p. 2. Compare with these conclusions of Rao the mostly supportive evidence in Varma's Columbia dissertation (*Dissertation Abstracts*, 19, No. 9 [1959]: 2404–5). Another very interesting note on developmental communication within Asia is Lucian Pye's comparison of the old and new communication systems in Burma (*Politics, Personality, and Nation Building*, especially pp. 20ff).
40. Doob, *Communication in Africa.*
41. *Ibid.*, p. 372.   42. *Ibid.*, p. 289.
43. *Ibid.*, p. 158.   44. *Ibid.*, p. 286.
45. *Ibid.*, p. 327.   46. *Ibid.*, pp. 316–17.
47. *Ibid.*, pp. 330–31.   48. *Ibid.*, p. 372.
49. See Holmberg, pp. 63–107. Dr. Holmberg is professor of anthropology at Cornell.
50. *Ibid.*, p. 79.   51. *Ibid.*, p. 105.

CHAPTER 2

1. This was a joint project of the Institut Français de Presse of the University of Paris and the Institute for Communication Research of Stanford University. It has not yet been published because the untimely death of Jacques Kayser left some of the important work unfinished.

The countries and newspapers represented are as follows: Argentina: *La Prensa, La Razón, Los Andes.* Australia: *Geelong Advertiser, Melbourne Age, Daily Mirror.* Brazil: *O Globo, O Estada de São Paulo.* Egypt: *Al Jomhouria, Al Ahram, Al Ayyam.* France: *Le Monde, Le Progrès, Le Parisien Libéré.* India: *The Times of India, Amrita Bazar Patrika, Hindustan Times.* Italy: *Il Mattino, Il Messagero, Corriere della Sera.* Japan: *Asahi, Mainichi, Hokkaido Shimbun.* Pakistan: *Dawn, Khyber Mail, Times.* Poland: *Trybuna Ludu, Zycie Warszawy, Trybuna Robotnicza.* United Kingdom: *The Times of London, The Daily Express, The Scotsman.* United States: *New York Times, New York Daily News, Des Moines Register.* USSR: *Pravda, Vechernaya Moskva, Kazakhstanskaya Pravda.*

31. See Festinger; also Lazarsfeld, Berelson, and Gaudet; and Berelson, Lazarsfeld, and McPhee.

32. See Cooper and Jahoda; also Kendall and Wolf.

33. See Kelley, "Salience of Membership and Resistance to Change of Group-Anchored Attitudes."

34. The most complete treatment of "influentials" is to be found in Katz and Lazarsfeld. There is a somewhat later review of the literature by Katz in "The Two Step Flow of Communication."

35. Many a political figure has said that he would willingly give up the editorial endorsement of a newspaper if he could frequently make news that appeared on the news pages. One political figure who expressed himself in that way was Franklin D. Roosevelt, who was elected to four terms in the United States Presidency despite editorial opposition by a great majority of newspapers.

36. Lazarsfeld and Merton, in Schramm, *Mass Communications,* p. 498. They add to what we have already quoted: "The operation of this status conferral function may be witnessed most vividly in the advertising pattern of testimonials to a product by 'prominent people.' Within wide circles of the population (though not within certain selected social strata), such testimonials not only enhance the prestige of the product but also reflect prestige on the person who provides the testimonials. They give public notice that the large and powerful world of commerce regards him as possessing sufficiently high status for his opinion to count with many people. In a word, his testimonial is a testimonial to his own status. The ideal, if homely, embodiment of this circular prestige pattern is to be found in the Lord Calvert series of advertisements centered on 'Men of Distinction.' The commercial firm and the commercialized witness to the merit of the product engage in an unending series of reciprocal pats on the back. In effect, a distinguished man congratulates a distinguished whisky which, through the manufacturer, congratulates the man of distinction on his being so distinguished as to be sought out for a testimonial to the distinction of the product. The workings of this mutual admiration society may be as nonlogical as they are effective. The audiences of mass media apparently subscribe to the circular belief: 'If you really matter, you will be at the focus of mass attention and, if you *are* at the focus of mass attention, then surely you must really matter.' "

37. For an illustration of mass media dialogue in one country, see Kraus.

38. Lazarsfeld and Merton, in Schramm, *Mass Communications,* p. 499.

39. See Cantril, *The Invasion from Mars.*

40. For a discussion of the "canalizing" effect of mass media, see Klapper, *The Effects of Mass Communication,* and Lazarsfeld and Merton in Schramm, *Mass Communications.*

41. Henry R. Cassirer, "Radio and Television in the Service of Information and Education in Developing Countries," typescript prepared for *World Radio Handbook,* 1963.

42. See, for example, Schramm, "What We Know about Learning from Instructional Television."

43. For a summary of research on programmed instruction until about January of 1963, see Schramm, *An Annotated Bibliography of the Research on Programmed Instruction.*

44. For more detail on this classification, see Schramm, "The Newer Educational Media in the United States."

45. Cassirer, "Radio and Television."

46. Cassirer suggests, "Under extreme circumstances of lack of school facilities, broadcasting . . . can create 'out of the air' a school system which is lacking on the ground."

CHAPTER 5

1. Dumont, "Accelerating African Agricultural Development."
2. *Ibid.*
3. For example, Rogers, *The Diffusion of Innovations.*
4. Ensminger, p. 25.
5. *Ibid.*, pp. 27, 32.
6. *Ibid.*, pp. 27, 28, 32.
7. Schramm and Winfield. With the consent of Dr. Winfield, I have borrowed quite closely in places from this paper.
8. For example, a very large survey of the use of different communication channels in agricultural adoption in the United States is reported in Wilkening. See also Rogers.
9. See Nicol, Shea, Simmins, and Sim.
10. Louis and Rovan; also Dumazedier.
11. Unesco, *Rural Television in Japan.*
12. Mathur and Neurath. Also Krishnamoorthy.
13. Mathur and Neurath.
14. Hodgdon, p. 7.
15. Report to US/AID.
16. Winfield and Hartman.
17. Reported in Foster, pp. 138–39.
18. Paper prepared by the French National Commission for Unesco.
19. *Ibid.*, p. 4.
20. See Tarroni; also Puglisi.
21. See two useful publications by Unesco, *Publications for New Literates: Seven Case Histories,* and *Publications for New Literates: Editorial Methods.*
22. For a review of research on the effectiveness of audiovisual materials, see Allen.
23. See Schramm and Winfield, p. 13.
24. Dieuzeide, pp. 45–58.
25. *Ibid.*, p. 46.
26. See the report submitted by the Soviet delegates to the expert conference on new media for education, March 1962, in Unesco, *New Methods and Techniques in Education,* pp. 35–40.
27. NHK, *The Listening Effects of "Radio English Classroom."*
28. NHK, *The Effects of "Radio Japanese Classroom."*

29. Xoomsai and Ratamangkala.

30. National Institute of Audio-Visual Education, *Effectiveness of Films in Teaching.*

31. See *Istanbul Physics Film Report.* This account follows closely the United Nations paper by Schramm and Winfield.

32. Femenías Loyola, pp. 37–43.

33. Personal report from Mr. Douglas Ensminger.

34. Arms, *End of Tour Report to US/AID.*

35. Cassirer, in *Report of International Seminar on Instructional Television,* p. 112.

36. See *Program Bulletin of the Asia Foundation,* 26 (1963): 3.

37. Reported in *Unesco Features,* No. 424, September 20, 1963, pp. 12–14.

38. Hadsell and Butts, pp. 28, 31.

39. Behrman, "The Faith That Moves the Mountains," in *When the Mountains Move,* pp. 31–44.

40. *Unesco Features.*

41. Henry R. Cassirer, "Radio and Television in the Service of Information and Education in Developing Countries," typescript prepared for *World Radio Handbook,* 1963.

42. Dieuzeide, p. 56.

43. Lefranc, p. 39.

CHAPTER 6

1. For a discussion of this, see the article by Hyman and Sheatsley.

2. Arms, "Diary from Nigeria."

3. For a description of the more common methods of communication research, see Nafziger and White. A useful handbook of social research in general is Leon Festinger and Daniel Katz, eds., *Research Methods in the Behavioral Sciences* (New York: Dryden Press, 1953). Another useful volume is Samuel P. Hayes, Jr., *Measuring the Results of Development Projects* (Paris: Unesco, 1959). For a review of communication research, see Schramm, "Mass Communication" *Annual Review of Psychology,* 13 (1962): 251–84.

4. Harold Lasswell, "The Structure and Function of Communication in Society," in Schramm, *Mass Communications,* p. 117.

5. Margaret Clark, p. 221.

6. Cooper and Jahoda.

7. Spurr, "Some Aspects of the Work of the Colonial Film Unit in West and East Africa."

8. Examples of such studies are the BBC Audience Studies; the *Continuing Study of Newspaper Readership,* published by the Bureau of Advertising, American Newspaper Publishers Association; Jacques Kayser's studies of the content of the French press; and program ratings for broadcasting.

9. See the review by Schramm, "Mass Communication," in *Annual Review of Psychology.* Also Hovland, Janis, and Kelley. Others of the Yale series are listed in the Schramm review.

10. Katz and Lazarsfeld.

11. Foster, pp. 137–38.

12. See Rogers.

13. Personal communication from Linwood Hodgdon, Ford Foundation and Ministry of Community Development, New Delhi, India.

14. Mead, *Cultural Patterns and Technical Change*, p. 185.

15. Redfield and Warner, p. 989.

16. Doob, *Communication in Africa*, pp. 159–60.

17. Beach, p. 468.

18. Doob, *Communication in Africa*, pp. 270–75.

19. *Ibid.*, p. 72.

20. Mead, *Cultural Patterns and Technical Change*, p. 255.

21. Foster, p. 132.

22. *Ibid.*, pp. 128–29.

23. Philips, p. 91; quoted in Foster, p. 129.

24. R. D. Linton and W. M. Hailey, quoted in Mead, *Cultural Patterns and Technical Change*, p. 184.

25. Doob cites this example (*Communication in Africa*, pp. 181–82) from Fortes, pp. 158–59, 211.

26. See Doob, *Communication in Africa*, pp. 182–83.

27. Quoted by Foster (pp. 127–28) from Margaret Clark, p. 232.

28. Wilson, "Problems of Survey Research in Modernizing Areas."

29. Wilson (*ibid.*, p. 232), discusses these problems. They are also mentioned by every social researcher who describes his technical problems in developing countries. For example, see Rudolph and Rudolph; Ralis, Suchman, and Goldsen; and Girard, all in *Public Opinion Quarterly*, 22, No. 3 (1958).

30. Rudolph and Rudolph.

31. *Ibid.*, p. 239.

32. Rao, in his study of two Indian villages.

33. Rudolph and Rudolph.

34. Rao.

35. Wilson, p. 234.

CHAPTER 7

1. Primary enrollments 40 to 51 per cent; secondary enrollments, 3 to 9 per cent.

2. *World Campaign for Universal Literacy*, United Nations Economic and Social Council, doc. E/3771, May 15, 1963, p. 55; and Corr. 1 and 2.

3. Pool, p. 235. There are now *five* radio receivers per 1,000 persons in India.

4. A developing country concerned with providing training for its communication personnel will be interested in Unesco's *The Training of Journalists: A World-wide Survey on the Training of Personnel for the Mass Media* (Paris, 1958). The volume is not restricted entirely to "journalists." It contains also some material on the training of broadcast and film personnel, and

describes all the main types of mass media training, along with specific descriptions of a number of national training patterns.

5. Unesco's handbook, *The Training of Journalists*, contains a great deal of information on journalism schools and curricula.

CHAPTER 8

1. Unesco, *Trade Barriers to Knowledge*, p. 5.
2. Lefranc, p. 39.
3. Francis Williams, *Transmitting World News*, pp. 79ff.

Bibliography

Adams, H. S., G. M. Foster, and P. S. Taylor. *Report on Community Development Programs in India, Pakistan and the Philippines.* Washington, D.C.: International Cooperation Administration, 1955.

Adams, R. N., *et al. Social Change in Latin America Today.* New York: Vintage Books, 1960.

Adiseshiah, Malcolm. "Education and Development," in Council on World Tensions, *Restless Nations.*

——. "Human Resources and the Development Decade" (mimeo.). Paris: Unesco, 1962.

Agarwala, A. N., and S. P. Singh. *The Economics of Underdevelopment.* Bombay: Oxford, 1958.

Allen, W. H. "Audio-Visual Communication Research," in *Encyclopedia of Educational Research.* New York: Macmillan, 1960.

Allport, Gordon, and Leo Postman. *The Psychology of Rumor.* New York: Holt, 1947.

Almond, Gabriel S., and James S. Coleman, eds. *The Politics of the Developing Areas.* Princeton, N.J.: Princeton University Press, 1960.

Aloba, Abiodan. "Journalism in Africa," *Gazette* (Leiden), 5, No. 4 (1960): 409–12.

Arms, George L. "Diary from Nigeria," *NAEB Journal,* September–October 1961, pp. 11–21.

——. *End of Tour Report to US/AID.* Nigeria, 1962.

Aronson, A. *Europe Looks at India: A Study of Cultural Relations.* Bombay: Hind Kitabs, 1946.

Asia Foundation. *Program Bulletin,* 26 (1963): 3.

Avery, Ronald W. "Management Training in Developing Countries," *New Commonwealth,* 21 (1955): 3.

Badiane, E. "Les Problèmes de l'information au Sénégal," *Le Mali* (Dakar), 5 (January 1960): 42–43.

Banfield, E. C. *The Moral Basis of a Backward Society.* Glencoe, Ill.: Free Press, 1958.

Barnett, H. G. *Innovation: The Basis of Cultural Change.* New York: McGraw-Hill, 1953.

Batton, T. R. *School and Community in the Territories.* London: Oxford University Press, 1959.

Bauer, P. T., and B. S. Yamey. *The Economics of Underdeveloped Countries.* Cambridge Economic Handbooks. Chicago: University of Chicago Press, 1957.

Baumann, H., and D. Westermann. *Les Peuples et les civilisations de l'Afrique, suivi de Les Langues et l'éducation.* Paris: Payot, 1948.

Beach, Harlan P. *A Geography and Atlas of Protestant Missions.* New York: Student Volunteer Movement for Foreign Missions, 1901.

Bebey, F. "L'Afrique de l'ouest et la télévision," *Afrique Nouvelle* (Dakar), June 1961.

Beck, Ursula. "Fernseh-Probleme an der Donau," *Fernseh-Rundschau,* 10, No. 11 (1960): 445–60.

Behrman, Daniel. *When the Mountains Move.* Paris: Unesco, 1954.

Belshaw, H. "Economic Development as an Operational Problem," *Civilizations,* 2, No. 2 (1952): 159–66.

——. *Population Growth and Levels of Consumption, with Special Reference to Countries in Asia.* New York: Institute of Pacific Relations, 1956.

Benham, F. "Education and Economic Development in the Underdeveloped Countries," *International Affairs,* 1959, pp. 181–87.

Berelson, Bernard, Paul F. Lazarsfeld, and William McPhee. *Voting.* Chicago: University of Chicago Press, 1954.

Bhat, A. R. "Development of a Multi-Language Press," in Unesco, *Developing Mass Media in Asia,* pp. 61–64.

——. Paper on Native-Language Press, submitted to Unesco Conference on Developing Mass Media in Asia. Bangkok, 1960.

Black, E. *The Diplomacy of Economic Development.* Cambridge: Harvard University Press, 1960.

Blin, Bernard. L'Information radiophonique dans les pays sous-développés. *Cahiers d'Etudes Radio-Télévision,* 1 (1957): 133–91.

Bocoum, M. "Le Role des moyens d'information dans les pays neufs," *Recueil des conférences faites au cours de la session de perfectionnement.* Strasbourg: International Center for Education in Journalism, 1959, pp. 190–96.

Boulahia, I. *Mémoire sur la presse en Afrique ou l'experience tunisienne.* Strasbourg: International Center for the Study of Journalism, 1961.

Brand, Willem. *The Struggle for a Higher Standard of Living.* Glencoe, Ill.: Free Press, 1958.

Brant, Charles S. *Tadagale: A Burmese Village in 1950.* Ithaca, N.Y.: Cornell University Press, 1954.

Bruk, S. I., and N. N. Cheboksarov. "National Development of Peoples of Asia and Africa," *Sovetskaya Etnografia,* 4 (1961).

Buchanan, N. S., and H. S. Ellis. *Approaches to Economic Development.* New York: Twentieth Century Fund, 1955.

Buitrón, A. "Problemas Económico-Sociales de la Educación en la América Latina," *América Indigena,* 20 (1960): 167–72.

Cannell, C. F., and J. C. MacDonald. "The Impact of Health News on Attitudes and Behavior," *Journalism Quarterly,* 33 (1956): 315–23.

Cantril, Hadley. *The Invasion from Mars.* Princeton, N.J.: Princeton University Press, 1940.

Cartwright, D. "Some Principles of Mass Persuasion," *Human Relations,* 2 (1949): 253–68.

Cassirer, Henry R. Address in *Report of the International Seminar on Instructional Television.* West Lafayette, Ind.: Purdue University. 1962.

———. *Television Teaching Today.* Paris: Unesco, 1960.

Celarié, A. *La Radiodiffusion harmonisée au service du développement.* Paris: Editions "Créations de Presse." *Les Cahiers Africains,* 6 (1962).

Clark, Colin. *The Conditions of Economic Progress.* 2d ed. London: Macmillan, 1951.

Clark, Margaret. *Health in the Mexican-American Culture.* Berkeley: University of California Press, 1959.

Codding, G. A. *Broadcasting without Barriers.* Paris: Unesco, 1959.

Coleman, James S. *Nigeria: Background to Nationalism.* Berkeley: University of California Press, 1958.

Coleman, J., E. Katz, and H. Menzel. *Doctors and New Drugs.* Glencoe, Ill.: Fress Press, 1962.

Comité pour les Relations Interafricaines. *Rapport sur la presse en Afrique de l'ouest.* Dolcar, 1960.

Coombs, Philip H. "The Economics of Educational Advancement and the Growth of Nations," in *Report of the International Seminar on Instructional Television,* October 8–18, 1961. West Lafayette, Ind.: Purdue University, 1961, pp. 14–19.

Cooper, Eunice, and Marie Jahoda. "The Evasion of Propaganda: How Prejudiced People Respond to Anti-Prejudice Propaganda," *Journal of Psychology,* 23 (1947): 15–25.

Council on Foreign Relations. *Social Change in Latin America Today.* New York: Vintage Books, 1960.

Council on World Tensions. *Restless Nations.* London: Allen & Unwin, 1962.

Cutlip, S. C. "Content and Flow of AP News—from Trunk to TTS to Reader," *Journalism Quarterly,* 31 (1954): 434–46.

Damle, Y. B. "Communication of Modern Ideas and Knowledge in Indian Villages," *Public Opinion Quarterly*, 20 (1956): 257–70.

DeFleur, M. L., and O. N. Larsen. *The Flow of Information: An Experiment in Mass Communication*. New York: Harper, 1958.

Deshmukh, C. D. "Tensions of Economic and Social Development in Southeast Asia," in Council on World Tensions, *Restless Nations*.

Dethoor, N. "A propos de 'Liberté I': Naissance du cinéma africain," *Croissance des Jeunes Nations* (Paris), 11 (May 1962): 22–28.

Deutsch, K. W. *Nationalism and Social Communication: An Enquiry into the Foundations of Nationality*. New York: Wiley, 1953.

———. "Shifts in the Balance of Communication Flows," *Public Opinion Quarterly*, 20 (1956): 143–61.

Deutschmann, Paul J. "The Mass Media in an Underdeveloped Village," *Journalism Quarterly*, 40 (1963): 27–35.

Deutschmann, Paul J., and Wayne A. Danielson. "Diffusion of Knowledge of the Major News Story," *Journalism Quarterly*, 37 (1960): 345–55.

Dieuzeide, Henri. "Notes for a Rational Theory on the Use of Radio and Television for Educational Purposes," *EBU Review*, 75B (1962), pp. 45–58.

Diouf, B. "L'Agence nationale de Presse dans un pays nouvellement indépendant" (roneo). Paper given at the conference of ministers of information of the Monrovia group, Dakar, September 1961.

Dollard, J. "The Acquisition of New Social Habits," in R. Linton, ed., *The Science of Man in the World Crisis*. New York: Columbia University Press, 1945.

Doob, Leonard W. *Becoming More Civilized*. New Haven: Yale University Press, 1961.

———. *Communication in Africa: A Search for Boundaries*. New Haven: Yale University Press, 1961.

Doucy, A., and P. Feldheim. *Problèmes du travail et politique sociale au Congo belge*. Bruxelles: Edition de la Librairie Encyclopédique, 1952.

Duarte, J. *El Diario Moderno*. Montevideo: Imprenta Tallares Graficas Sur, 1948.

Dube, S. C. *Indian Village*. London: Routledge & Kegan Paul, 1955.

———. *India's Changing Villages: Human Factors in Community Development*. London: Routledge & Kegan Paul, 1958.

———. "Some Problems of Communication in Rural Community Development," *Economic Development and Cultural Change*, 5 (1957): 129–46.

DuBois, Cora. *Social Forces in Southeast Asia: 1954–1958*. New York: Harper, 1958.

Dumazedier, J. *Television and Rural Adult Education.* Paris: Unesco, 1956.

Dumont, René. "Accelerating African Agricultural Development," *Journal of Agriculture,* 3 (1959): 231–53.

The Economist, Intelligence Unit, London. *The Problem of Newsprint and Other Printing Paper.* Paris: Unesco, 1949.

Ensminger, Douglas. "Ways of Overcoming Obstacles to Farm Economics Development in the Less-Developed Countries." Paper presented to American Farm Economics Association, Storrs, Connecticut, 1962.

Erickson, C. G., and H. M. Chausow. *Chicago's TV College—Final Report of a Three-Year Experiment.* Chicago: Chicago City Junior College, 1960.

Fall, M., *et al.* "Table ronde sur les problèmes de l'information," *L'Unité Africaine* (Dakar), March 6, 1962, pp. 11–14.

Feldmann, Erich. *Theorie der Massenmedien: Presse, Film, Funk, Fernsehen.* München: Dr. Hermann Jungck, 1962.

Femenías Loyola, María Teresa. "A Ten-Years Experiment in Chile," *Shiksha,* 11, No. 3 (1959): 37–43.

Festinger, Leon. *A Theory of Cognitive Dissonance.* Stanford, Calif.: Stanford University Press, 1962.

Film Centre, London. *The Use of Mobile Cinema and Radio Vans in Fundamental Education.* Paris: Unesco, 1949.

Fink, Raymond. *Information and Attitudes in Laos.* Washington, D.C.: Bureau of Social Science Research, American University, 1959.

Fortes, Meyer. *The Dynamics of Clanship among the Tallensi.* London: Oxford University Press, 1945.

Foster, George M. *Traditional Cultures and the Impact of Technological Change.* New York: Harper & Row, 1962.

Fourastié, Jean. *Le Grand Espoir du XX siècle: Progrès technique, progrès économique, progrès social.* 3d ed. Paris: Presses Universitaires de France, 1952.

——. *La Productivité.* Paris: Presses Universitaires de France, 1952.

Frankel, S. H. *The Economic Impact on Underdeveloped Societies.* Cambridge: Harvard University Press, 1953.

Fraser, A. K. *The Teaching of Healthcraft to African Women.* London: Longmans, Green, 1932.

Frederix, P. *Un Siècle de chasse aux nouvelles; de Havas à l'AFP, 1835–1957.* Paris, 1958.

Free, Lloyd. *Some International Implications of the Political Psychology of Brazilians.* Princeton, N.J.: Institute for International Social Research, 1961.

French National Commission for Unesco. Paper prepared for the Meeting of Experts on Development and Use of New Methods and Techniques in Education, at Unesco House, March 12–20, 1962. Paris: Unesco, ED/New Meth/62/5.

Friedrich-Ebert-Stiftung. *Der Beitrag der Massenmedien zur Beziehungsarbeit in den Entwicklungsländer.* Hannover: Verlag für Literatur und Zeitgeschehen GMBH, 1960.

——. *Fragen der Entwicklungshilfe aus soziologischer Sicht.* (Hectographed.) Bonn: Friedrich-Ebert-Stiftung, 1960.

——. *Literatur über Entwicklungsländer.* 2 vols. Hannover: Verlag für Literatur und Zeitgeschehen, 1961.

Geertz, Clifford. *The Development of the Javanese Economy: A Socio-Cultural Approach* (mimeo.). Cambridge: Center for International Studies, Massachusetts Institute of Technology, 1956.

Gerschenkron, A. "Economic Backwardness in Historical Perspective," in B. F. Hoselitz, *Progress of Underdeveloped Areas.*

Ghose, H. P. *The Newspaper in India.* Calcutta: University of Calcutta, 1952.

Gina, A. *The New Role of the Ministry of Information* (roneo). Lagos: Ministry of Information, 1961.

Ginsburg, N., ed. *Atlas of Economic Development.* Chicago: University of Chicago Press, 1961.

Girardeau, E. "Les Télécommunications de l'Union Française," *Nouvelle Revue Française d'Outre-Mer* (1955): 375–80.

Golden, H. H. "Literacy and Social Change in Underdeveloped Countries," *Rural Sociology,* 20 (1955): 1–7.

Goldsen, Rose, and Max Ralis. *Factors Related to Acceptance of Innovation in Bang Chan, Thailand.* Ithaca, N.Y.: Cornell University Press, 1957.

Gourou, P. *The Tropical World, Its Social and Economic Conditions and Its Future Status.* Translated by E. D. Laborde. London: Longmans, Green, 1958.

Grace, H. A., and J. O. Neuhaus. "Information and Social Distance as Predictors of Hostility toward Nations," *J. Abnorm. Soc. Psychol.,* 47 (1952): 540–45.

Greenberg, B. S. "Additional Data on Variables Related to Press Freedom," *Journalism Quarterly,* 38 (1961).

Hadsell, R. S., and G. K. Butts. "Educational Television in Iran," *The Multiplier,* 4 (1961): 28, 31.

Hagen, E. E. *On the Theory of Social Change.* Homewood, Ill.: Dorsey, 1962.

Hall, E. T. *The Silent Language.* Garden City, N.Y.: Doubleday, 1959.

Hall, E. T., and W. F. Whyte. "Intercultural Communication: A Guide to Men of Action," *Human Organization,* 19 (1960): 5–12.

Halley, Lord. *An African Survey. A Study of Problems Arising in Africa South of the Sahara.* London: Oxford University Press, 1957.

Halpern, J. M. *Aspects of Village Life and Culture Change in Laos.* New York: Council on Economic and Cultural Affairs, 1958.

Harrell, T. W., D. Brown, and W. Schramm. "Memory in Radio News Listening," *Journal of Applied Psychology,* 33 (1949): 265–74.

Heidermann, Horst. *Erwachsenenbildung in Entwicklungsländern Afrikas und Asiens* (hectographed). Bonn: Friedrich-Ebert-Stiftung, 1960.

Heilbroner, Robert L. *The Great Ascent.* New York: Harper & Row, 1963.

Hickey, Gerald. *The Study of a Vietnamese Rural Community—Sociology.* East Lansing: Michigan State University, Vietnamese Advisory Group, 1960.

Hirabayashi, Gordon K., and M. Fathalla El Khatib. "Communication and Political Awareness in the Villages of Egypt," *Public Opinion Quarterly,* 22 (1958): 357–63.

Hirschmann, A. O. *The Strategy of Economic Development.* New Haven: Yale University Press, 1960.

Hoban, C., and E. Van Ormer. *An Inventory of Instructional Television Research, 1918–1950.* Port Washington, N.Y.: U.S. Special Devices Center, 1951.

Hodgdon, Linwood L. "Psychological and Sociological Factors in Rural Change." Paper presented to the 16th general assembly of the World Medical Association, November 13, 1962, Bombay, India.

Holmberg, Allan R. "Changing Community Attitudes and Values in Peru: A Case Study in Guided Change," in Council on Foreign Relations, *Social Change in Latin America Today.*

Hoselitz, B. F. "Noneconomic Barriers to Economic Development," *Economic Development and Cultural Change,* 1 (1952): 8–21.

Hoselitz, B. F., ed. *Progress of Underdeveloped Areas.* Chicago: University of Chicago Press, 1952.

Hoselitz, B. F. *Sociological Aspects of Economic Growth.* Glencoe, Ill.: Free Press, 1960.

Hoselitz, B. F., and W. E. Moore, eds. *Industrialization and Society.* Paris: Unesco-Mouton, 1963.

Houn, Franklin W. *To Change a Nation.* Glencoe, Ill.: Free Press, 1961.

Hovland, Carl J. "The Effects of the Mass Media of Communication," in Gardner Lindzey, ed., *Handbook of Social Psychology.* Boston: Addison-Wesley, 1954.

Hovland, Carl, Irving Janis, and Fred Kelley. *Communication and Persuasion.* New Haven: Yale University Press, 1954.

Huan, Nguyen-Cong. "Les Astres et le paysan vietnamien," *France-Asie*, April 1955, pp. 449–64.

Huard, M., and M. Durand. *Connaissance du Viet-Nam*. Paris: Ecole Française d'Extreme Orient, 1954.

Huth, Arno G. *Communication and Economic Development*. New York: Carnegie Endowment for International Peace, 1952.

———. *Communications Media in Tropical Africa*. Washington, D.C.: International Cooperation Administration, 1960.

Hyman, Herbert, and Paul H. Sheatsley. "Some Reasons Why Information Campaigns Fail," *Public Opinion Quarterly*, 11 (1947): 412–23.

Iguchi, I. *Masu Kominyukeishon*. Tokyo: Kobunsha, 1951.

Ingram, James C. *Economic Change in Thailand since 1850*. Stanford, Calif.: Stanford University Press, 1955.

Institute for International Economic Studies. *The Place of Paper in Development and Foreign Aid*. Stockholm: The Institute, with the assistance of the FAO and Unesco, March 1963.

International Press Institute. *The Flow of the News*. Zurich, 1953.

———. *The Press in Authoritarian Countries*. Zurich, 1959.

International Public Opinion Research, Inc. *A Survey of Cabinet Officials of Member Countries in the United Nations on World-wide Freedom of Information*. New York, 1952.

Isaacs, H. *Scratches on Our Minds*. New York: John Day, 1958.

Istanbul Physics Film Report. Technical Report and General Report. Ankara, 1961.

Ito, Kinji. *An Experimental Study with Programmed Instruction in Geography*. Tokyo: Komatsunagi Elementary School, 1961.

Janis, I. L., C. I. Hovland, *et al. Personality and Persuasibility*. New Haven: Yale University Press, 1959.

Janvier, J. "Une Expérience africaine: Le Ministère de l'information, de la radiodiffusion et de la presse de la république du Sénégal," *L'Enseignement du Journalisme* (Strasbourg, International Center for Education in Journalism), Autumn 1960, pp. 51–70.

———. "Rapport pour la réunion d'experts sur la constitution d'une agence interafricaine de presse." Dakar, December 1961.

Joos, L. C. D. "La Radio en Afrique," *Recueil des conférences faites au cours de la session de perfectionnement*. Strasbourg: International Center for Education in Journalism, 1959, pp. 217, 225.

Katz, Elihu. "The Two Step Flow of Communication," *Public Opinion Quarterly*, 21 (1957): 61–78.

Katz, Elihu, and Paul F. Lazarsfeld. *Personal Influence*. Glencoe, Ill.: Free Press, 1955.

Kayser, Jacques. *One Week's News*. Paris: Unesco, 1953.

Kelley, Harold H. "Salience of Membership and Resistance to Change of Group-Anchored Attitudes," *Human Relations*, 8 (1955): 275–89.

Kelley, Harold H., and E. H. Volkart. "The Resistance to Change of Group-Anchored Attitudes," *American Sociological Review*, 17 (1952): 453–65.

Kendall, Patricia L., and Katherine M. Wolf. "The Analysis of Deviant Cases in Communication Research," in P. F. Lazarsfeld and F. E. Stanton, eds., *Communication Research, 1948–49*. New York: Harper, 1949, pp. 152–79.

Khudiakov, E. L. *Theory and Practice of the Party-Soviet Press*. Moscow: Moscow University Press, 1957.

Kimble, G. H. T. *Tropical Africa*. New York: Twentieth Century Fund, 1960.

Kitchen, Helen, ed. *The Press in Africa*. Washington, D.C.: Ruth Sloan Associates, 1956.

Klapper, Joseph T. *The Effects of Mass Communication*. Glencoe, Ill.: Free Press, 1960.

——. "Mass Media and the Engineering of Consent," *American Scholar*, 17 (1948): 419–29.

Kluckhohn, F. R. "Dominant and Substitutive Profiles of Cultural Orientations (Values)," *Social Forces*, 28 (1950): 376–93.

Kraus, Sidney J., ed. *The Great Debates*. Bloomington: University of Indiana Press, 1962.

Krishnamoorthy, P. V. "Broadcasts for Rural Audiences in India," *Rural Broadcaster*, September 1962, pp. 11–12.

Kruglak, T. E. *The Foreign Correspondents*. Geneva: Librairie E. Dorz, 1955.

Larson, O. N., and R. Hill. "Mass Media and Interpersonal Communication in the Diffusion of a News Event," *American Sociological Review*, 19 (1954): 426–33.

Lazarsfeld, Paul, Bernard Berelson, and Hazel Gaudet. *The People's Choice*. New York: Columbia University Press, 1948.

Lazarsfeld, Paul F., and Robert K. Merton. "Mass Communication, Popular Taste, and Organized Social Action," in Schramm, *Mass Communications*, pp. 492–512.

Leauté, J. "Le Développement des moyens d'information et de la formation professionnelle en Afrique," *L'Enseignement du Journalisme* (Strasbourg), Autumn 1961, pp. 26–50.

Lefranc, Robert. "The Audio-Visual Media: Their Place in the School," *World Screen*, 3 (1961), 39.

Lerner, Daniel. *The Passing of Traditional Society*. Glencoe, Ill.: Free Press, 1958.

Levine, J., and J. Butler. "Lecture vs. Group Decision in Changing Behavior," *Journal of Applied Psychology*, 36 (1952): 29–33.

Lewin, Kurt. "Channels of Group Life," *Human Relations*, 1 (1941): 145.

——. "Group Decision and Social Change," in T. M. Newcomb and E. L. Hartley, eds., *Readings in Social Psychology*. New York: Holt, 1947, pp. 330–44.

Lewis, Oscar. *Life in a Mexican Village: Tepoztlan Restudied*. Urbana: University of Illinois Press, 1951.

Lewis, R., and J. Rovan. *Television and Teleclubs in Rural Communities*. Paris: Unesco, 1955.

Lewis, W. Arthur. "Education and Economic Development," *International Social Science Journal*, 14 (1962): 688ff.

Lucas, D. B., and S. H. Britt. *Advertising Psychology and Research*. New York, McGraw-Hill, 1950.

Ly, A. *Les Masses africaines et l'actuelle condition humaine*. Paris: Présence Africaine, 1956.

McClelland, David C. *The Achieving Society*. New York: Van Nostrand, 1961.

McCormack, W. G. "Mysore Villagers' View of Change," *Economic Development and Cultural Change*, 5 (1957): 257–62.

McDermott, W., K. Deuschle, J. Adair, H. Fulmer, and B. Loughlin. "Introducing Modern Medicine in a Navajo Community," *Science*, 131 (1960): 197–205, 280–87.

McFadden, T. J. *Daily Journalism in the Arab States*. Columbus: Ohio State University Press, 1953.

MacMillan, R. "L'Enseignement du journalisme au Ghana," *Recueil des conférences faites au cours de la session de perfectionnement*. Strasbourg: International Center for Education in Journalism, 1959, pp. 197–204.

Macquet, J. J., and D'Herteflet. *Elections en société féodale: Une Etude sur l'introduction du vote populaire au Ruanda-Urundi*. Bruxelles: Académie Royale des Sciences Coloniales, 1959.

Manevy, R. "L'Evolution de la presse africaine et l'histoire de la presse." *Recueil des conférences faites au cours de la session de perfectionnement*. Strasbourg: International Center for Education in Journalism, 1959, pp. 205–16.

Mankekar, D. R. "The Journalist's Role in Emergent Countries," *The Journalist's World* (Brussels), April–June 1963, No. 2, pp. 1–2, 16.

Marris, P. *Family and Social Change in an African City: A Study of Rehousing in Lagos*. London: Routledge & Kegan Paul, 1961.

Marshall, A. *Principles of Economics*. 8th ed. London: Macmillan, 1930.

Martin, Ferrer S. *Muestra Piloto de las Escuelas Radiofónicas Rurales. Acción Cultural Popular, Escuelas Radiofónicas de Sutatenza* (Colombia). Paris: Unesco, 1951.

Martin, L. "Influence de l'humidité relative sur les propriétés physiques des papiers," *L'Imprimerie Nouvelle* (Paris), September and December, 1959.

Marx, K. *Capital*. Edited by F. Engels. Chicago: Kerr, 1926.

———. *A Contribution to the Critique of Political Economy*. New York: International Publishing Company, 1904.

Mathur, J. C., and Paul Neurath. *An Indian Experiment in Farm Radio Forums*. Paris: Unesco, 1959.

M'Baye, A. "Radiodiffusion et Développement," *L'Unité Africaine* (Dakar), November 21, 1959.

Mboya, Tom. "Tensions in African Development," in Council on World Tensions, *Restless Nations*.

Mead, Margaret. "Applied Anthropology, 1955," in *Some Uses of Anthropology: Theoretical and Applied*. Washington, D.C.: Anthropological Society of Washington, 1956.

Mead, Margaret, ed. *Cultural Patterns and Technical Change*. New York: Mentor (for Unesco), 1955.

Meier, G. M., and R. F. Baldwin. *Economic Development, Theory, History, and Policy*. New York: Wiley, 1957.

Merton, R. K. *Mass Persuasion*. New York: Harper, 1946.

Morocco, Kingdom of, Ministry of National Education. *Cinéma et Education Populaire*. Rabat, 1949.

Morris, C. *Varieties of Human Value*. Chicago: University of Chicago Press, 1956.

Morton-Williams, P. *Cinema in Rural Nigeria*. Zaria: Federal Information Service, 1953.

Myrdal, G. *Economic Theory and the Underdeveloped Regions*. London: Duckworth, 1957.

———. *Rich Lands and Poor: The Road to World Prosperity*. New York: Harper, 1958.

Nafziger, Ralph O., and David Manning White. *Introduction to Mass Communication Research*. Baton Rouge: Louisiana State University Press, 1963.

Nair, Kusum. *Blossoms in the Dust*. New York: Praeger, 1962.

National Institute of Audio-Visual Education. *Effectiveness of Films in Teaching*. New Delhi, India, 1961. Abstracted in Benjamin Duke, ed., *Survey of Educational Media Research in the Far East*. (Washington, D.C.: U.S. Office of Education, 1963), p. 136.

Nehru, J. *The Discovery of India.* London: John Day, 1946.

Neill, S. *Survey of the Training of the Ministry in Africa: Part I.* London: International Missionary Council, 1950.

Neisser, C. S. "Community Development and Mass Education in British Nigeria," *Economic Development and Cultural Change,* 3 (1955): 352–65.

Nelson, L. "The Financing of Educational Television," in *Educational Television: The Next Ten Years.* Stanford, Calif.: Institute for Communication Research, 1962.

Nesmeyanov, A. N. "The Tasks and Possibilities of Modern Science in Overcoming the Economic Backwardness of Certain Countries," *Vestnik Academii Nauk SSSR,* 12 (1959).

NHK Radio-Television Cultural Research Institute (Japan Broadcasting Corporation). *The Effects of "Radio Japanese Classroom," April 1954–December 1955.* Tokyo, 1956. Abstracted in Benjamin Duke, ed., *Survey of Educational Media Research in the Far East* (Washington, D.C.: U.S. Office of Education, 1963), pp. 102–3.

———. *The Listening Effects of "Radio English Classroom," April 1954–March 1955.* Tokyo, 1956. Abstracted in Benjamin Duke, ed., *Survey of Educational Media Research in the Far East* (Washington, D.C.: U.S. Office of Education, 1963, pp. 103–4.

Nicol, J., A. A. Shea, G. J. P. Simmins, and R. A. Sim. *Canada's Farm Radio Forum.* Paris: Unesco, 1954.

Nobecourt, J. "La Presse quotidienne au Congo belge: Situation au début, 1959," *Techniques de Diffusion Collective* (Paris), October 1959.

Nove, A. *The Soviet Economy.* New York: Praeger, 1961.

Nurkse, Ragnar. *Problems of Capital Formation in Underdeveloped Countries.* Oxford: Blackwell, 1953.

O'Leary, Hans D. "Die Filmarbeit der Britischen Kolonialverwaltung," *Kulturarbeit,* 12 (1960): 191–95.

Opler, M. E., and R. D. Singh. "Economic, Political and Social Change in a Village of North Central India," *Human Organization,* 11 (1952): 5–12.

Ozdil, Ilhan. "A Causative Diagnostic Analysis of Turkey's Major Problems and a Communicative Approach to Their Solution," *Dissertation Abstracts,* 20, No. 8 (1960).

Osmánczyk, Edmund. *Publicystyka w kraju budującym socjalizm* (Publication in a country building socialism). Warsaw: Czytelnik, 1952.

Paul, B. E., ed. *Health, Culture and Community: Case Studies of Public Reactions to Health Programs.* New York: Russell Sage Foundation, 1955.

Pentony, DeVere, ed. *The Underdeveloped Lands.* San Francisco: Chandler, 1960.

Philips, Jane. "The Hookworm Campaign in Ceylon," in Howard M. Teaf, Jr., and Peter G. Franck, eds., *Hands across Frontiers: Case Studies in Technical Cooperation.* Ithaca, N.Y.: Cornell University Press, 1955.

Piaget, J., and A. M. Weil. "The Development in Children of the Idea of the Homeland and of Relations with Other Countries," *International Soc. Sci. Bull.,* 3 (1951): 561–76.

Pool, Ithiel de Sola. "The Mass Media and Politics in the Modernization Process," in Lucian Pye, ed., *Communications and Political Development.*

Powdermaker, Hortense. *Copper Town: Changing Africa.* New York: Harper & Row, 1962.

Les Problèmes de l'information officielle au Congo. Report of a conference of Directors of Information held at Lovanium University, Leopoldville, 1960.

Puglisi, Maria Grazia. "The Contribution of Italian Television to the Campaign to Eradicate Illiteracy through TV Broadcasts: 'It's Never Too Late.'" Paper presented to the Unesco Meeting of Experts on New Methods and Techniques in Education, March 12–20, 1962.

Pye, Lucian. "Administrators, Agitators, and Brokers," *Public Opinion Quarterly,* 22 (1958): 342–48.

———. "Communication Patterns and the Problem of Representative Government in Non-Western Societies," *Public Opinion Quarterly,* 20 (1956): 250–51.

Pye, Lucian, ed. *Communications and Political Development.* Princeton, N.J.: Princeton University Press, 1963.

Pye, Lucian. *Politics, Personality and Nation Building.* New Haven: Yale University Press, 1962.

Queensland Institute for Education Research. *An Experimental Investigation of Method in School Broadcasting.* Queensland, Australia, 1956.

Rao, Y. V. L. "The Role of Information in Economic and Social Change: Report of a Field Study in Two Indian Villages." Doctoral dissertation, University of Minnesota, 1963.

Redfield, Robert, and W. Lloyd Warner. "Cultural Anthropology and Modern Agriculture," in *Farmers in a Changing World,* 1940 Yearbook of Agriculture, U.S. Department of Agriculture. Washington, D.C.: Government Printing Office, 1940.

Rizzuto, F. A. "Con Paso Firme hacia la Libertad Absoluta," *Veritas* (Buenos Aires), October 1960, p. 584.

Roberts, D. B. *Types of Organizations in Adult and Mass Literacy Work*. Sydney, Australia, 1952.

Rogers, Everett M. *Diffusion of Innovations*. Glencoe, Ill.: Free Press, 1963.

Rosenblum, L. *Newspaper Typesetting Cost Survey*. Report of a study carried out for the Graphic Arts Research Institute, Cambridge, Mass., (offset), 1959.

Rostow, W. W. *The Stages of Economic Growth*. Cambridge, England: Cambridge University Press, 1960.

Rudolph, Lloyd, and Suzanne H. Rudolph. "Surveys in India: Field Experience in Madras State," *Public Opinion Quarterly*, 22 (1958): 235–44.

Schramm, Wilbur. *An Annotated Bibliography of the Research on Programmed Instruction*. Washington, D.C.: U.S. Office of Education, 1964.

———. "Mass Communication," *Annual Review of Psychology*, 13 (1962): 251–84.

———. *Mass Communications*. 2d ed. Urbana: University of Illinois Press, 1960.

———. "The Newer Educational Media in the United States." Working paper for Paris Conference of Experts on Educational Media, March 1962. Published in Unesco, *New Methods and Techniques in Education*, pp. 5–17.

———. "Newspapers of a State as a News Network," *Journalism Quarterly*, 35 (1958): 177–82.

———. *One Day in the World's Press*. Stanford, Calif.: Stanford University Press, 1960.

———. "What We Know about Learning from Instructional Television," in *Educational Television: The Next Ten Years*. Stanford, Calif.: Institute for Communication Research, 1962, pp. 52–76.

Schramm, Wilbur, and R. F. Carter. "Scales for Describing National Communication Systems" (mimeo.). Stanford, Calif.: Institute for Communication Research, 1959.

Schramm, Wilbur, and G. F. Winfield. "New Uses of Mass Communication for the Promotion of Economic and Social Development." Paper presented at the United Nations Conference on the Application of Science and Technology for the Benefit of the Less Developed Areas, Geneva, 1963. Washington, D.C.: *U.S. Papers for the Conference*, Vol. 10, 1963.

Schultz, T. W. "Education and Economic Growth," in Nelson B. Henry, ed., *Social Forces Influencing American Education*. Chicago: University of Chicago Press, 1961.

Schumpeter, J. A. "Economic History and Entrepreneurial History," in *Change and the Entrepreneur.* Cambridge: Harvard Research Center in Entrepreneurial History, 1949.

———. *The Theory of Economic Development.* New York: Oxford University Press, 1941.

Shannon, L. W., ed. *Underdeveloped Areas: A Book of Readings and Research.* New York: Harper, 1957.

Sibley, W. E. "Social Structure and Planned Change: A Case Study from the Philippines," *Human Organization,* 19 (1960–61): 209–11.

Sigmund, P. A., Jr., ed. *The Ideologies of the Developing Nations.* London: Praeger, 1963.

Smith, Adam. *An Enquiry into the Causes of the Wealth of Nations.* New York: Random House, 1927.

Spicer, Edward H., ed. *Human Problems in Technological Change.* New York: Russell Sage Foundation, 1952.

Spurr, Norman E. "Some Aspects of the Work of the Colonial Film Unit in West and East Africa," in *Visual Aids in Fundamental Education.* Paris: Unesco, 1952, pp. 37–44.

Staley, Eugene. *The Future of Underdeveloped Countries: Political Implications of Economic Development.* New York: Harper, 1954.

Steinberg, D. J. *Cambodia. Its People, Its Society, Its Culture.* New Haven: Human Relations Area Files Press, 1959.

Strumilin, Stanislav. "The Economics of Education in the USSR," *International Social Science Journal,* 14, No. 4 (1962): 633–46.

Tarroni, Evelina. "A Programme on the Struggle against Illiteracy," *Television and Adult Education,* 6 (1962): 3–8.

Technology and Economic Development. Special issue, *Scientific American,* 209, No. 3 (September 1963).

Terrou, F., and L. Solal. *Legislation for Press, Film, and Radio: Comparative Study of the Main Types of Regulations Governing the Information Media.* Paris: Unesco, 1951.

Thomason, F. S., and R. A. Wolcott. *Breaking the Illiteracy Barrier through Radio.* Washington, D.C.: Government Printing Office, 1960.

Tyaguneko, V. "The Tendencies of Social Development in the Liberated Countries in the Contemporary Era," *Mirovaya Ekonomika i Mezhdunarodnye Otnosheniya,* 3, 1962.

Unesco. *Adult Education Groups and Audio-Visual Techniques.* Paris, 1958.

———. *L'Analphabétisme dans le monde au milieu du XXème siècle.* Paris, 1957.

———. *Developing Information Media in Africa.* Paris, 1962.

———. *Developing Mass Media in Asia.* Paris, 1960.

———. *Education for Journalism*. Paris, 1954.

———. *Illiteracy at Mid-Century*. Paris, 1957.

———. *Mass Media in the Developing Countries*. Paris, 1961.

———. *New Methods and Techniques in Education*. Paris, 1963.

———. *News Agencies. Their Structure and Operation*. Paris, 1953.

———. *The Problems of Transmitting Press Messages*. Paris, 1956.

———. *Publications for New Literates: Editorial Methods*. Reports and Papers on Mass Communication, No. 22. Paris, 1957.

———. *Publications for New Literates: Seven Case Histories*. Reports and Papers on Mass Communication, No. 24. Paris, 1957.

———. *Report on World Social Situation*. Paris, 1961.

———. *Rural Television in Japan*. Paris, 1960.

———. *Social Education through Television*. Reports and Papers on Mass Communication, No. 38. Paris, 1963.

———. *Social Implications of Technical Advance in Underdeveloped Countries: A Trend Report and Bibliography*. Paris, 1954.

———. *Space Communication and the Mass Media*. Reports and Papers on Mass Communication, No. 41. Paris, 1963.

———. *Trade Barriers to Knowledge*. Paris, 1955.

———. *World Communications*. Paris, 1956, 1964.

———. *World Survey of Education*. 3 vols. Paris, 1955, 1958, 1961.

United Nations. *Aspects of Economic Development: The Background to Freedom from Hunger*. New York, 1962.

———. *The Capital Development Needs of the Less Developed Countries*. New York, 1962.

———. *Compendium of Social Statistics*. New York, 1963.

———. *Demographic Yearbook*. New York, to 1962.

———. *Per Capita National Product of Fifty-five Countries, 1952–54*. New York, 1957.

———. *Statistical Yearbook*. New York, to 1962.

———. *Yearbook of Labour Statistics*. New York, through 1962.

Vaizey, J. Introduction to "Economics of Education," *International Social Science Journal*, 14 (1962): 627–28.

Van Bol, J. M. *La Presse quotidienne au Congo belge*. Bruxelles: La Pensée Catholique, 1959.

Van der Kroef, Justus M. "Southeast Asia—Some Anthropological Aspects," *Human Organization*, 10 (1951): 5–15.

Victorian School Broadcasts Advisory Committee. *Television for Schools. Report on Experimental Mathematics Programmes*. Victoria, Australia, 1961.

Vieyra, P. "Responsabilités du cinéma dans la formation d'une conscience nationale africaine," *Présence Africaine* (Paris), No. 27, 1960.

Voss, Harald. *Rundfunk und Fernsehen in Afrika.* Köln: Verlag Deutscher Wirtschaftsdienst, 1962.

Wagley, Charles. "The Brazilian Revolution," in Council on Foreign Relations, *Social Change in Latin America Today,* pp. 177–230.

Waples, Douglas. *Los Problemas de la Comunicación Pública en el Perú.* Lima: Instituto de Relaciones Humanas y Productividad, 1959.

Waples, Douglas, Bernard Berelson, and Franklin Bradshaw. *What Reading Does to People.* Chicago: University of Chicago Press, 1940.

Weber, Max. *The Protestant Ethic and the Spirit of Capitalism.* New York: Scribner, 1930.

White, L., and R. D. Leigh. *Peoples Speaking to Peoples.* Chicago: University of Chicago Press, 1938.

Wilkening, E. A. "Roles of Communicating Agents in Technological Change in Agriculture," *Social Forces,* 34 (1956): 361–67.

Williams, Francis. *Transmitting World News.* Paris: Unesco, 1953.

Williams, J. G. *Radio in Fundamental Education in Undeveloped Areas.* Paris: Unesco, 1950.

Wilson, Elmo C. "Problems of Survey Research in Modernizing Areas," *Public Opinion Quarterly,* 22 (1958): 230–34.

Winfield, G. F., and P. Hartman. "Communications—The Way to Health Improvement," *The Multiplier,* 4, No. 3 (1961): 2113.

Wolseley, R. E. *Journalism in Modern India.* Bombay: Asia Publishing House, 1953.

Worthington, G. B. *Connaissance scientifique de l'Afrique.* Paris: Berger-Levrault, 1960.

Xoomsai, M. L. Tooi, and P. Ratamangkala. *A Survey of Results of Using School Broadcast as a Teaching Method.* Bangkok: Department of Educational Research, College of Education, 1960.

Yang, C. K. *A Chinese Village in Early Communist Transition.* Cambridge, Mass.: Technology Press, 1959.

Yur'yev, I. G. "Laws and Characteristics of the Transition to Socialism in Socially and Economically Retarded Countries," *Vestnik Moskovskogo Universiteta,* 1, 1959.

Zimmerman, C., and R. A. Bauer. "The Effect of an Audience upon What Is Remembered," *Public Opinion Quarterly,* 20 (1956): 238–48.

Zinkin, Maurice. "What the Underdeveloped Countries Have to Do," *India Quarterly,* 8 (1952): 132–41.

Zischa, A. "Der Film in der Asiatischen Welt," *Aussenpolitik,* 5 (1954): 112–16.

Index